CLIPS FROM A LIFE

CLIPS FROM A LIFE

DENIS NORDEN

FOURTH ESTATE · *London*

First published in Great Britain in 2008 by
Fourth Estate
A division of HarperCollinsPublishers
77–85 Fulham Palace Road, London W6 8JB
www.4thestate.co.uk

1

A catalogue record for this book is available from the British Library

ISBN 978-0-00-727795-7

Typeset in Minion and Trade Gothic
Printed in Great Britain by Clays Ltd, St Ives plc

Mixed Sources
Product group from well-managed
forests and other controlled sources
www.fsc.org Cert no. SW-COC-1806
© 1996 Forest Stewardship Council

FSC is a non-profit international organisation established to promote the
responsible management of the world's forests. Products carrying the FSC
label are independently certified to assure consumers that they come
from forests that are managed to meet the social, economic and
ecological needs of present and future generations

Find out more about HarperCollins and the environment at
www.harpercollins.co.uk/green

For
Max and Angus
(Latest in series)

CONTENTS

LIST OF ILLUSTRATIONS

All photographs are from the author's private collection, unless otherwise credited.

Frank Muir, Charles Maxwell and DN. Photograph © BBC Photo Library.

Take It From Here: Wallas Eaton, Dick Bentley, Alma Cogan, Jimmy Edwards and June Whitfield. Photograph © BBC Photo Library.

Take It From Here: Frank and DN. Photograph courtesy of Popperfoto/Getty Images.

Bernard Braden. Photography courtesy of The Kobal Collection/ Melina Prods.

What's My Line: Frank, Lady Isobel Barnett, Barbara Kelly and DN. Photograph © BBC Photo Library.

London Laughs.

PLATE TWO

Whack-o!: Jimmy Edwards. Photograph © BBC Photo Library.

My Word!: Frank Muir and Dilys Powell. Photograph © BBC Photo Library.

Inspirational sheet-music for *My Music*.

My Music: Steve Race, Frank, Ian Wallace and John Amis. Photographs © BBC Photo Library.

Looks Familiar. Courtesy of FremantleMedia Ltd.

Looks Familiar: Dickie Henderson, Diana Dors and Danny La Rue. Photograph courtesy of BFI Stills.

Looks Familiar: Alec McCowen, DN, Pat Phoenix and Eric Sykes. Photograph courtesy of BFI Stills.

Looks Familiar: Alice Faye. Photograph © FremantleMedia Ltd.

Looks Familiar: David Niven. Photograph © FremantleMedia Ltd.

Looks Familiar: Sammy Davis Jr. Photograph courtesy of BFI Stills.

Our Kid.

PLATE THREE

Melvin Frank. Photograph courtesy of Brut Productions/Ronald Grant Archive.

Buona Sera, Mrs Campbell.

A Thurber original.

It'll Be Alright on the Night.

It'll Be Alright on the Night cartoon.

The Crazy Gang: Bud Flanagan, Charlie Naughton, Jimmy Gold, Jimmy Nervo and Teddy Knox. Photograph by Houston Rogers courtesy of the Mander & Mitchenson Theatre Collection, © V&A.

'Monsewer' Eddie Gray.

Chesney Allen and Bud Flanagan.

DN and the Brylcreem touch. Photograph courtesy of Ronald Grant Archive.

Sanders of the River. Photograph courtesy of London Film Productions/Ronald Grant Archive.

Moore Marriott. Photograph courtesy of BFI Stills.

Countdown: Richard Whiteley, Carol Vorderman and DN. Photograph © ITV/Granada.

The young DN.

FOREWORD

In a long-ago *New Yorker* cartoon, a publisher is seen advising the anxious author whose slim volume of memoirs he has just tossed aside, 'Cut out all the insights and beef up the anecdotes.'

And insofar as I have followed any guiding principle for the ensuing ruminative rummage, that injunction would more or less cover it.

No other discipline was observed. For some eighteen months or so, I simply set down each recollection as it arrived, making no attempt to impose any order, merely letting them pile up without regard for chronology or variousness. The process was so similar to the way we used to gather in clips for the TV shows from which I had been earning my bread and non-fat butter-substitute over the past forty-some years, it seemed appropriate to acknowledge the resemblance in the book's title. At the very least, that gave me an excuse to abandon *This is On Me*, *The Story Thus Far*, *Innocent Bystanding* and *Some of the Bits Frank's Book Left Out*.

As might have been expected, the project ended up as a higgledy-piggledy mishmash of moments that had amused or impressed me over the course of my working life, each complete in itself but in aggregate an undisciplined jumble of 250-plus jottings as disconnected and random as the wisps and scraps of memory that delivered them.

'Do you want me to rearrange them so that they make more of a straight line across the decades?' I asked Louise Haines, my infinitely patient editor.

'I'm not averse to a bit of backwards and forwards zig-zagging,' she replied. 'We might even make some kind of virtue of it.'

Thankful for this – you only have to Google my screenplay credits to see how small a gift I have for sustained narrative – I was even more grateful when she added, 'If you could just work out a separate timeline for me, I'll try to put the bits and pieces into some kind of minimally coherent order, then chop it into chapters.'

This she proceeded to do, with considerable diligence and ingenuity, in the process achieving an agreeable (to me, anyway) reversal of Life's customary running order by positioning my chronicles of childhood up towards the book's rear end. Incidentally, that timeline, for those who feel the need of it, can be found on page xvii.

But in addition to Louise, there are several others to whom I owe a debt of gratitude for helping me get the thing finished. Foremost among them is Avril, my wife, who not only painstakingly scrutinised and proofed each paragraph as it was hewn from the living rock, she managed the some would say impossible task of keeping my spirits up throughout.

I'm also indebted to Maggie, my daughter, Nick, my son, and his wife Elspeth, whose unfaltering encouragement, reinforced by offerings from all manner of recherché delis, acted as a constant spur. Nor could I have done without the clear-eyed interventions of Zoe and Katy, my grand-daughters, and the long-distance support of Jamie, the grandson.

My warmest thanks also go to Brenda Talbot, my secretary from way back, who, with her husband, John, performed miracles of delving and digging; to Norma Farnes, my literary agent, and April Young, my everything-else agent, for taking care of the hard-headed stuff; to Doctor Paul Blom, for keeping me near enough seventy per cent road-worthy and Kieran Pascal for performing roughly the same function with my IT equipment.

I would add a further thank-you note to Jamie Muir, for giving me permission to quote one of Frank's *My Word!* stories and to Messrs Eyre Methuen for allowing me to reprint bits from *Coming To You Live!* and the *My Word!* books.

But enough now of the Opening Titles. Cue Clips.

TIMELINE

1922 Born 6 February, Mare Street, Hackney, within the sound of Bow Bells.

1927 Craven Park Elementary School.

1933 City of London School.

1939 Joined Hyams Brothers Gaumont Super Cinemas at State, Kilburn.

1940 Transferred to Trocadero, Elephant & Castle, as Assistant Manager.

1941 Gaumont, Watford, as General Manager ('Youngest Cinema Manager in the country').

1942 Also managed Town Hall Music Hall, Watford.
Wrote *History of the Holborn Empire* (radio), six programmes presented by Sidney Caplan, Musical Director at Holborn Empire, then Watford.
Left to join RAF.

1943 Married Avril.

1944 To France on D-Day; thence Belgium, Holland, Germany.

1945 Demobbed; joined Hyman Zahl Variety Agency as staff writer.

1946 Joined Ted Kavanagh Associates, a cooperative of writers.
Wrote *Bentley in London* for Australian radio.

1947   Son Nicholas born.

Wrote links for *Beginners Please* (radio), Variety series introducing new performers fresh out of the forces; producer Roy Speer.

Met Frank Muir.

1948   *Take It From Here* (radio), written with Frank for ten years. We collaborated for seventeen years, writing film scripts, stage revues, TV series; appeared together on panel games, including *My Music* (radio and TV), *My Word!* (radio), *What's My Line* (TV), *The Name's the Same* (TV).

Wrote Bernard Braden programmes (radio and TV).

Wrote links for *Show Time* (radio), Variety programme showcasing newcomers; presenter Dick Bentley; first broadcasts included Bob Monkhouse; producer Roy Speer.

Starlight Hour (radio), sixty-minute series; written with Frank and Sid Colin; starred Alfred Marks, Benny Hill, Geraldo and orchestra.

1949   *Third Division* (radio), written with Frank, with contributions from Paul Dehn. First comedy show allowed on 'highbrow' Third Programme; included *Balham: Gateway to the South*; with Robert Beatty, Peter Sellers, Harry Secombe, Michael Bentine, Benny Hill, Robert Moreton; producer Pat Dixon.

1950   *Breakfast with Braden* (radio), written with Frank; live Saturday mornings; with Bernard Braden, Barbara Kelly, Benny Lee, Pearl Carr, Nat Temple and orchestra. Series became *Bedtime with Braden*, then *Between-times with Braden*.

1951   *Here's Television* (TV), one-off, one-hour sketch show, written with Frank. First programme to send up TV.

Maggie born.

Gently, Bentley (radio), written with Frank. Performed in Australia on ABC, with Australian cast.

1952 *In All Directions* (radio); the first radio comedy series the BBC allowed to be aired without a script. Frank and I devised and edited it into coherence. Starred Peter Ustinov and Peter Jones, who played all the characters and most of the sound effects.

London Laughs (revue), Adelphi Theatre; with Jimmy Edwards, Tony Hancock, Vera Lynn (later Shirley Bassey); ran two years.

1953 *Barbara with Braden* (TV), written with Frank; with Barbara Kelly, Bernard Braden; producer Brian Tesler.

The Name's the Same (radio), panel game; with Frank, myself, Fanny Craddock and Frances Day. In 1954, it won National Radio Award as the Most Promising New Programme. Programme didn't make it to 1955.

1954 *And So to Bentley* (TV), b/w live; written with Frank; with Dick Bentley, Peter Sellers, Bill Fraser, Jackie Collins.

Between-times with Braden (radio); written with Frank.

1955 *Bath-night with Braden* (TV), b/w, live; written with Frank; with Bernard Braden; produced by Brian Tesler.

Began writing sketches, with Frank, for George and Alfred Black's *Blackpool Summer Shows*, continued until 1963. Arthur Haynes starred in one revue.

1956 *Whack-o!* (TV), written with Frank; 63 episodes to 1972, 47 live and b/w. Set in Chiselbury School.

Finkle's Café (radio), 'where the posh squash to nosh', written with Frank. Based on American series, *Duffy's Tavern*, 'where the elite meet to eat'. With Peter Sellers, Sid James, Avril Angers, Kenneth Connor; producer Pat Dixon.

1957 *My Word!* (radio), panel game; other panellists included Nancy Spain, E. Arnot Robertson, Anne Scott James, Antonia Fraser and Dilys Powell. Ran for over thirty years. We published seven books of *My Word!* stories (1974–91).

1960 'Consultants and Advisors, BBC TV Light Entertainment'. Left in 1964. Frank stayed on.

Bottoms Up!, movie version of *Whack-o!*, written with Frank and Michael Pertwee.

Became one of the founder members of The Writers' Guild of Great Britain.

1961 *The Seven Faces of Jim* (TV), written with Frank; introduced Richard Briers and Ronnie Barker to TV.

The Writers' Guild of Great Britain Award for Best Contribution to Light Entertainment.

1962 *More Faces of Jim* (TV), written with Frank.

Brothers in Law (TV), written with Frank and Henry Cecil.

1963 *Mr Justice Duncannon* (TV), written with Frank and Henry Cecil.

1964 *How to Be an Alien* (TV), written and presented with Frank; based on George Mikes' book of the same name.

The Big Noise (TV), b/w; written with Frank; starring Bob Monkhouse.

Hazel Adair and myself joint chairmen of The Writers' Guild.

1965 *My Music* (radio and couple of seasons on TV) panel game; with Frank, myself, Ian Wallace, David Franklin followed by John Amis, chairman Steve Race. Ran till 1993.

1967 *At Last the 1948 Show* (TV), 'Script Referee'.

1968 *The Bliss of Mrs Blossom* (movie); written with Alec Coppel; starring Shirley MacLaine, Richard Attenborough; director Joe McGrath.

Buona Sera, Mrs Campbell (movie), written with Melvin Frank, Sheldon Keller; starring Gina Lollobrigida, Shelley Winters, Lee Grant, Phil Silvers, Peter Lawford, Telly Savalas; Academy Award nomination for Best Original Screenplay.

1969 Wrote *The Best House in London* (movie); starring David Hemmings, George Sanders; director Phillip Saville.

1970 *Every Home Should Have One* (movie), written with Barry Took and starring Marty Feldman.

1971 *The Statue* (movie), written with Alec Coppel; starring David Niven.

1973 *Looks Familiar* (TV), nostalgia panel game; wrote and presented 195 episodes to 1987 for Thames TV.
During this time, wrote cartoon sequence of *The Water Babies* (movie). Also wrote, under the name of Nicholas Roy, *Confessions of a Door to Door Salesman* (movie).
You Can't Have Your Kayak and Heat It (book), with Frank; collected *My Word!* stories.

1974 *Upon My Word!* (book), with Frank (*My Word!* stories).
Take My Word for It (book), with Frank (*My Word!* stories).

1977 *It'll Be Alright on the Night* (TV), wrote, selected and presented to 2006. Second *It'll Be Alright on the Night* won Silver Rose of Montreux. Its twenty-nine year run, earned me entry in the *Guinness Book of Records*.

1978 Frank and I jointly won Variety Club Award for Best Radio Personality.

1979 *The Glums* (book), with Frank.

1980 Awarded CBE.
Oh, My Word! (book), with Frank (*My Word!* stories).

1983 Wrote and presented *It'll Be Alright on the Day* (TV); all sport cock-ups pre-Cup Final.

The Complete and Utter My Word! Stories (book), with Frank.

1984 Royal Variety Show (theatre), introduced Robert Dhéry's bell-ringer sketch.

1985 *Coming To You Live* (book), behind-the-scene memories of fifties and sixties Television.

1988 Wrote and presented *In On the Act* (TV), short nostalgia series; with Roy Castle, Bernie Winters and others.

Wrote and presented *Pick of the Pilots* (TV), six episodes; all failed pilot programmes.

Wrote and presented *With Hilarious Consequences* (TV), twenty-one years of Thames Television sitcoms ('It was the best of Thames, it was the worst of Thames').

1989 *You Have My Word* (book), with Frank (*My Word!* stories).

1991 Selected, wrote and presented *Denis Norden's Laughter File* (TV); ran till 2005.

1992 Wrote and presented *Denis Norden's Trailer Cinema* (TV); one-off.

1993 Selected, wrote and presented *Laughter by Royal Command* (TV); based on Royal Variety Shows.

1995 Selected, wrote and presented *40 Years of ITV Laughter* (TV); three sixty-minute programmes.

Wrote and presented *Legends of Light Music* (radio).

1996 Selected, wrote and presented *A Right Royal Song and Dance*, based on Royal Variety Shows.

1999 The Writers' Guild of Great Britain Comedy Award for Lifetime Achievement.

2000 Royal Television Society Lifetime Award.

2006 Wrote and presented *All the Best* (TV); farewell round-up programme.

MOSTLY CINEMAS AND CINE VARIETY

As an insomniac from as far back as I can remember, I have always kept in mind a story I heard about Ronald Knox. At the age of six he was a solemn, clever child but could not sleep at night. When someone asked him, 'What do you think about when you're lying awake?' he replied, 'I think about the past.'

In 1938, age sixteen, having opted for Spanish rather than German at City of London School, I used to spend my free Wednesday afternoons acting as interpreter at a hostel the Salvation Army had set up in Clapton to house refugee children from the Spanish Civil War. In order to keep up with the questions the kids used to ask me, I paid close attention to the war reports from Sefton Delmer, the distinguished foreign correspondent of the *Daily Express*. I had long been attracted by the term 'Foreign Correspondent' and when I noticed that the photographs of Sefton Delmer invariably showed him wearing a belted raincoat with epaulettes, that clinched it. I wrote to him, outlining the marks I had been getting for Conversational Spanish and English Essay and asking whether there was any chance of joining him out there as an apprentice.

A little to my surprise, his reply was favourable. Less surprisingly, the reaction of my parents was not. Reasonably enough, they pointed out the sacrifices they had made to send me to a public school and the strong likelihood of my perishing on some foreign field before I reached seventeen.

As it was impossible for me to go to Spain without their consent, I went into a sulk and decided to leave school anyway. Rather than go on to university, I would start paving the way towards my next-on-the-list ambition, to become a highly paid Hollywood screenwriter.

The only person I could think of who might possibly have some access to Hollywood was the father of a girl I had recently taken out. His name was Sid Hyams, one of three brothers who owned and operated a small chain of London's largest cinemas. He agreed to see me and suggested I come along to his office at the Gaumont State, Kilburn ('Europe's Newest, Largest and Most Luxurious Cinema').

Having learned that the Hyams brothers also owned a film studio, I brought with me the synopses for two screenplays I had roughed out between making the appointment and setting out to meet Mr Sid, as he was called on his own turf; his two brothers being Mr Phil and Mr Mick.

I think he must have had a word with my parents in the interim, because he nodded my manuscripts into an in tray and made a counter-proposal. Before launching into a career as a writer for the cinema, might it not be prudent to spend some time learning the preferences and predilections of cinema audiences? And surely the best way to do that, he ventured, would be to work for a while as a cinema manager.

With that end in mind, he was prepared to put me through a training programme that would leave me conversant with every aspect of the cinema. Starting with a course in looking after the boilers, I would progress to electrician, stagehand, projectionist, member of the front-of-house team, thence to Assistant Manager and, finally, General Manager.

My apprenticeship began at the Gaumont State in 1939, when my blue boiler suit brought my mother close to tears every time she saw me leave the house in it. ('Is this what all the sacrifices have been for?') In 1941, I was transferred from Assistant Manager at the Trocadero, Elephant & Castle, to General Manager at the Gaumont, Watford. A few weeks after I arrived there, our feature film was Alfred Hitchcock's first Hollywood movie, *Foreign Correspondent*. It starred Joel McCrea, wearing a belted raincoat with epaulettes.

The Gaumont Super Cinemas, built by the Hyams brothers, were palaces of Renaissance-style grandeur located in some of the poorest and dreariest parts of London. They included the Troxy, Commercial Road, the Trocadero, Elephant & Castle, the Regal, Edmonton, and the brothers' proudest achievement, the Gaumont State, Kilburn, a 4,000-seater, the largest cinema in Britain ('In Europe!' insisted Mr Phil), with a tower you could see from miles away.

Mr Sid was the quiet, reflective brother, Mr Mick was the youngest, a restlessly energetic go-getter and Mr Phil was the power-house, loving the limelight and constantly proclaiming the role their Super Cinemas played in furnishing drab suburbs with buildings that reawoke magical expectations.

The larger cinemas in the chain featured Cine Variety, combining films with three or four top-line Variety acts. In addition to the two big general release movies and the stage show, you were offered a newsreel, an organ solo and a cartoon or 'short', not to mention the trailers. Sometimes the stage element would be in the form of a touring revue, a circus, a pantomime or even, though rarely, an opera.

CLIPS FROM A LIFE

All this for sixpence. Occasionally the full programme lasted over four hours, every minute of which, Mr Phil would warn his managers, had to live up to those magical expectations.

To a great extent, this meant observing certain rules of showmanship that are now considered irrelevant. 'Never open the curtains on a white screen' was one I remember, and today's disregard for it can still irk me occasionally. Mr Phil held the view that allowing that large white oblong to glare at our patrons before they saw it occupied by a film image impeded their passage from reality into illusion, in those days the main reason for going to the pictures. We used to protect the illusion by making sure the curtains in front of the screen were closed when we projected the preliminary Censor's Certificate, never revealing the screen until it was filled by the MGM lion or the Universal biplane and our patrons were well on their way to Hollywood.

While I was serving my time as Assistant Boilerman at the Gaumont State, we were sometimes told to raise the temperature inside the cinema in order to promote the sales of ice cream and soft drinks. It would generally happen when the feature film was set in the tropics or the desert and it always resulted, I was told, in a noticeable rise in sales.

When I came to the Trocadero as Assistant Manager, one of my more difficult duties was to superintend these sales. In addition to my less than perfect grasp of the monetary side, I had the daily responsibility of nominating the usherettes charged with carrying the ice cream trays.

When fully loaded with tubs and wafer-bars, the trays were a considerable weight, so it was a job the girls hated. To alleviate this, we had instituted an alphabetical rota system to ensure the work was shared out fairly.

For me, the snag in this system was that, as P. A. (known as Bill) Fowler, the General Manager explained, a girl could be excused ice cream tray duty and the rota bypassed if it happened to be her 'time of the month'. Accordingly, at the daily general assembly in the main foyer before the doors opened, when all the front of house staff would be inspected for clean uniforms and fingernails, I would consult my rota-list and read out, 'Miss Robinson, your turn for the front stalls ice cream tray.'

Not infrequently, Miss Robinson would answer, 'Not today, sir. Time of the month.'

I would consult my list again. 'But, Miss Robinson, you said that two weeks ago.'

Like as not, she would fix me with that bold Elephant & Castle stare and answer, 'So?'

Barely eighteen years old and wearing my father's dinnersuit, I was aware – as were they all – that I did not know enough about the mechanics of the matter to pursue it. 'All right, Miss Robinson. Excused ice cream tray.'

The Hyams brothers enjoyed their reputation as 'the last of the great showmen' and never neglected an opportunity to live up to it. Of the three, Mr Phil was the most flamboyant and forceful. A tall, heavy-set man with hunched shoulders, he always seemed to be in a hurry, glowering and snapping out his words, although at unexpected times he would suddenly bestow a surprisingly friendly grin. The eldest of the brothers who had given London its most spectacular suburban cinemas, he acted on snap decisions and hunches, most of which worked out as anticipated. And while there would be some fearsome scowling when they failed, he would still flash the occasional conspiratorial grin.

I liked him enormously and jumped at the chance of attending his 100th birthday party, at which he sat in a very fancy wheelchair attended by two trim, short-skirted nurses, like old Mr Grace in *Are You Being Served?*. When I commented on this, I was given the same grin as sixty-odd years ago.

One of Mr Phil's dicta that he and his brothers managed to live up to most of the time was, 'Always give an audience everything they expected to see plus something they weren't expecting.' Sometimes he would couch it as 'If they've paid sixpence for their seat and you give them nine-pennorth of entertainment, you can hold your head up with anybody in any business.'

The other lesson he taught me was 'Never be slowed down by a cup of tea.' What this meant in practice was learning how to drink a cup of tea while it was still scalding hot, never wasting valuable time waiting for it to cool down.

Among the Gaumont State's wondrous new technical amenities was the 'rising mike' system, a set of microphones positioned at various places underneath the stage floor. Operated by remote control, each of them could rise silently into view through a small hidden trapdoor to whatever heights had been preselected, then just as silently slide down out of sight again, leaving the floor of the stage as flat and smooth as before.

Soon enough, that inconspicuousness was to provide its own hazards. I recall one of the big dance bands that played a week there when I was a stagehand. For reasons I never discovered, the bubbly blonde vocalist who was one of the band's main attractions missed the rehearsal call on Monday morning and arrived only just in time for the opening show in the afternoon.

She bounded on stage for her first number dressed in a long, full skirt and, smiling radiantly, stood directly over the little trap door through which the rising mike slid upwards …

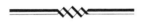

In 1939 the next Royal Command Performance was due to take place in November and, for the first time, the Hyams brothers were being given a chance to produce it.

Their plans for it were typically ambitious. It would be staged at the Gaumont State and, with the intention of bringing Hollywood to Kilburn, Eddie Cantor would be flown over to compère a bill that would include Shirley Temple, a song-and-dance duet by Judy Garland and Mickey Rooney, comedy from Laurel and Hardy and a sketch by the cast of MGM's enormously successful series of Andy Hardy films. In addition, there would be lavish numbers from four West End musicals and contributions from whoever was topping the bill at the Palladium.

For the finale, we would see Deanna Durbin, alone on a darkened stage and lit only by a pin-spot, singing 'Ave Maria', while 400 choirboys, each bearing a lighted candle, would descend from the upper circle to the stage on specially built ramps attached to the side walls of the vast auditorium.

That was the scene I was looking forward to most. But then, along came 3 September …

The Trocadero, Elephant & Castle, where I graduated to Assistant Manager in 1940, had one of the most elaborate interiors in the Hyams brothers' cinema chain. The auditorium, seating 3,500, was resplendently Italianate, sumptuously decorated, the marble columns and pink mirrors extending to the waiting rooms and loos.

On the second Sunday after I arrived, the General Manager left me in sole charge, a responsibility I shouldered fairly adequately until we came to the stage show.

Sunday nights were Amateur Talent Night and by the second performance, it was plain that things were slipping beyond my control.

On the stage, a thin blonde girl was trying to get through 'Alice Blue Gown', to the accompaniment of Bobby Pagan at the organ, but the audience was becoming restive. As I watched helplessly from the back of the stalls, the whistles and barracking grew louder and the girl's voice was becoming ever more quavery.

How it would have ended I don't know, but I suddenly became aware that a bulky figure in a heavy overcoat and with a pushed-back black Homburg on his head was standing beside me. It was Mr Phil. 'What's happening? What's going on?'

I could only gesture, 'I'm sorry. They just won't – I don't quite –'

But he was gone, striding down the aisle towards the steps that led up to the side of the stage. Mounting them, he came to the mike and motioned to the girl and Bobby for silence. As the noise from the audience died away, he stood centre-stage and, taking off his black Homburg, addressed them. 'You all know who I am.'

Indeed they did. Mr Phil often took the opportunity to talk to an audience from the stage and sometimes he would stop by the six-penny queue to solicit their opinions individually. Tonight, they gave him an encouraging round of applause. He stilled them.

'I want to tell you something that happened here a few years back. I dropped into the Troc, as I often do, but this time I came in through the stage door. And as I came up the steps, I heard the sound of sobbing coming from one of the dressing rooms. I went to investigate and there sat a young girl crying her eyes out. I said, "What's the matter?" and she said, "It's them. That audience. I can't do it. I just can't face them. I'm sorry."

'So I said to her, "Listen. I'll tell you about the Elephant & Castle audiences. Yes, they're hard. They're the toughest audience in the country. But let me assure you of one thing. However hard they are, they're fair. They'll give you a chance. Will you take my word?"

'She nodded and, sure enough, she went on. And, ladies and gentlemen, may I tell you that girl's name? That girl's name was Gracie Fields.'

There was a respectful silence. Then from the audience came a yell of appreciation and a storm of applause. Mr Phil nodded to the girl, gave Bobby the go-ahead sign, descended the steps and rejoined me at the back of the stalls. The audience heard the girl out in a silence that was almost reverent and rewarded her with another vociferous round of applause.

When we had retired to the office to inspect the night's takings, I ventured, 'That was a wonderful story, Mr Phil. I'll remember that.'

He gave me that sudden, unnerving grin. 'Pack of lies.'

A prodigious amount of eating went on during the early evening programmes in thirties and forties suburban cinemas. Mothers with basketfuls of food would pick up their children from school and feed them their tea while they were all watching the movie. The consequent chomping, munching, slurping, rustling and muttered instructions was often so distracting to other patrons, someone at one of our weekly managers' meetings suggested dividing the stalls into eating and non-eating areas, as some cinemas went on to do with smoking and non-smoking.

Nor did the families dutifully deposit their detritus in the rubbish bins provided, as happens (sometimes) with later generations. The result was that when the cleaners came in at the end of the day to vacuum the stalls' carpeting, their first task was to pick up the overlay of eggshell, orange peel, apple cores, biscuit wrappers and the scattered assortment of bread crusts which, thanks to the surrounding darkness, children had found it so easy to leave uneaten. These were in addition to the ever-present topping of monkey nut shells, which always made walking between the empty rows sound like a giant eating celery.

It was, though, another measure of the way in which going to the pictures in those days was regarded as a family experience. Indeed, there were many mothers who used their local cinema as a crèche, a warm and safe place to deposit their young whenever there was a need to offload them for a few hours. I still treasure the memory of a small boy tugging at the sleeve of one of our tall Trocadero doormen to ask, 'Please, Mister. Mum says what time is the big picture over three times?'

The great majority of men wore hats of one kind or another in those days, placing them carefully on their laps when they sat in the cinema. As it was also a time when cigarette smoking was so prevalent as to be practically compulsory, Frank Muir and I found great satisfaction many years later in combining the two habits for one of the many Sherlock Holmes pastiches we wrote back then.

'Something else I observed, Watson, was that our quarry had recently been to the cinema?'

'Good Heavens, Holmes, how did you discern that?'

'There was ash in the crown of his trilby.'

In forties cinema-going, there were more scenes of a sexual nature enacted in the audience than on the screen. B-movie scenes that were played in shadow or darkness were the most conducive to back-row action and I have sometimes wondered whether that might account for the prevalence of 'film noir' during that decade.

It was an era when the local picture-house was about the only place that offered affectionately disposed couples both warmth and darkness, particularly the back row, known among the GIs as Hormone Alley. None of the theatres I worked in had installed the special banquette-style 'Couples Seats', a purpose-built facility that was often a feature of North of England cinemas, but every usher and usherette on the Hyams Brothers circuit was instructed to exercise discretion when shining their torch along that area.

Among the more venturesome males of the period, a body of back-row folk-wisdom had gradually developed, some of its tips more helpful than others. Of the only two I remember, one was the initiatory manoeuvre that could be described as 'slide of hand', while the other strongly recommended beginning the proceedings by kissing the nape of her neck. Not only was it believed to promote arousal, it also allowed you to watch the picture at the same time.

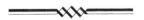

When I arrived at the Trocadero, the General Manager was Bill Fowler, a large, easy-going man with huge hands and amused eyes. He was unfailingly forbearing with me, allowing me completely free rein except on one point. At five o'clock every evening he would go up to his office, lock the door and I had to make sure no one on any account disturbed him. At half past five I had to go round to the side-door of the adjoining Rockingham pub and collect 'Bill Fowler's usual', a quarter bottle of Scotch. Concealing this under my jacket, I would return to the cinema and knock softly on his office door. It would open just wide enough for his hand to take the bottle from me.

At a quarter past six, he would reappear, in evening dress, freshly shaven, good-humoured and ready to take his place in the foyer to welcome incoming patrons. 'I was born three double Scotches under par,' was the only confidence I had from him about our nightly procedure. 'If anything happens to the Rockingham, stay clear of me.'

As things worked out, I had been transferred to the Gaumont, Watford, by the time the Blitz started in earnest, the Rockingham got hit and the wartime whisky shortage began to bite. I can only report that Bill Fowler continued to turn up at all the managers' weekly meetings, as good-humouredly imperturbable as ever and still surveying the world with an expression of private amusement.

It was an afternoon in June 1940 and a two-thirds full house at the Trocadero, Elephant & Castle, was under my sole command, Bill Fowler having decided to take a day off. So when the telephone call came from Head Office I had to deal with it on my own.

The voice at the other end was both grim and urgent. 'The news has just come through that France has surrendered. That means England is on its own, so you'd better let the audience know straightaway.' I quickly alerted the projection room to stand by and hurried into the auditorium.

Making my way down the side of the stalls to the door leading into the back-stage area, I reached the organ pit and, from there, phoned projection to stop the film and bring up the houselights. Then, eighteen years old and dimly aware this was some kind of historic moment, I pressed the organ's Up button and ascended with it to stage level.

A spotlight hit me as soon as I came into view. With a preliminary cough to make sure the mike was working, I said, 'Ladies and gentlemen, I have to inform you that France has fallen and Britain is now fighting the War alone.'

I paused, uncertain how to continue. There was a moment of complete silence, then from somewhere at the back came a solitary shout that was immediately taken up by the rest of the audience. 'Put the bleeding picture back on.' As the shouting increased, I signalled the projection box, the houselights went down and the picture was resumed.

When, many years later, I described this incident to Dilys Powell, soon after she joined *My Word!*, her immediate response was totally characteristic. 'What was the picture?'

Fortunately, its title was difficult to forget. 'It was *Old Mother Riley in Society.*'

She nodded understandingly. 'Well, there you are,' she said. 'Arthur Lucan. He really was very good.'

In the years before the Clean Air Act, fog could be a cinema-going hazard. On the Hyams Brothers' circuit, whenever there was a particularly dense one, a commissionaire would go up and down the outside queue shouting, 'Owing to the fog penetrating the hall, the clearness of the picture cannot be guaranteed.'

This was not a universally followed procedure. Indeed, a cinema in Norwood, known locally as 'Ikey's Bug Hole', would put out a placard proclaiming, 'It's clearer inside.'

After one of his appearances on *Looks Familiar*, Larry Adler told me that his earliest London date had been in Cine Variety at the Troxy, Commercial Road, another of the Hyams Brothers' cinemas. Nobody had warned him that it was a custom at the Troxy to allow the first row of the stalls to be occupied by nursing mothers, their prams in front of them. Even more disconcertingly, when they were feeding their babies, they would turn themselves sideways on to the stage and continue watching from that position. It presented performers with a spectacle Larry had never encountered before or since.

At the Trocadero, we had a 'Barred List', a not very extensive assortment of minor miscreants whose descriptions and (rarely) photographs were pinned on the inside of the cashier's window for easy reference.

Among the more persistent offenders was 'Tossoff Kate', a mild-mannered, middle-aged lady with a greasy black fringe. If she managed to evade the cashier's scrutiny, she was still fairly easy to spot as her line of work necessitated constantly changing her seat. Moving from row to row, she would, I discovered, adjust her fees to match the seat prices she found herself in. While offering the same service all over the cinema, she charged more for it in the one-and-nines than she did in the sixpennies.

I found this graduated tariff rather admirable and would have liked to put some questions to her about her specialised trade. Had she found, for instance, that one type of movie was better for business than others? Did the contents of the newsreel affect customer demand? Did takings tend to peak during the trailers?

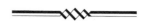

During my time as a Cinema Manager, none of the illicit practices I had to contend with proved more intractable than what became known as the 'Untorn Tickets Fiddle', 'fiddle' being the forties word for 'scam'.

When you bought a ticket at the cinema box office in those days, the cashier receiving your money would push a button on the Automaticket machine in front of her and up through a little metal trapdoor would pop a numbered ticket, differently coloured for the various prices.

You took this ticket to the door of the stalls or circle, where a uniformed member of the front of house staff would tear it in two, handing you one half and, using a bodkin, thread the half he retained on to a length of string.

At the end of each day, the ticket strings would be collected, placed in a sack and dispatched to a place in Crediton, Devon, where Entertainment Tax officials would, I presumed, count them and check their numbers against those shown on the Automaticket machine. (How anybody had the patience, let alone the eyesight, for this task I never discovered.)

The flaw in the system was this: ninety-nine per cent of patrons on receiving their half of the ticket would let it flutter to the floor once they had entered the auditorium's darkness. The cleaning staff would, of course, vacuum up the discarded half-tickets the following morning – but not before certain members of staff with a mercenary turn of mind had scooped up a few and pocketed them.

Now the fiddle came into play. The next time one of them was allocated ticket-tearing duties, he – in practically all the cases I came across, it was a 'he' – would take up his position at the stalls or circle door with a quantity of his collected half-tickets secreted somewhere nearby. Careful to select patrons who were engaged in conversation, or were in other ways inattentive, he would take their proffered ticket and, with a show of tearing it in half, 'palm' it and hand them back one of the half-tickets from his secret cache.

Later in the day he would take his collection of untorn tickets to the girl in the box office – again, they were practically always girls – and she would dispose of them one at a time to the next lot of patrons arriving at her desk; generally on the pretext that it had been handed back by someone who had mistakenly asked for too many, something that happened frequently enough to be unremarkable. At the end of the day, the pair would split the take, in what proportions I never found out, but over the course of weeks, the two of them could net a tidy amount.

They were always careful not to make their substitutions when the manager or anybody supervisory was about, so it was a difficult operation to police. At the Hyams Brothers weekly meeting of managers we would discuss ways of getting on top of it, sometimes going to the lengths of using 'dummy' patrons. We finally had to agree to concen-trate on the scheme's main weakness, which was the degree of com-plicity it required between female cashier and male ticket-taker. With this in mind, we paid close attention to any such pairings, keeping a special eye out for the emotional outbursts the stress of that kind of relationship could lead to. Occasionally this watchfulness would turn up a culprit, but not often.

All in all, it was a fiddle we never even came close to mastering. In fact, I have it on good authority that, to a lesser degree, it's still being played today.

At the State, Kilburn, my training as a projectionist included operating a Stelmar spotlight during the stage shows. As the 'spot room', a little space high up in the cinema's roof, was above the projection booth, manipulating the bulky Stelmar's powerful white beam to capture one of the tiny figures capering on the stage far below was a singularly empowering experience for a teenager.

And there were circumstances when one's prowess could really be put to the test. If a performer suddenly decided to make an unrehearsed entrance from the wings, it needed something special in the way of reaction speed and accuracy of aim to make sure he was spotlit the moment he appeared and didn't have to take his first few steps on-stage unnoticed.

Most satisfying of all were the occasions when I was called on to help bring about an affecting finish to a sentimental song. To achieve this direct assault on the audience's emotions, nothing worked better than having the stage lighting slowly fade while, gradually and imperceptibly, I dwindled my spotlight's circle down till it became no more than a pin of light on the singer's face. Then, as the last note died, my headphones would relay the Stage Manager's whispered 'Dead Blackout' and, 'snap!' – all was darkness.

A second of deep silence, then – if everyone concerned had done it right – up would come the roaring applause. I would hear the Stage Manager's urgent 'Full Up White!', and it would be 'snap!' again as the whole stage became ablaze with light.

Umpteen years later, when David Bernstein and I planned our yet-to-be-staged 'Festival of Schmaltz', we agreed this was a moment that had to be included.

The week the Trocadero offered a full-scale circus as its on-stage attraction was a unique one in many ways. The first problem was finding suitable accommodation for all the performers and animals in wartime South-East London. This our never-fazed Stage Manager, Jim Pitman, accomplished successfully until it came to the question of housing the three 'forest-bred lions'.

It was wintertime and their trainer refused point-blank to even consider housing them anywhere outdoors. After being turned down by every warehouse and factory in the neighbourhood, Jim was driven to keeping their cages in the back-stage area, flush up against the rear wall.

When a boilerman experienced the heart-stopping sensation of a large, furry paw silently reaching out to him while he was going from one side of this darkened area of the stage to another, I had notices hastily printed warning staff and visitors to exercise caution when crossing the stage.

What made this makeshift arrangement really memorable, however, was that we were showing an MGM movie that week. Every time the film's opening came on screen and MGM's Leo emitted his trademark roars, from somewhere behind him came a trio of answering roars.

It impressed audiences no end, while Jim and I enjoyed some time-wasting sessions trying to guess what the visitors were saying to Leo.

Among the acts we played in Variety or Cine Variety, one that has lodged himself securely in my memory is Olgo, the Mathematical Genius. He was a refugee from Nazi Germany, a charming little man who could square any three-figure number instantaneously in his head.

Unfortunately, first house Monday, when he explained his special powers and asked for volunteers to call out three-figure numbers for him to square, nobody in the audience had the faintest idea what he was talking about. His request was met by a silence, which grew and grew. As manager, I had to be out front during the first performance of every programme, so I hastily shouted, 'Three hundred and forty-six', to which he snapped out the answer while I hurried over to the other side of the auditorium and shouted, 'Seven hundred and nineteen.' I kept this up until someone in the stalls grasped the idea and called out, 'Nine hundred and ninety-nine.' Other members of the audience caught on and shouted their own numbers out and soon the act took on a brisk pace and the Mathematical Genius was beaming.

As the week went on, I had to break the ice in this fashion for him at the start of every performance, with the organist taking over my role on my day off. Audiences never failed to pick up on it and, as far as I could verify, his answers were always correct. It was a rare talent, though I sometimes wonder how he adjusted to the introduction of the pocket calculator.

Another sharply etched memory is the unusually amusing con-juror who turned up for one of our Sunday Night Amateur Talent competitions at the Gaumont, Watford. While I was watching him from the back of the stalls, two uniformed military policemen appeared at my side. They told me that he was an Army deserter and would I give them permission to go backstage, in order to arrest him? As we made our way together down the side-aisle to the pass door, I could see him watching us from the stage, although his patter did not falter. Arrived in the prompt corner, the redcaps agreed to let him finish his act and, while we waited, told me that he had been on the run for more than six months, picking up money to live on by going from one talent show to another across the home counties.

Well aware we were waiting there for him, he brought his performance to a smooth finish and as he came off-stage held his hands out good-naturedly. Snapping handcuffs on them, one of the redcaps said, 'Okay, Houdini, let's see you get out of these.'

I had been secretly hoping he would make his exit on the other side of the stage, where a panic-bolt door would have taken him straight out into the High Street and on to a passing bus.

Another memory that has remained undimmed is the act performed by Edna Squire Brown. She was a dignified lady who did a genteel striptease, employing trained white doves. They would flutter above her, only alighting on her whenever and wherever concealment was required.

Although it didn't happen on my watch, I was warned about certain occupants of the sixpenny seats who used to turn up for her Saturday night performances carrying packets of birdseed.

If there was such a thing as a 'resident' band on the Hyams Brothers circuit during the time I served there, it was the one conducted by

Teddy Joyce. An almost forgotten name now, he was a Hyams Brothers' favourite and hugely popular with South London audiences.

For my money, he led the best stage band I ever saw, with the possible exception of Jack Hylton's. But while Hylton himself did little more than stand in front of the band looking benevolent, Joyce was at all times the centre of attention, using the band as background to his own antics, very much as Cab Calloway did in America.

A Canadian, tall, slim, narrow-faced, slicked-back black hair, Joyce's customary costume of high-waisted, tight-fitting black dress trousers and equally tight-fitting black bolero jacket made his legs seem endless. He would put this to good effect in his snake-hips style of dancing, particularly when, as he often did, he performed alone on a darkened stage in front of a white screen, dropped in to mask off the band. Lit only by a small spotlight shining up from the centre of the footlights, the silhouette of his undulating figure would be projected on the screen behind him, elongating to giant size as he advanced, diminishing to human proportions as he retreated.

It was as skilful as it was effective. For another of his showpieces, the band left their instruments on the rostrum, came downstage and formed a tight semicircle around Joyce, who was seated on a low stool, his back to the audience. The band thrust out their hands towards him, revealing that they were all wearing white gloves, each finger of which had a thick, black line along the top. The picture it presented was that he was seated at the keyboard of a three-rank organ. Joyce would then complete the picture by 'playing' their outstretched hands, each touch producing a sonorous hummed response. It was an illusion I have never seen duplicated, its music so carefully orchestrated and rehearsed, the effect was irresistible.

He was full of novel presentation ideas, though not all of them worked out as planned. I'm thinking of a surprise opening he devised for one of his early visits to the State, Kilburn. The audience heard the Teddy Joyce signature tune, 'The World is Waiting for the Sunrise', coming from behind the closed front curtains. But when the curtains rose, the stage was empty. Then, from somewhere above the top of the proscenium arch, the band slowly descended into view, seated on a platform hung on wires, its leading edge decorated by a bank of plywood clouds.

Slowly, if a little fitfully, they came down, their unusually spectacular entrance winning an appreciative round of applause. Then, about four feet from the floor, the platform began to tilt sideways ...

A firm favourite with the Trocadero's patrons was Jack Doyle billed as 'The Singing Boxer'. Less than highly successful in the ring, he toured in Variety, singing sentimental Irish ballads, thus inspiring Tommy Trinder's observation that 'Instead of singing Mother Machree, Jack Doyle'd do better fighting her.'

On the Trocadero stage Jack usually appeared with his wife, the sexy Mexican film star Movita. They would perform romantic duets, always ending with 'by popular request', the 'Come, Come, I Love You Only' ballad from *The Chocolate Soldier*. This they would sing standing face to face, gazing into each other's eyes, and, on the final fervent 'Come, Come!', clutch each other convulsively, groin to groin. It was a finish that never failed to stir the Troc audience.

I had never heard of the touring revue that was to be our next on-stage attraction at the Trocadero. It bore the unpromising title of *Red Hot & Blue Moments* and this was its first London date after going round the provinces for months. Consequently, when I found myself a seat in the stalls the following Monday afternoon to watch it, I knew nothing about its principal comedian, Sid Field.

No point in making a meal of this. From the moment Sid Field made his first entrance, I was entranced. For the rest of the week, I not only watched every one of his three-a-day performances, I came in on my day off to see two more of them.

It's an abiding shame that no trace of his quality remains on film. Do not, I implore you, assess him on the basis of what you see of him in *London Town*. Shot in an empty studio without an audience, his reproduced stage sketches are given a stilted, not to say embalmed, look, offering no hint of the delicacy of his comic touch.

Months later, whenever I came home on leave, I would go to see him in his hugely successful revues at the Prince of Wales Theatre. He repeated several of the sketches I had first seen him perform in *Red Hot & Blue Moments*. But when it came to his portrayal of 'Slasher Green', the archetypal spiv, nothing in the West End could match the additional ingredient the Trocadero lent to it.

Hobbling awkwardly in an ankle-length, wide-shouldered black overcoat, knotted white scarf and turned-down black trilby, he would wring tears of laughter from the packed Elephant & Castle audiences, most of them dressed in long black, wide-shouldered overcoats, knotted white scarves and turned-down black trilbies.

Phil Park, for many years the organist at the Regal, Edmonton, was more than just a gifted musician. A superb showman at the organ, he also composed much of the music for some of the London Palladium's most successful revues and brought to the Wurlitzer a keen grasp of technical innovation.

In a bid to replace the narrow bench on which organists sat, occasionally sliding sideways along it to reach one of the end foot-pedals, he sought a means by which they could remain in one position. He came up with the idea of a seat fashioned along the lines of that used in boats by solo scullers. It consisted of two cunningly shaped halves, one for each buttock, connected by a central spring. Seated on this, the occupant was no longer obliged to slide his whole body sideways, he merely stretched out a leg.

A prototype was built and, a few weeks later, the Monday first house audience heard the opening notes of Phil's signature tune and saw him rise slowly into view upon his new seating arrangement. Then, as the music was reaching a crescendo, it suddenly stopped, and in its place came a shrill cry of agony.

As Phil himself good-humouredly agreed afterwards, the strength of the spring appeared to need something of a rethink. He never entrusted himself to it again, however, leaving his invention to live on in cinema organ folklore as 'The Nutcracker Seat'.

My earliest venture into what I suppose, stretching it a bit, you could call 'writing for the screen' was at the Trocadero, when I found myself providing the words for the slides that were projected on the iron curtain during the organ interludes.

In those days, the Mighty Organ was a popular element in the cinema-going ritual, though admittedly, it could drive some people to distraction. (Graham Greene called it 'the world's wet mouth drooling'.) At the time, it was the loudest musical noise around, always in danger of sounding overwrought, bombastic or syrupy, but in the hands of a Quentin MacLean or a Sidney Torch it would offer a pleasurable quarter of an hour.

The organ interlude's place on a cinema's list of attractions may well have been prompted by the prevailing Fire Regulations. These demanded that the proscenium-size fireproof curtain separating the stage from the auditorium (the 'iron') be lowered at least once during each programme.

It was sometimes a laboriously slow process so, as the iron descended, up from the circular pit in front of it, to the strains of the organist's signature tune, would rise the mighty Wurlitzer. (There has never been a better illustration of the phrase 'to come up smiling' than the cinema organist.)

The organ itself could verge on the spectacular. Shaped like an enormous, intricately fluted jelly mould, its panels were illuminated from within in constantly changing pastel colours that nicely set off its occupant's white dinner jacket.

As for the content of the interlude, that would take the form of either a recital or a sing along (in those days known as 'community singing'). One of the most frequently requested items in the repertoire was 'In a Persian Market', with its tinkling bells and dramatic cymbal clashes. Another crowd-pleaser was 'Coronation Scot', in which some organists would ostentatiously hold their hands above their heads and use only the foot-pedals to play the opening 'puffing out of the station' bit. It invariably drew a round of applause.

Whatever the music, it would be illustrated, and occasionally enhanced, by a succession of slides projected on the iron. These would bear text appropriate to the musical theme and we ordered them from Morgan's Slides of Gray's Inn Road at a cost of ninepence per slide.

One week at the Trocadero, Bobby Pagan, 'popular broadcasting organist', didn't have time to write the linking text for his interlude and asked me to help out. It was a medley entitled 'Memories of Albert Ketèlbey' and as my knowledge of the composer was something less than sketchy, I suggested to Bobby that I convert the recital into a sing along by fitting words to all the melodies. I feel it is to my credit that I can recall nothing of this desecration, except that I opened one of his flimsier pieces with the words, 'When Ketèlbey's feeling bright, / He will write Something light. / Dainty dances, melodies sweet, / Making your feet tap to their beat.' Nevertheless, Bobby was pleased with the package and recommended it to the other organists on the circuit. So, within weeks, my writings were achieving a kind of syndication, displayed to audiences in Edmonton, Commercial Road, Norwood, Kilburn and far-flung Watford.

I continued working in this now vanished area of literary endeavour until my managerial duties left no time for it. This was despite the fact that, in addition to my shameful ignorance of musical matters, I was so totally unaware of copyright laws, I never even considered applying for permission whenever I set about parodying current popular songs. We found these were what went down best with wartime audiences, so I wrote umpteen of them, without ever receiving one reprimand from any publisher. As always happens, the only example Time has not scrubbed from my memory is one hardly worth preserving, a version of an almost totally forgotten 'Last Waltz' of the period, 'Stay in My Arms, Cinderella'. Its new words were projected against a background photograph of Neville Chamberlain and began 'Stay on my arm, Umbrella'.

Perhaps the reason why that one has remained with me is that it was, I believe, the first time I saw an audience laugh at something I had made up.

An incident that revealed the Wurlitzer could occasionally be something less than Mighty happened at the Troxy one afternoon when I was acting as relief manager. At the end of the interlude, the organ's lift mechanism failed and the organist had to remain perched up in the air during the ensuing film, while all available staff searched the cinema for the winch handle that would wind him down manually.

The bomb that destroyed the Holborn Empire fell on the night of 11 May 1941. Probably the best loved of London's Variety theatres, next in prestige to the Palladium as a showcase for top-line stars, it was also the annual home of the children's patriotic Christmas classic, *Where the Rainbow Ends*. For me, it was where I gained my first glimpse of such favourites as Max Miller, Teddy Brown, Max Wall, Jimmy James, Caryll and Mundy, Hutch, Eddie Gray. (For descriptive matter on such imperishables, I refer you to Roy Hudd's excellent *Cavalcade of Variety Acts* and John Fisher's equally loving *Funny Way to be a Hero*.)

With the Holborn Empire gone, its long-time Musical Director, Sidney Caplan, moved to the Watford Town Hall Music Hall, where I was General Manager. Sidney was not an easy man to get close to but if you caught him at the right moments, his stories of the Holborn Empire's great names could be fascinating, especially if, like me, you believed Variety to have been the most pleasurable of public entertainments.

After I had wrung a sizeable number of these reminiscences from him – it entailed sieving out a certain amount of malice – I asked him whether he would be prepared to relate some of them on radio, using gramophone records of the artists concerned by way of illustration. After obtaining his slightly grudging consent, I contacted Anna Instone, the Head of the BBC's Gramophone Record Department at the time, and asked her if she would be interested in putting on six radio half-hours entitled *A History of the Holborn Empire*, with none other than the theatre's Musical Director as narrator, the script to be supplied by a newcomer to the broadcasting medium.

Thus was born my first BBC radio series. Transmitted early 1942, all that remains of it is a mention somewhere in the archives of *Radio Times*.

During the early forties I did some RAF training in Blackpool, where I discovered the cinemas were in the habit of interrupting the main feature sharp at 4 p.m. every day, regardless of what point in the storyline had been reached, in order to serve afternoon tea. The houselights would go up and trays bearing cups of tea would be passed along the rows. After fifteen minutes, the lights would dim down again, the trays would be passed back and the film would resume. Anyone unwise enough to be sitting at the end of a row at that point could be left holding stacks of trays and empty cups.

When I began my stint as General Manager of the Gaumont, Watford, they had only recently discontinued the practice of serving afternoon teas while the film was still showing. The cessation of this amenity was, I soon discovered, much regretted by various members of the front of house staff. Prior to my arrival, the Gaumont's patrons could, by giving their order to one of the ushers or usherettes on their way in, enjoy a choice of four types of afternoon tea. Without taking their eyes off the big picture, they could partake of a plain pot of tea, a pot of tea with a sandwich, a pot of tea with a piece of cake, or a Full Cinema Tea, which consisted of a pot of tea with both sandwich and piece of cake.

A few of the more observant front of house staff had noted that many patrons who ordered the Full Cinema Tea did not consume both the accompanying items. If they ate the sandwich, they left the cake; if they ate the cake, they left the sandwich.

As a consequence, before certain ushers and usherettes returned a tray to the cinema café, they would lift off any unconsumed item and stow it behind the small velvet curtains that masked the back-stalls radiators. The next time a patron asked for a Full Cinema Tea, they would relay the order to the kitchen as a plain pot of tea, make up the deficiencies from the supplies they had secreted behind the radiator curtains, accept payment for the Full Cinema Tea and pocket the difference.

Our wartime cinema-goers would sit there in the darkness, munching on a sandwich and/or cake which had sometimes been gathering dust under a radiator for days and, to the best of my knowledge, we had not received one complaint.

Rarely were there any empty seats in places of entertainment during wartime. There were, however, certain differences in cinema-going habits. At the larger inner city houses, such as the Trocadero or the State, Kilburn, audiences went to see a particular film or a particular star in the accompanying Variety show. At the Gaumont, Watford, on the other hand, I found that, irrespective of what was showing, they liked to go to the same cinema every week, on the same day, at the same time and, not infrequently, many of them expected to sit in the same seat.

To meet this need, we had inaugurated a kind of unofficial Advance Booking System. It included me being in the foyer as they arrived, welcoming them by name, leading them upstairs to the Circle (most of them preferred the Circle), showing them into the seats that had been kept empty for them and leaving them with a warm 'Enjoy the show.' For their part, if there was any week they couldn't make it, they would punctiliously telephone the cinema and let us know.

But the protocol did not end there. When the programme was over, they would expect me to be in the foyer as they came out, both to let them know if it was raining outside and to receive their reasoned critique of the programme.

For them, it was all part of their weekly cinema-going ritual and I can't deny there were aspects of it that I found equally pleasing. For one thing, I always used to enjoy watching audiences emerge from the darkness after a movie. In those more innocent days, their faces would still have that tranced, slightly dazed look as they struggled to get into their coats, some of them unconsciously adopting the mannerisms of whatever big star they had just been watching.

My other reason was slightly more shady. There was a small cash sum I could draw on for 'Entertaining regular patrons'. What this meant in practice, was delivering an ice cream tub to a few of them during the intermission, 'With the Management's compliments.' As my Ice Cream Sales Account rarely seemed to balance, this could prove very useful for remedying deficiencies.

One mystery I never managed to solve was the inordinate number of ladies' shoes that found their way into the cinema's Lost Property cupboard at the end of each day. My apprenticeship as an usher had shown me how many female patrons would gratefully slip off one or both of their shoes as soon as they'd settled in their seats, while the variety of other items that turned up in the cupboard had demonstrated how the steep rake of the auditorium floor could cause any objects placed under a seat to slide forward beneath the row in front, and sometimes further.

I could understand why the retrieval of some of these might be neglected as not worth the trouble, but shoes? To deepen the mystery further, in all the hours I spent bidding a managerial farewell to patrons as they made their way out of the cinema, I never came across one who emerged shoeless.

What's more, although a regular Saturday night patron known to the Gaumont, Watford, staff as 'Rear Row Rita' once contacted our Lost Property with a view to recovering a missing pair of pale pink panties, we never once received an enquiry in respect of missing shoes. They would pile up in the cupboard and every now and again we sent a representative batch of them to the Salvation Army.

After I had been at the Gaumont, Watford, for a while, *Kine Weekly* printed a few paragraphs about me, headed 'Britain's Youngest Cinema Manager'. If that was so, it was mainly because most of the other managers were now in the forces and, sure enough, late in 1942, I received my own call-up papers.

The Gaumont staff, plus those at the Town Hall Music Hall, which I was also managing by then, combined to present me with a splendid fitted leather suitcase as a leaving present. We had a boisterous party and the following noon, I turned up, as ordered, at the Induction Centre, RAF Padgate.

Two days later, I was back in the Gaumont foyer. Padgate, for their own good and sufficient reasons, had deferred my enlistment, instructing me to return whence I came, holding myself ready for recall at twenty-four hours' notice. The Hyams Brothers had not yet found a replacement, so they asked me to stay on until the RAF was once again ready for me.

The fitted leather suitcase was an embarrassment. I offered it back but, on behalf of all of them, Sidney Courtenay the organist, who had been acting as my stand-in, insisted I keep it. A couple of months later, when the RAF hauled me back again, this time for keeps, the staff of the two theatres clubbed together again and I found myself trying to wave away a pair of silver hairbrushes. When I pitched up at Padgate again, I must have been the most luxuriously equipped recruit in the intake.

MOSTLY
WORLD WAR TWO

For several years I dickered with a screenplay based on an encounter I had during my initial RAF training at Blackpool. It happened after I woke up one morning to find my face and entire upper body had turned bright red overnight.

Realising it was some kind of rash, and remembering the instructions they had dinned into us for such emergencies, I packed what they were pleased to call my 'small kit' and took myself off to the downtown Medical Inspection room.

This was a former lock-up shop where, after waiting an hour or so, I exhibited my reddened areas to a bored Medical Officer. He took a cursory glance, lifted a phone, muttered into it, 'I'm sending you a recruit with rubella' and turned me over to his orderly.

In the outer office the orderly explained that rubella was German measles, then gave me a chit and told me to make my way with it, preferably not by public transport, to the RAF hospital at Lytham St Annes.

And it was on my recollections of what I found when I arrived there that I wanted to base a film story. As soon as I presented my chit, a nursing orderly conducted me to a small ward and suggested I get into bed. As I did so, I noticed that the ward contained three other occupants, all of them congregated in silence at the other end of the room, eyeing me attentively. As soon as the orderly left, one of them – I later discovered his name was Smithy, a tall, skinny fellow, with a long, melancholy face and a lantern jaw – asked me, a little apprehensively, what brought me there. Opening my pyjama jacket, I displayed my gently glowing torso, adding, 'It's German measles.'

They came closer and inspected it with considerably more care than the Medical Officer had done. Then, as one, they moved away again and held a long, whispered discussion. Finally they returned to my bedside and introduced themselves. The other two were named Olly and Ted, but it was Smithy who, with some hesitation, announced that they had agreed to risk taking me into their confidence.

Lowering his voice he explained that the reason they were there was that the three of them were in the final stages of 'working their ticket'. The phrase employed to describe activities aimed at illegally obtaining a premature discharge from the Services. They had all chosen to take a medical route towards this objective and, as each of them had now spent several weeks building up an elaborate case history, they were understandably apprehensive that I might in some way upset their plans. I gave them what reassurance I could and spent the rest of my hospital stay watching their meticulous charades with some fascination.

For Olly, an ebullient Londoner pining for the delights of Tottenham Court Road ('To think that right now me and my bird could be tanning the floor of the Paramount'), was aiming to make his escape on the grounds of a sudden loss of hearing, brought about by a bomb explosion while he was on leave. To this end he was training himself not to register any change of expression at sudden, loud noises and to gaze uncomprehendingly at any remark addressed to him. The other two were assisting his deception by unexpectedly banging mess tins together nearby, or sharply calling out his name when he had his back to them, monitoring his neck muscles to make sure they betrayed no involuntary twitch. They rarely caught him out.

Ted had set himself a more uncomfortable task. Finding he had a facility for vomiting at will, he had decided to starve his way out of the RAF, throwing up at the first swallow of any food they placed in front of him. He subsisted on midnight snacks made up of scraps the other two secreted from their own meals and chocolate bars from their sweet rations. By the time I joined them, he was looking a little gaunt and his complexion was an unhealthy yellow.

Smithy had chosen the loneliest path. Electing to make his escape by the psychiatric route, he would feign sudden raging outbursts, become prostrated by violent headaches and was given to prolonged and inexplicable bouts of silent weeping. 'Always real tears,' he told me proudly, indicating the streaks they made down his cheeks.

For three days I watched them playing their parts, becoming more and more intrigued by their ingenuity and their attention to the fraudulent detail they brought to their individual stratagems. Then just as I was finding myself totally caught up in their efforts, I woke up one morning to find my skin had returned to its customary porcelain hue. The moment the medical staff saw this, I was told to gather up my small kit and ordered to return to my unit forthwith.

From that point on, my participation in their story ceased, leaving me feeling both disappointed and frustrated. Over the weeks, months, then years that followed, the three of them still lurked in my thoughts and I never stopped wondering if all that carefully plotted dissembling had produced results and which, if any, of them got away with it.

That concept of 'getting away successfully' came back to my mind when, sometime in the early sixties, I saw *The Great Escape*, probably the best of many 'breaking out of prisoner of war camp' movies we were being treated to at that time. I came out of it mulling over the scrap of an idea that perhaps the story of Smithy, Ted and Olly could be presented as a kind of upside-down version of that theme. Not a tongue-in-cheek rendering, but the true story of three likeable deceivers bent on outwitting the intractable regime that was confining them.

The trouble was, of course, that I didn't know how far they had succeeded and I was reluctant to fabricate anything. Nevertheless, I began to make notes.

Then, in the late seventies, we had just finished a recording of *Looks Familiar* and the audience were filing out, when I noticed that one of them was lingering behind, trying to catch my eye. I recognised that jaw immediately. It was Smithy. With much hand-shaking and shoulder-gripping he joined me for a drink in Hospitality. Here, by ourselves at a small table, I plied him with questions, hoping for details that might provide me with a climax for my story, even perhaps a denouement.

His response was discouraging. He told me that no more than a week after I left the ward, an examining board had come round to evaluate the trio's medical condition. Telling Smithy that they would defer a verdict on him until a psychiatrist could join them, they concentrated on Olly and Ted, the bogus hearing loss and the sham stomach disorder. In both cases their claims were accepted without a moment's quibble and in no time at all the two of them had departed, vanishing immediately into deepest Civvy Street, whence Smithy had not heard a word from either of them since.

'So much for dramatic conflict then,' I remember thinking. 'Not even any irony.' Grasping at straws, I asked him, 'How about you? How did you get on?'

Sensing my anticipation, he looked apologetic. 'I didn't. I never did go in front of them.' He then explained that after the other two left, he became so bored that he began having second thoughts about the whole venture. On the house doctor's next round he declared himself suddenly free of all his troubling symptoms and assured him he was feeling so much better, he would like to be returned to his unit. With visible relief they granted his request and by the end of that week he was back in training.

That was the point where I decided to place the putative screenplay into the Discarded File. However, noticing my downcast reaction, Smithy ventured, 'But I did have another go at it.'

I brightened. Smithy was far the most appealing character of the three, his air of gentle melancholy lending him an extra dimension. Perhaps the screenplay might still be salvageable. 'When?' I asked. 'Where?'

He went on to recount how he had had, by any standards, an eventful War. Posted to the Western Desert, he moved on to Sicily and thence to Northern Europe where, after VE Day, with the rank of Sergeant, he became part of the Occupying Forces in Germany.

'That was when the boredom set in again,' he recalled. 'It was bitterly cold and all we were really doing was just hanging around waiting for our demob number to come up. I got so fed up that when a couple of blokes in my mob got out ahead of time on what I knew were faked compassionate grounds, I decided I'd have another go at taking a short cut.'

So, once again, he reported sick with violent headaches and bouts of uncontrollable weeping. As these symptoms were by now greeted with a greater degree of understanding and sympathy, in no time at all Smithy was put on a plane bound for a specially adapted psychiatric hospital in Norfolk.

And here chance decreed that his case was assigned to a particularly caring doctor, an elderly refugee whose unstinting concern for his patients was a byword. Having tut-tutted over Smithy's symptoms, he confided that his own family had all been killed by the Nazis, including a son who would have been about Smithy's age had he lived. 'So I know how your family would feel if I sent you back to them in that condition.' And, ignoring Smithy's protestations, the saintly old man solemnly promised that under no circumstances would he allow Smithy home until his recovery was complete.

'Result?' Smithy said, his voice betraying only a slight trace of bitterness. 'I didn't get out till at least six months later than if I'd waited for my demob number to come up.'

Mentally I sent the notes for my escape story back into the Discarded File. True it might be, but who would believe it?

To gain my Wireless Operator badge, I had to pass an Aldis lamp test. This entailed standing on top of a hill and writing down a Morse message as it was blinked on and off at me from the top of a neighbouring hill.

There was absolutely no chance I would be able to decipher it. My Morse was adequate, but my eyesight was such that the dots and dashes of light merged into an undifferentiated blur.

My only recourse was to have a chum, skilled in the Aldis arts, conceal himself in a bush a yard or so away with a long stick. This he jabbed into my leg as the flashes were being transmitted, a hard jab indicating a dash, a soft one a dit.

Luckily, we were only required to reach a fairly modest speed at Aldis reading, so I managed a pass. To this day, I don't know why my crouching accomplice didn't just call the letters out to me. Possibly it was because the painful jabs I had to endure in some way made it seem less like cheating.

Anyway, I paid my respects to Samuel Morse years later when

I suggested he could have entitled his autobiography, *I Dit-Dit My Way.*

During my time moving round Britain with the RAF, a popular trick for saving money on the obligatory telephone call home to let them know you were safe was to make it a personal call to your own name. That way your family knew it was you putting in a call and in reply to the operator's 'I have a personal call for Mr D. Norden', they would simply deny you were there and the call would cost nothing. It worked several times for me, though I gave it up after my mother answered the call and said to the operator, 'No, I'm sorry he's not here but please tell him he should wear his overcoat in this weather.'

My mother never really mastered communication aids. Long after the War, when my parents were living in one of the ground-floor flats in a large four-flat converted house, they became worried about a spate of local burglaries, so my sister Doreen and I persuaded the landlord to install an entry-phone system.

I spent some time explaining to my mother how to make the best use of it. 'When the front-door buzzer goes, pick up that phone and ask "Who is it?" And only when they've stated who they are do you press the button to let them in. Never,' I emphasised, 'never ever press that button till whoever's outside has told you exactly who they are.'

My mother followed these instructions unfailingly. The trouble was that whenever she asked 'Who is it?' just as unfailingly the people who came calling on her would answer, 'Me', whereupon my mother would press the button that opened the door.

Prior to landing in Normandy on D-Day, my unit (554B Mobile Signal Unit 83 Group 2nd Tactical Air Force) was confined to a vast military encampment on the coast somewhere between Portsmouth and Southampton. Thousands of troops, of all types and nationalities, were assembled there, in preparation for the imminent invasion.

I have never known boredom like it. Under strict orders to keep ourselves in readiness to move at any moment, we were not allowed to stray further than five yards from our tents and the whole site was surrounded by barbed wire bearing starkly worded signs, 'If you go any further, you will be shot.' With no wireless sets or newspapers permitted, we could only sit around outside the tent all day, with occasional trips to the latrines or mess tent.

On the third morning I took a chance and went for a little wander. Within a few yards, I found myself in the middle of a group of large unoccupied tents emblazoned with the American stars and stripes. It looked to be some kind of supply point, so I nosed around a bit.

And that was when I chanced on my most unforgettable discovery of World War Two. At the far end of one of the empty tents, I saw a wooden crate marked USO. It was crammed to the top with books, pocket-size editions of what seemed to be all that was best in current American writing. These editions were specially printed for the

American forces and really were pocket size, measuring no more than half the vertical length of our Penguins. When I picked up a few to glance at the names, there they all were. Steinbeck, dos Passos, Benchley, Wolfe, Ferber, Dreiser, Woollcott, Perelman … One hundred and thirty in all.

I hurried back to where the rest of my unit was dawdling about and, within moments, the books were nestling at the back of our tent under some RAF greatcoats. We spent the next couple of days lying on the grass in sunlit content, reading the best America had to offer. When our embarkation order came, we divvied up the books between us and they went with us on the landing-craft.

They accompanied us all the way through France, Belgium, Holland and into Germany, functioning as a kind of mobile lending library for the various other units we became associated with. I still treasure a tattered half dozen of them.

My family took a somewhat guarded view of my Uncle Jack, partly because he smoked a pipe and was headmaster of a notoriously rough and tumble 'elementary' school in Islington, but also because he was given to agnostic opinions and spent his holidays taking solitary walking tours across Europe.

He was always one of my favourite relatives and I think I may have been one of his, because when I was on leave in 1944 and went to see him, he presented me with a souvenir of his walking trips, a small blue volume entitled *Baedeker's Guide to Northern France*. 'This might possibly come in handy,' he said and quoted me that line about War being a brutal way to learn geography.

No more than a few weeks later, it was D-Day and Dick Organ and I were in the cab of a water bowser about to land on the beach in Normandy. After a beach-head had been established, it wasn't long before we found ourselves in more settled conditions, a tented encampment among the Normandy apple trees.

As I was lolling outside our tent, immersed in a Robert Benchley pocket book and contentedly enjoying what seemed to be the continuous sunshine of that summer, a visit from Flying Officer Brown, our Squadron CO, had me scrambling to my feet.

'You're always reading,' he said. 'So I'm volunteering you to get a wall newspaper started while we're here.'

My response was instinctive. 'Will it get me off guard duties, sir?'

A deal was agreed and I set to. The contents of the paper, typed on a large oblong arrangement of blank message pads pinned to an improvised easel, were confined to gossipy items about the personnel on the camp, because nothing of the remotest military significance could be included in case the Germans launched a counter-attack and the newspaper fell into enemy hands. So I operated under a rigorous censorship.

In fact, I was beginning to doubt that I could rustle up sufficient material to fill the space available when I suddenly remembered that Uncle Jack's Baedeker was still at the bottom of my kitbag. Having learned that we were only a few miles away from the town of Bayeux, I looked it up. And, sure enough, there it was.

Within a few hours, the wall newspaper was completed. Its centrepiece was an article on the Bayeux Tapestry. It was a descriptive essay, so detailed in its command of dates and names that F/O Brown came over with a confidential message. His superiors had instructed him to find out how an ordinary AC2 came to be so well up on French cultural history.

I was aware that at the beginning of the War everybody had been asked to hand in their copies of Baedeker so, not wishing to drop Uncle Jack in it, I merely confessed that 'One of my family used to go on walking holidays round here.'

Although I felt sure this didn't satisfy them, they still suggested I apply for a transfer to Military Intelligence.

'He's always been a vivacious reader,' an aunt of mine used to say. Eric Sykes mentions in his autobiography that when we were first together in the RAF, stationed at Swaffham in Norfolk, I would read a book while marching the mile and a half from the barracks to the Mess Hall every morning for breakfast. I managed it, as I recall, by falling in behind a cooperative fellow airman of suitable height and on the command 'Forward march', I would tuck an opened book between the straps of the haversack on his back and, for the rest of the journey, tread his footsteps well.

While we were making our way across Holland and Germany, we had occasional visits from the mobile cinemas sent out by AKS.

These film shows were always welcome, although there seemed to be a somewhat tactless preponderance of those patriotically gung-ho military adventures Hollywood was churning out at the time.

However, the sceptical chi-iking with which our lads received such posturings more than made up for their heavy-handed heroics. One I remember with particular pleasure had a scene in its final reel where the gallant GI hero was sent back from the front-line to have his wounds treated in his Mid-West home town. After undergoing a tense time in the operating theatre and a spell in a wheelchair, comes the day when he must face a special medical examination to determine whether or not he is fit enough to return to the battlefield.

We saw his hopeful face as he disappeared into the doctor's consulting room, his college sweetheart anxiously waiting outside. After a while, the door opened again and there he stood, the very picture of dejection and dismay.

As he sagged miserably against the doorway, almost with one voice the RAF audience exclaimed, 'He's passed!'

When Bill Fraser made his West End debut in 1940, he was acclaimed as the most talented new revue comedian for years. The show was *New Faces*, the one that introduced Eric Maschwitz's 'A Nightingale Sang in Berkeley Square', and I can remember being enthralled by its wit and sophistication. Before Bill had time to take advantage of, let alone revel in, his new-found fame, he was called into the RAF. By the time he came out five years later, *New Faces* had been forgotten and he had to start the painful clamber to the top from the beginning again. Indeed, the next time I saw him on the professional stage, he was part of a concert party at Westgate-on-Sea.

In the interim, we had become well acquainted. Not long after D-Day, while my Signals Unit were bedded down for a while in Normandy, a notice went up on the Orderly Room board, calling for volunteers willing to help form an RAF entertainment unit. When I went along to offer my services, I found that the CO of the unit was Pilot Officer Bill Fraser. After I showed him a few lyrics and sketches I had written, very much under the influence of *New Faces*, he appointed me a sort of unofficial PA and we conducted the auditions together.

One of the first to turn up was a Sergeant in the RAF Regiment who told us he had an act that would 'knock 'em out of their seats'. He then took a razor blade from his tunic pocket, popped it in his mouth and began chewing. After bringing the microphone nearer to his face, so that we could hear the metallic crunching sounds more clearly, he beckoned Bill closer. Motioning him to put his hand out, he opened his mouth and dribbled a mixture of metal fragments and saliva into his outstretched palm.

At his expectant look, Bill said apologetically, his eyes seeking somewhere to wipe his hand, 'I think it's more cabaret than revue.'

Fortunately, the next group of hopefuls included a gleam of pure gold by the name of LAC Eric Sykes. In his warm-hearted auto-biography, *If I Don't Write It, Nobody Will*, Eric has given such an engaging account of the shows we did, the places we toured and the people we met over the ensuing fifteen months, I find it hard to recall any incident he failed to cover.

Come to think of it, there was one. After celebrating VE Day on Lüneburg Heath, then hearing the proclamation of VJ Day, most of us became preoccupied with speculations about how soon our demob numbers would come up. In a bid to sustain unit morale, Bill organised a totally unauthorised trip into Denmark. We were stationed in Schleswig-Holstein by this time, occupying a former German seaplane base, so the border wasn't that far. We commandeered a truck and, after selling its spare tyre to defray expenses, we made for Aabenraa, the nearest Danish town of any size.

Arriving there at midday, we installed ourselves in the dining room of an old-fashioned wood-timbered auberge just in time for lunch. The twelve of us were led to a table in the centre of the room, while the respectable Danish businessmen and merchants sitting at tables round the walls kept their eyes politely on their plates. Although we must have been the first British servicemen to come their way, they confined their curiosity to the occasional surreptitious glance.

Denmark, which Hitler had dubbed 'the storehouse of Europe', knew nothing of food shortages. For us, on the other hand, who had known only rationing and dried eggs for the past five years, the lavish abundance of the food now set before us not only widened our eyes, it silenced all conversation between us as we ate. All that could be heard was an occasional rapturous moan. The well-mannered Danes around us betrayed no reaction to these noises, apart from a lifting of the eyebrow here and there, as if to acknowledge our English right to behave eccentrically.

They received the ultimate confirmation of this eccentricity when the dessert trolleys were paraded for our inspection. One of them was devoted solely to cream flans, saucer-size cream flans, tea-plate-size cream flans, soup-plate-size cream flans, all of them topped with an inch-high layer of whipped cream sculpted with intricate hillocks and pyramids.

We could only gaze in fascination. This was 1945, remember, and we had not seen as much as a teaspoonful of cream since 1939.

'The middle-size one, I think, gentleman,' Bill said, to break the spell. When we each had one sitting on the table in front of us, we could still only stare at it, unwilling to disturb its creamy lusciousness. Bill stood up. 'Gentlemen,' he said and motioned all of us to be upstanding. 'Under the circumstances, there is only one thing to do.'

With which, he placed his hand underneath his plate and balanced it on his palm while he waited for us to do the same. Then, as one, the twelve of us raised our hands and sploshed a plateful of cream flan full in our faces.

As we stood stock-still, cream dripping from our eyebrows, noses and cheeks down on to our blue uniforms, we heard a sudden little spattering of applause. Those good Danish burghers were thanking us for allowing them to witness what was surely some traditional old English ritual.

The three *Bags of Panic* shows I wrote in the RAF, to star Bill Fraser and Eric Sykes, with Corporal Ron Rich, later to become the Reverend Ronald Rich, supplying the music, were all in the nature of what were then known as 'revues'. They consisted of sketches, songs, 'point numbers' and 'quickies'.

Each show ran for upwards of two and a half hours, making it all the more odd that when I consider the stack of material required to fill the three of them, I can now recall no more than two items. One was a song Ron and I sang called 'After I've Liberated Europe' ('Who's going to liberate me?') and even there Eric can remember more of the words than I can.

The other half-forgotten unforgettable was a joke Bill was so fond of he referred to it as his 'all-time top Service gag', insisting that, in one form or another, it be included in every edition. This was not easy as, unlikely as it may seem today, none of the revues incorporated what is now known as a 'standup'. So the joke had to be either enacted by two performers as a quickie or sneaked in somewhere during the course of a sketch.

Fortunately, it dealt with a situation which, for Service audiences, worked even better when acted out than narrated. So, in three different versions, they saw a Cockney airman arrive back at barracks after a forty-eight-hour leave, dripping wet from head to foot. 'Blimey,' says one of his mates. 'Is it still raining in London?' 'No,' the airman replies. 'When I got home, the wife was in the bath.'

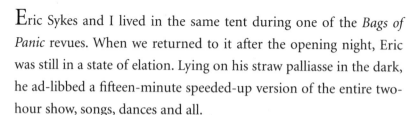

Eric Sykes and I lived in the same tent during one of the *Bags of Panic* revues. When we returned to it after the opening night, Eric was still in a state of elation. Lying on his straw palliasse in the dark, he ad-libbed a fifteen-minute speeded-up version of the entire two-hour show, songs, dances and all.

It was the most glorious piece of sustained comic improvisation I have ever witnessed and nothing since has left me so exhausted with laughter.

Nineteen forty-five. We were under canvas in some meadows outside Brussels and eager to get away from camp and sample the city's
fleshpots, I took a short cut across the area designated as our parade
ground. I was chancing my luck because this was prohibited territory
unless one was on duty and, sure enough, halfway across I was halted
by a familiar roar. 'Airman!'

It was the Station Warrant Officer, a bristling little man and a
stickler for the niceties. Marching up to me, he said, 'And just where
do you think you're going?'

'Sorry, sir. I was in a hurry to get on the transport for Brussels.'

He looked me up and down. 'With a dirty cap-badge?' As I winced,
he passed sentence. 'Crossing the parade ground and dirty badge?
You are confined to camp, my son.'

With which he stumped off. I wandered back to my tent and
found I was the only one there. Everyone else was on their way to
Brussels. On an impulse, I went round the back of the tent and cut
across the field to the perimeter hedge. I made my way along it till
I found a hole through which I could squeeze. On the other side was
a narrow country road and I started to walk along it in the direction
of Brussels, hoping to hitch a lift.

After no more than a couple of minutes, I heard the sound of an
engine approaching from behind me and when I turned, there was
an RAF 15-hundredweight truck. I stuck out my thumb and it pulled
up. Gratefully, I went to climb in and only then noticed who the
driver was. It was the Station Warrant Officer.

We gazed at each other. Then very deliberately, he said, 'You done
it all wrong, aincha.'

The remark struck me as so apt that, quite involuntarily, I found
myself smiling. He bristled. 'What's so funny?'

'What you just said, sir. It's so spot-on.'

'It is indeed,' he said. Then, 'Jump in.' And we were off to Brussels.

Since that day, 'You done it all wrong, aincha' has headed my list of benign reproaches.

Contrary to the present-day belief, implanted by a regrettable number of popular films, World War Two did not occur as a series of zooming headlines. It dragged on for year after wearisome year.

My own generation, whose early years were spent in a confused synthesis of Hollywood and reality, was left with a similar set of misconceptions. Thanks to the films of the thirties and forties, I grew up firmly believing that:

Driving a car entails continuously half-turning the steering wheel from one side to another.

Shaving consists of two vertical strokes of the razor down each cheek, followed by patting the face with a towel.

Girls close their eyes when kissing, lifting their heels and occasionally kicking one shoe off behind them.

Childbirth requires lots of hot water.

MOSTLY
POST-WAR AND
VARIETY

There was a spell after the War when I was employed by the Hyman Zahl Variety Agency as a trainee agent and writer-in-residence. The latter duty entailed writing any scripts the comedians on his books needed for their 'spot' broadcasts. There were any number of those one-off radio spots available in programmes such as *Variety Bandbox, Workers' Playtime, Henry Hall's Guest Night, Music Hall, Northern Music Hall*, etc., and as Hymie represented some sixty-three comedians at that time, I did very little agenting.

To be fair, the writing chores were not quite as onerous as they first seemed. This was partly because most of the comedians arrived with a selection of jokes they refused to be parted from, which saved me a fair amount of work. But mainly it was because, in those days, every comedian was expected to finish his act with a song, which carved another helpful chunk out of his allotted seven or eight minutes. These songs were generally of a sentimental nature, giving rise to the axiom that the perfect solo broadcast spot was 'Five minutes of gags about mother-in-law followed by two minutes of song about mother.'

As payment for supplying the script for such occasions, I would be given whatever 'plug' money the comedian would (illicitly) receive from the song's publisher for performing it. It was not a princely sum, three or four guineas was the norm, but if it was a romantic number, you could sometimes augment it by finding an excuse to repeat part of the song again. This was generally achieved by following the first chorus with a fervently delivered 'recitative', an over-heated monologue in which the song's romantic theme would be comedically underlined before a return to its last eight bars. ('You may not believe me, but I tried everything with that girl. Everything, I tell you! Flowers, chocolates, jewellery ... They all worked.')

By far the most profitable comedian to write for proved to be Issy Bonn. Besides being a top-of-the-bill comedy name, he enjoyed considerable recording success as a singer. Consequently, the BBC allowed him to finish with a medley. Three songs, three lots of plug money.

One of Hymie Zahl's judgements that has stayed with me was addressed to a comedian whose full name those same years have erased but whose first name was Harry.

Harry had been one of Hymie's artists throughout the War years and he was a byword in the Zahl office as 'the comic who played Dover more times than any other performer'. During that period, many artists did not welcome being booked for a week at Dover because the town was within range of the German heavy guns across the Channel as well as being a regular target for bombing raids. The sound of the air-raid siren was frequently heard and theatre performances were regularly halted for an announcement offering audiences the choice of going down to the shelter or remaining in their seats for the rest of the show.

In most cases, they elected to remain and the performers would keep going until the 'All Clear' sounded. Harry, a stubby, cheery little man, would sometimes entertain audiences for hours at a time on his own, getting them singing and laughing, in complete disregard of the thuds and explosions that could be heard outside. In consequence, he became a local favourite and something of a legend.

When the War ended and I joined the office, he was fulfilling dates around the North of England – Halifax, Huddersfield, Attercliffe, etc. Unfortunately, their reports on his act were less than flattering and Hymie was obliged to call him into his office to discuss his future.

When Harry came in, his spirits were noticeably drooping and I can still remember the fragment of conversation I heard before they closed the door.

'I don't understand it,' Harry said. 'Does the fact that I played Dover more times than any other comic count for nothing, Hymie? Doesn't what I did with those audiences down there mean anything these days?'

'Of course it does,' Hymie said. 'But I'm afraid the time has come when you have to face the truth. What it amounts to, Harry, is that you are an artist who is only at his best during heavy shelling.'

At the Variety agency, Hymie allowed me to make occasional minor bookings off my own bat, especially where little or no money was involved. Thus it was I was able to book Harry Secombe into his first West End date, a prestigious charity show sponsored by the Albany Club. He performed the hilarious 'shaving' act that later became his trademark and it went down so well, he was given a string of bookings across the North of England.

At the first one, unfortunately – as I recall, it was either Huddersfield or Halifax – the manager came round after his opening performance. 'You're not shaving on my bloody time,' he growled and paid him off.

My usual response to magic tricks is boredom if I can work out how they are done and sullenness if I can't. However, while I was in the employ of the Hyman Zahl Variety Agency, one of my duties was to make weekly visits to the Nuffield Centre, a servicemen's club which had become London's foremost showcase for new acts. On one visit, I saw a magician whose final feat I found so totally baffling, it left me in a state just short of awed.

To demonstrate his exceptional powers of memory, he passed down to an ATS girl in the audience a copy of the London Telephone Directory – back then, you could get all the numbers in one book – and invited her to open it anywhere at random. After she had done so, he asked her to look at the two pages she could now see, choose one of them and tell him what page number it was.

'Page 273.'

'Page 273?' He frowned thoughtfully for a moment. 'Would you now look at the three columns of names on that page and select one of the columns.'

'Okay.'

'Would you tell me which column you've decided on?'

'The middle column.'

'Page 273, second column … All right? Next thing I'd like you to do is run your finger down the names in that column till you come to one you'd like me to try and recall. Tell me when you've picked it.'

'Right … Got one.'

'Good. Then all I need you to do now is, counting from the top, tell me how far down the column that name comes.'

'It's – the fifteenth name down.'

'So – the fifteenth name down the second column of page 273.' He closed his eyes and put both hands to his temples, as though at a sudden headache. Then, relaxing, 'That name is Jarvis, Kenneth. The address is 23 Springfield Road, N16, and, just to round it off, the telephone number is Clissold 6232.'

When the answer was confirmed, the applause was so vociferous he repeated the trick several times, only going wrong once on a detail of the address. Next morning I wrote such a glowing report on his performance, Hymie told me to go back that evening and sign him up.

This time I entered the Nuffield by way of the Stage Door, which meant crossing the backstage area to get into the audience. I could hear the voice of my magician in front of the curtain asking someone to pick a column. But now I could see that, behind him, with only the thin curtain between them, sat a man with a London Telephone Directory on his lap, turning the pages as the directions were given and murmuring the information in a voice audible only to his employer standing the other side of the curtain.

My disillusionment was total, but the trick's simplicity was so irresistible, I remained impressed. Sad to tell, however, it didn't stand the test of the subsequent Moss Empires booking we got him. The curtains were too thick.

I would often eat at Olivelli's, the famous theatrical digs in Store Street, London, not simply for the quality of their pasta but also for such titbits as the one I gleaned from Jack Wilson. He told me that one of the first things the Nazis did when they came to power in the early thirties was to ban Wilson, Keppel and Betty from appearing anywhere in Germany.

Apparently they objected to the bare legs.

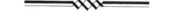

There was no end to the amount of time, patience and planning some Variety performers put into perfecting a comedy routine. Payne and Hilliard were a prime example. They were a male and female double act, she large and commanding, he short and fierce.

A staple of their well-established act was 'our impression of Napoleon crossing the Alps'. For this, he would don an overlong military coat and equally oversized Napoleonic hat, while the curtains behind them opened to reveal a painted backcloth of a magnificent mountain range, the peaks capped with snow. After an exchange of pseudo-French dialogue, he would bark an order and, at his imperious gesture, the whole backcloth would drop to the floor. He would step over it and, at another gesture, the mountain range would rise up again behind him.

It never failed to get a laugh – even with audiences who had seen it several times before. But I always found myself marvelling at the logistics and ongoing expense it involved. As well as the considerable cost of a specially painted full-stage backcloth, there was the weekly outlay and worry of getting it transported from theatre to theatre. All that for one gag …

I had the same feelings about a moment in one of Sid Field's sketches, where a yelping group of dogs would run on stage towards him. When they were halfway across, he would point a finger and say, 'He went that way!' Whereupon, the entire pack turned around and ran the other way.

The whole incident took no more than half a minute. But how many hours of effort and training went into making sure it worked every time?

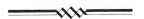

Another couple of Variety acts my memory still curls around are Owen McGiveney and the Nicholas Brothers. McGiveney was a quick-change artist, a 'Protean' act, as they were called in American vaudeville. English by birth, he enjoyed enormous success in the States.

For a typical performance, he would offer a scene from Dickens, in which he would play all the characters himself, changing from one to another in lightning succession, altering not only his voice but also his clothes and entire physical appearance. He would scurry on and off stage, or sometimes nip behind a piece of furniture and re-emerge split seconds later with a completely different costume and make-up. Obviously, there was an army of hidden helpers accelerating his changes but nothing I have seen since has been so brilliantly timed and executed.

As for the Nicholas Brothers, they were far and away the most spectacular dancing act I ever saw, repeatedly doing the splits at high speed, and finishing by bumping down a flight of steps, hitting each step with legs wide apart in the 'splits' position. To this day I cannot believe there is any way that this doesn't hurt.

There was a time when comedians would move into their obligatory closing song by way of a formalised comic introduction, generally incorporating something along the lines of: 'And now, ladies and gentlemen, I'd like to finish with a beautiful little song entitled "If I Had My Life to Live Over – I'd live it over a pub".'

These 'little song' titles were in brisk demand. They were a useful linking device and any of them that proved particularly successful tended to be jealously guarded. They were often hotly fought over, accusations of 'pinching' being levelled and occasionally submitted for arbitration by a sub-committee of the Variety Artists' Federation. Whenever an American comedian visiting the Palladium happened to promulgate a brand-new 'little song entitled', it would be heard in provincial theatres around the country within days, American sources being regarded as public domain.

It may be of interest that out of the hundreds of such song titles in service at that time, the few that remain lodged in my memory all illustrate that useful aid to comic timing, the comma in the middle. Thus, a little song entitled:

'Don't Play Marbles With Father's Glass Eye, He Needs It To Look For Work.'

'Get Off The Table, Mabel, The Sixpence Is For The Waiter.'

'Will You Love Me Like You Used To, Or Have You Found A Better Way?'

'She's Only Been Gone For Seven Days, But Already It Feels Like A Week.'

'You Made Me Do You, I Didn't Want To Love It.'

'When You Were Nine And I Was Eight, And We Were Seventeen.'

My memory mechanism is one that tends to retain words, rather than images. But a scene that has remained in sharp focus derives from a weekend Avril and I had at Knocke-le-Zoute, Belgium, in 1945, not that long after the end of hostilities.

For some reason, the local casino invited us to visit the only gaming room that had remained open during the War years. Its vaulted and chandeliered interior was in complete darkness, except for a pool of light at the far end where one green-shaded lamp shone down on a solitary roulette table. All the surrounding tables were shrouded in heavy linen sheets, while this one had only two white-haired women and three elderly men sitting at it. All were in full evening dress, the women in jewellery, the men with white bow-ties, and not a word or a glance passed between them.

As they sat staring at the table, the room's silence was broken only by the roulette ball's clattering around the wheel and the muttered announcements of the croupier. After five minutes, we tiptoed away, wondering whether that tableau had remained thus throughout the War.

For many years, I used to read imported copies of weekly *Variety* from cover to cover, devouring with special pleasure its lengthy reviews of vaudeville bills around the USA. Although I was unfamiliar with practically every name they mentioned, the characteristically pithy descriptions of their acts offered by *Variety*'s team of critics usually allowed me to construct a pretty clear picture of them.

Not always, though. Joe Cook was a frequently mentioned comedian, and while his *Variety* notices were always approving, they never failed to mention one detail that defeats me to this day. His write-ups would invariably run something along the lines of 'As ever, Joe Cook was received with much joyous mitt-pounding, garnering special plaudits for his hilarious impersonation of four Hawaiians.'

Even now, I find myself puzzling over that last reference. How do you impersonate four Hawaiians? Yes, all right. But 'hilariously'?

One further *Variety* memory. W. C. Fields took a full page ad in a Christmas edition that read, 'A merry Christmas to all my friends except two.'

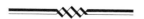

When Hyman Zahl's top-line Variety artists were touring the country 'on percentage', the company manager would send Hymie the figures for each night's theatre takings by coded telegram. It was a simple code based on the phrase, 'Money Talks', with each letter representing a digit (M = 1, O = 2, N = 3, and so on).

When a key figure in the Zahl office left for another agency, the security of the code was considered compromised, so Hymie deputed me to come up with another easily memorised ten-letter phrase in which no letter was repeated. After about ten minutes, I suggested – 'Grand Hotel'. His admiration was so unbounded, he could hardly speak for a moment. Then he straightaway commissioned 'at least three' spares to cover any future defections.

It cost me a sleepless night, but next morning I arrived with 'Dirty Jokes', 'Jack Hylton', 'Spanish Fly' and 'Mind The Gap'. He applauded them all, but I sensed a slight touch of disappointment.

Never mind. Over the intervening years, each of them has proved more than useful for encoding PIN and credit card numbers.

Manny Jay, another Variety agent, occupied an office on the floor above Hyman Zahl. A brooding, heavily built man, one of the cornerstones of his empire was the Ben Abdrahman Wazzan Troupe, a seven-man family of acrobats, much given to quarrelling violently with each other. Every few weeks I would hear a loud pounding of footsteps descending the wooden stairs and when I opened the door, there would be Manny brandishing a railway ticket to some remote provincial town and panting as he thudded downward, 'Just got a phone call. More trouble with the bloody Arabs.'

Some imperfectly remembered scraps from my days in the world of Variety theatre:

The juggler who performed his act standing beside a screen prominently marked 'Swearing Room'. Every time he dropped something, he would momentarily retire behind it. His re-emergence was always greeted with applause.

A musical act who dressed as a waiter and had a white-clothed table on stage, immaculately laid out as for a banquet, complete with bottles and bowls of fruit. He produced musical sounds from each item on display, skipping from one to the other, squeezing piping notes from oranges and apples, whistling down knives and forks, treating groups of wine bottles as a xylophone, revealing the hidden harmonica in a lamb chop. I was impressed not only by the complex dashing to and fro his act demanded, but also by the fact that he was always on-stage a good hour before he was due to go on, to make sure no one disturbed his meticulously positioned table layout.

The magician, rendered similarly nameless by my faltering memory, who would mutter admiringly to himself throughout his fairly run of the mill act, expressing astonishment at his own skills every time he completed a trick. He was also a favourite with Tony Hancock, who recalled hearing him murmur, after completing an elementary 'disappearing an egg from a black velvet bag' effect, 'The man must be in league with the Horned One, a follower of the Left Hand Path.'

Looking back on it, Variety was really an inter-War phenomenon. In essentials, it came to an end on 3 September 1939. While it lasted, it was the most consistently successful and fulfilling family entertainment this country has known. After the War, it died of Television, nude shows and the indifference of the young.

MOSTLY
RADIO, FRANK AND
CENSORSHIP

I joined Ted Kavanagh Associates at roughly the same time as Dick Bentley. He had been one of the biggest radio stars in Australia and when he came over here, the Australian Broadcasting Commission booked him for a twice-weekly series of fifteen-minute dispatches from London and I was given the job of researching and writing them for what was, even for those days, a spectacularly paltry fee.

I enjoyed it, though. Dick himself was an amiable fellow, dapper and good-humoured, and in the year or so that the series ran I met and got to know just about every Australian showbusiness immigrant, from Peter Finch to Kitty Bluett.

If any programme failed to turn up a suitable visiting Australian, I had Dick out on the street interviewing whichever colourful London characters I could rope in. One of the best of these turned out to be Mike Stern, an amusingly voluble market trader, who claimed to have 'the only market stall in Petticoat Lane with a fitting room'. He scored such a hit with Australian listeners, the ABC sent a cable asking me to look out any other lively East End personages we could feature.

There were many, of course. I took to prowling the little streets round the Lane in search of them and it was in one of those – Stoney Lane, I believe it was called – that I had my most arresting encounter.

The narrow thoroughfare was empty, except for one man sitting on a Bentwood chair outside a small lock-up shop. He was staring down moodily at the pavement but, as I passed, he glanced up and his whole expression changed. Leaping to his feet in disbelief, 'I can't believe it,' he muttered, staring at me, 'I just don't believe it.'

'What is it?' I asked. 'What's the matter?'

'Nothing, sir,' he said hastily. 'Nothing that need concern you. Except –' he hesitated. 'Could I ask you a favour, sir, a small favour?'

'What sort of favour?'

'If you could stand there a minute. I just want my brother to –'
And, raising his voice, 'Stanley! Stanley!'

A muffled, bad-tempered voice from somewhere inside the shop
bellowed back, 'What is it now?'

'Outside! Just come outside a mo.'

From within the lock-up emerged a second man, an ill-humoured
version of the first. 'What now?' he growled. 'What do you want of
my –' then, catching sight of me – well, I won't say he staggered back,
but he definitely shifted. A hand went up to his mouth and he
gasped. 'Oh, my God!'

'What is it?' I said again. 'What's the matter?'

The first man had recovered himself by now. 'Nothing that need
trouble you, sir,' he said soothingly. 'Just a family difference of opin-
ion. Thank you for your time.'

He moved to his brother and, frequently darting a furtive glance
in my direction, the two began a fierce, whispered argument, inaudible to me but obviously a matter of urgent concern.

By now I had become extremely curious. I had to learn more.
'Can't you tell me what this is about?'

The first man – I later discovered his name was Lammy – hesitated, then, with obvious reluctance, said, 'Well, you see, sir, it's to do
with the Duke of Northumberland.'

Seeing my blank response, he hurried on. 'Or perhaps I should say,
the late Duke of Northumberland. As you no doubt know, the gentleman passed away last month and her Ladyship had the task of dis-
posing of his clothing. As is our custom, my brother travelled up
there to inspect what was on offer and what does he come back with?
Out of all His Lordship's extensive wardrobe, one suit. Goes all the
way up there and comes back with just one suit!'

'If you're going to tell it, tell it properly,' interjected Stanley. 'It was a brand new Savile Row suit that His Lordship, God rest his soul, never even had the chance to put on his back.'

'I give you that,' admitted Lammy, 'but the important thing is, that suit was made so exactly to the Duke's measurements, the chance it will fit anyone that comes to this shop is no more than one in a million. I could sit outside here in the street for a year without seeing anybody exactly the right size for it.' Turning to me, 'Then, blow me, this morning, no more than two days later, along you come!'

'Now tell me there's no such thing as coincidence!' said Stanley.

Then they played what I later decided was their masterstroke. With a word of thanks for my patience, they both left me and went inside their shop.

Of course, I followed them. And, of course, I bought the suit.

It fitted me no better than adequately. But I never put it on without experiencing a wave of fellow feeling for the two brothers and the skill with which they performed their neatly crafted playlet.

Ted Kavanagh, whose wartime radio series, *It's That Man Again*, was listened to by every wireless set owner in the British Isles, became the first scriptwriter to attain national recognition. An endearing man, on the tubby side, not at all assertive, he had a ginger moustache, prominent ginger eyebrows, a rolling gait, wore jaunty brown trilbies and there was more than a touch of Fred Emney about him.

A steady rather than a heavy drinker, he was also a chain-smoker, given to patting up and down his pockets in search of cigarettes. Occasionally, the search would bring to light a packet of the expensive black-and-white Markovitch brand, whereupon his whole face would crumple into rueful dismay. 'Oh, Lor'! Where was I last night?'

Early in the post-war era, Billy Butlin laid on a special train to take an imported Italian Opera Company, plus some invited guests, up to his Skegness holiday camp for a one-night performance of *La Bohème* to an audience of end-of-season campers.

None of the company could speak English but on the morning after their arrival, we watched a bunch of them set out to explore the camp, commenting excitedly as they inspected the chalets, mess halls, children's amenities.

At one outdoor compound, however, they fell silent.

A group of women campers, dressed in vests and bloomers, were performing keep fit exercises to the shouted commands of a rollneck-sweatered Redcoat. As they panted and laboured, their legs blue with the cold, I watched the singers shake their heads sympathetically. Obviously they'd wandered into some harsh kind of punishment area.

Soon after I joined Ted Kavanagh Associates, the office put together a revue, headed by Peter Waring, to tour military bases overseas. It fell to me to assemble the supporting cast, so I put an advertisement in the 'Singers Wanted' column of *The Stage*. I received a quite disproportionate number of applications from sopranos, a few of which bore the letters 'MPR' under the signature.

When we auditioned them and I asked one of those who had appended the letters what they stood for, she muttered 'Management's Privileges Respected.' I am still not sure whether that meant what I hesitated at the time to think it meant.

The band leader Maurice Winnick, in his capacity as an impresario, bought the English rights of an American radio comedy series he renamed *Ignorance is Bliss*. At every stage of its performance he made his presence felt, notably, as Sid Colin, its scriptwriter, reported, after the final rehearsal of each show. While the performers were sitting waiting for the recording to begin, Maurice used to fidget about, anxious to cram in some last-minute gags. Finally he would instruct one of his entourage, 'Nip out and get an evening paper. There might be something topical in it.'

Much has been made of the implicit lack of logic in *Educating Archie*, which had Peter Brough indulging in ventriloquism on radio. Equally dotty, though, was *Monday Night at Seven*, where a conjuror named Sirdani displayed card tricks over the air.

On the only occasion I flew Concorde, I was very flattered when the Captain invited me on to the flight deck. After exhibiting various complicated instruments and dials, he said, 'It's difficult for most people to grasp the concept of really high speed, so we lay on a simple demonstration. In the time it takes me to say your name, we will have travelled a mile. Ready?'

'Ready,' I said.

'Right,' he said. 'Stand by … Frank Muir.'

I first met Frank in early 1947. Like me he was ex-RAF, had risen to the similarly dizzying rank of Leading Aircraftman and, as in my case, spent the latter part of his service career writing shows to entertain the troops. Two years almost to the day older than me, elegantly moustached and tweeded, insouciant owner of a Singer sports car, he was six foot four, one and a quarter inches taller than me – not two inches as he always averred; I am six foot two and three-quarters – and he had the same willowy, some would say skinny, build with, as he liked to put it, 'shoulders like a hock bottle'.

The meeting was engineered by Charles Maxwell, the producer of *Navy Mixture*, a radio programme to which we had both contributed 'spots', for Jimmy Edwards in Frank's case, for Dick Bentley in mine. Charles thought it might be refreshing to combine the two then relatively unknown comedians in a programme of their own, spicing it with another little-known Australian, the lively Joy Nichols. To explore this possibility he took us to lunch at a staggeringly expensive Jermyn Street restaurant, where he outlined his ideas for the show, concluding, 'Would you two be averse to writing the script together?'

Instantly and in almost perfect unison, we replied, 'Not a whit averse.' Some forty or so years later, when Frank was reconstructing the occasion for his autobiography, he rang me to confirm that simultaneous response. Musing on it, we agreed that, for each of us, the relish with which we had both brandished the same out-moded locution gave us our first hint that our minds might run on parallel tracks.

Regrettably, on the question of what happened after that, our recollections parted company. According to Frank, when the meal ended the two of us strolled round the corner to my office at Kavanagh Associates where, after meeting Ted Kavanagh, he left to finish a script he was writing for *Oliver's Twists*, while I returned to a *Northern Music Hall* piece I was knocking out for one of the agency's comedians, and we didn't meet again until later that week.

Which is not how I remember the rest of the afternoon. What I can still picture clearly is that when Frank left the office, I began pecking at the comedian's solo piece but found myself too restless and excited to continue. After half an hour or so of screwing up pages, I went for a walk up Waterloo Place into Lower Regent Street, where immediate distraction presented itself in the shape of a large cinema.

Without hesitation I bought a ticket. Inside the stalls were well populated, but I was able to find an aisle seat midway down where I settled to watch the picture.

I had arrived near the end of the second feature, a typical slice of cut-price Hollywood toshery set in seventeenth-century France. Although its title has long fled, as has its plot, it contained one scene which remains clearly etched in my mind to this day.

It opened in a tavern, with the hero – we may as well call him Louis – sitting dejectedly at a wooden table. As he gazes mournfully into his tankard, a voice interrupts his reverie. 'You seem sad, M'sieur.'

The voice belongs to a white-bearded, white-haired old gentleman at the corner table, patently some kind of local sage. Louis, obviously acquainted with him, pours out his heart. She has left him! The only lady to whom he has ever given his heart! And all because of that stupid duel!

The old man is consoling. 'She will return,' he assures him. 'Where there is true love, there is always forgiveness.'

Louis shakes his head. 'Women are different from men,' he sighs.

'Ah!' observes the old man. 'M'sieur is a philosopher.'

At which two people in the cinema laughed. One was me. The other was someone sitting several rows behind me. When the lights came up, I looked round to see who it was and, sure enough, there sat Frank.

But here comes the depressing part of this story. Frank had absolutely no recollection of it. In fact, he would flatly deny that any of it ever happened. 'It's fiction,' he maintained. 'I never went to the pictures that afternoon. The whole thing simply swam up from somewhere in your subconscious.'

'But I've often heard you using that "M'sieur is a philosopher" line,' I would protest.

'Only because you are always using it.'

'But I can remember the whole scene so clearly.'

'It's that thing they call False Memory.'

Is it? Half a lifetime further on I'm still not a hundred per cent convinced.

Frank's birthday was on the fifth of February, mine is the sixth, a juxtaposition that served to strengthen our shared distrust of astrology. Two people born under the same sign and only one day apart, could not, in all the essentials, have been more dissimilar. While Frank had an almost psychic gift of being able to repair or craft at first sight anything he turned his hand to, my handiness has never been anything but irretrievably cak. Had I been born in any other century but the twentieth, I wouldn't have lasted a month. Could either of us be expected to believe that if I had come into the world a day earlier, I would have been one and a quarter inches taller, able to turn a table leg on my own lathe and given to pink bow-ties?

Such were the sentiments we conveyed to a gentleman who wrote the horoscope page in a certain Sunday tabloid when he offered to give us a free reading in one of his forthcoming columns. What we hesitated to include was a tale that had recently come my way about one of my favourite science fiction writers, Isaac Asimov.

Accused by a young woman of displaying a bigoted attitude towards astrology, Asimov replied, 'Being human, Miss, I suppose I do contain a certain amount of bigotry within me. But I carefully expend it on astrology in the hope that I won't be tempted to use it on anything with a shadow of intellectual decency about it.'

Come right down to it, Frank and I could not have been more different in temperament. To give just one example: while he always laughed when the cast were rehearsing a script we had written, genuinely enjoying hearing our words, I was known as 'The Miserable One', sitting there scowling and worrying. Frank was never much of a worrier. I remember Sid Colin saying, 'Frank only worries to be sociable.'

In spite of those differences, we spent so many years sharing an area of our lives that could not be shared with anyone else, we took on the kind of affinities you associate with long-married couples. These included a form of non-verbal communication that enabled us to exchange complex messages without a word being spoken. You have no idea how many pungent remarks I was glanced.

In the first week that Frank and I began writing together, we came across a leading article in his local Leytonstone paper deploring the Council's decision to close down a park bandstand. In ringing phrases, it urged its readers to recall the purposes for which we had fought the recent War and the important part popular music had played in bringing about our final victory. It concluded with a clarion call in bold type that declared, 'Let the people snig!'

It was the first in the private repertoire of favourite phrases we built up over the years, as well as heading our list of useful misprints.

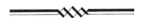

A fifties letter to *Radio Times* offered the following verse:

> Scriptwriters Norden and Muir
> Are said to be terribly pure
> Their jokes it is true
> Are not often blue
> But I wish they were just a bit newer

When Frank and I began writing *Take It from Here*, it was long before the advent of such life-support systems as the word processor, the electronic printer and the laser copier. Indeed, the most advanced item of technological gadgetry writers had at their disposal was the recently introduced biro pen. And even that was regarded with distrust by a generation brought up to revere expensive fountain pens.

In fact, from today's perspective, the procedures involved in getting our words from manuscript to performance copy now seem almost mediaeval in their laboriousness.

As both Frank and I were hopeless at typing, the first draft of a script would be painstakingly written out in longhand, a task that always fell to me because my crabbed and angular scrawl was that much faster than Frank's beautiful copperplate. We would sit facing each other across our wide office desk, batting the lines to and fro while, at intervals, Brenda, our secretary, would poke her head round the door to ask, 'Anything yet?'

As soon as there were a couple of pages ready for her to collect, she would take them back to her own office and convert my scribbles, blotches and marginal jottings into pages of neat, double-spaced print. On completion, these would be subjected to further alterations, crossings-out and scrunched-in additions, which as often as not entailed, as we were all still living without benefit of 'Delete' or 'Cut & Paste', typing the entire segment out again in full.

This was time-consuming enough, but made even more so by the related carbon-paper requirements. One disadvantage of collaboration was that we needed two copies of everything and in those days the only way to get two copies was to insert a carbon paper when typing. Any extra copies that were required entailed the use of additional carbon papers, with the result that long before anybody had a problem with carbon footprints we were having one with carbon handprints.

There was also an acknowledged hierarchy governing the

distribution of those carbon copies. The further up the pecking order someone was, the fewer carbons were inserted between his copy and the original. When we finally delivered the script to Charles Maxwell, our producer, he was handed the original or 'top' copy; his secretary got the first carbon copy, while Frank and I retained the smudged and fading copies three and four. An acceptable christening sentiment back then might have been 'May he grow up to be someone who only receives top copies.'

Once Charles had indicated his satisfaction with the script, a by no means inevitable reaction, BBC secretaries would begin transforming it into a number of performance copies. To this end, they had to retype the whole thing yet again, this time on to stencils. These were then fed into a large duplicating machine, known by the somewhat Waffen SS title of 'The Gestetner', whose operation resembled that of a barrel organ; i.e., you stood at the side of it with as cheerful an expression as you could muster and kept turning a handle for what seemed ages. The pages of the performance scripts that tumbled out, printed on unusually thick yellow paper, were collated and held together in the top left-hand corner by the type of large sharply pointed split-pin unlikely to meet today's Health and Safety requirements.

I have to confess, I do sometimes regret the passing of all that cumbersome palaver. Time-wasting it may have been, but it did instil one valuable discipline. It made you less inclined to go with the first thought that came into your head. When setting off on a false trail could lead to such excesses of retyping and rejigging, you were obliged to mull an idea over in a lot more detail before committing yourself to it.

It was, I suppose, akin to television watching in the days before the invention of the remote control. You tended to give the programme a bit more of a chance before hauling yourself up and walking across to change the channel.

On the other hand, all that carbon paper ...

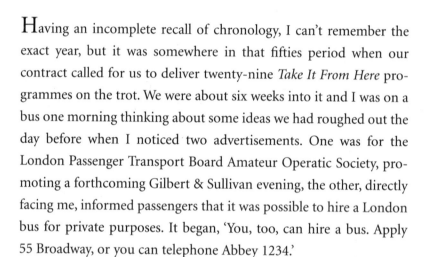

Having an incomplete recall of chronology, I can't remember the exact year, but it was somewhere in that fifties period when our contract called for us to deliver twenty-nine *Take It From Here* programmes on the trot. We were about six weeks into it and I was on a bus one morning thinking about some ideas we had roughed out the day before when I noticed two advertisements. One was for the London Passenger Transport Board Amateur Operatic Society, promoting a forthcoming Gilbert & Sullivan evening, the other, directly facing me, informed passengers that it was possible to hire a London bus for private purposes. It began, 'You, too, can hire a bus. Apply 55 Broadway, or you can telephone Abbey 1234.'

It must have been that first advert still ticking away at the back of my mind because I suddenly realised that 'You, too, can hire a bus. Apply 55 Broadway, or you can telephone Abbey One, Two, Three, Four' exactly fitted a popular G&S tune. At the time, I didn't know its title, never having been much of a G&S devotee, but I learned later on that it's 'Dance a Cachucha' from *The Gondoliers*.

The words were a perfect fit. Some years later, while I was chatting with Sammy Cahn after he had made an appearance on *Looks Familiar*, he mentioned the very particular pleasure of finding 'words that sit exactly on the music'. It was a pleasure which, like so many

others, I had first experienced in the sixth form, when I noticed that
Keats' 'Thou wast not born for death, immortal bird, / No hungry
generations tread thee down' could be sung to the tune of the verse
of Stanley Holloway's 'With Her Head Tucked Underneath Her Arm'.
More recently, there was a Radio 2 traffic bulletin that slotted comfortably into the melody of Judy Garland's 'I Was Born In A Trunk'.
It went, as I recall:

> There's a car broken down
> On the east-bound carriageway
> Of the elevated section
> Of the M22.

I mentioned the G&S find to Frank as soon as I got into the office
and we discussed how best to make use of it. He was as fired up about
it as I was and we came up with the notion of helping out the London
Passenger Transport Board Amateur Operatic Society by fitting bus-
based lyrics to some other well-loved G&S tunes.

There was a bus timetable in the office so, after sending out to
Chappell's in New Bond Street for a Gems from *Gilbert & Sullivan*
LP, we went at it.

By working through lunch, we had it finished by three in the
afternoon. It included parodies of 'With Catlike Tread' ('Don't cuss
the poor old bus, / Swearing at the drivers, / Wanting change for
fivers, etc.'); 'Take a Pair of Sparkling Eyes' ('Take a 6 to Kensal Rise,
/ Stopping off at Hackney Wick, etc.'); 'Three Little Maids from
School' ('One little lady bus conductress, / Leaping about like a gym
instructress, etc.'); plus three others and concluding with a completed chorus of substitute words for the rousing 'Dance a Cachucha'
('You, too, can hire a bus, etc.').

Fairly pleased with ourselves for finishing off a sizeable chunk of script so early in the week, we rang our producer, Charles Maxwell, to read it to him over the phone. We hadn't read him more than a couple of lines of the introduction when he interrupted. Were we seriously trying to put parodies of Gilbert & Sullivan on air? Surely we must know that all the G&S works were under a copyright so inviolable, no one had ever been granted permission to alter a syllable, let alone perpetrate a whole set of parodies. How could we have wasted a whole day on a piece the BBC could not possibly broadcast?

Good question. But we were so reluctant to abandon the idea, we rang another BBC department and asked how we could set about getting in touch with whoever was the current owner of Gilbert & Sullivan's copyright. It turned out to be Bridget D'Oyly Carte, granddaughter of Richard, founder of the D'Oyly Carte Opera Company. Where might she be found? Well, considering her relationship to the man who built the Savoy Theatre, we could try the Savoy Hotel.

We did. She had a suite there, and yes, she was a regular listener to *Take It From Here* and yes, she could see us in the morning, around eleven.

Should we immediately start work on an alternative piece so that if she gave us a thumbs-down, we would not have lost one and a half days? With a schedule that only allowed us four and a half days' writing time, come what may, the completed script for the whole show had to be in Charles' hands by 2 p.m. Friday. The possible loss of time would mean at least one session of working right through the night.

But we found ourselves totally unable to focus on any substitute for the G&S idea. Somewhere around nine that evening we gave up trying and arranged to meet in the Savoy entrance hall at a quarter to eleven the next morning.

Between us, we sang the whole thing through to Bridget D'Oyly Carte and heard her chuckle a few times. When we finished, she nodded cheerfully and gave us permission to broadcast it, moving across to her desk to confirm her agreement in writing.

While she was busy doing that, we took great satisfaction in telephoning Charles and singing it through to him again. This time, with a warning that if he was still minded to turn it down, he would be placing himself in mortal peril.

From a window of our fourth floor office in Conduit Street, you could look across Regent Street straight down into the ladies' changing room at Jaeger's. In addition to the obvious delights this afforded, there was the extra pleasure of spotting the moment when a visitor noticed it.

As he gazed down, remarking on the pleasing view of Regent Street that stretched out below, we would see the back of his neck suddenly tighten. Our standard drill then was to trump up an immediate excuse to get him back in the visitor's chair, where there was nothing to gaze at but the posters on our wall. Then we would wait to see how long it took him to concoct a reason to get back to the window.

Very few of them would come straight out with it and say they wanted to take another look at the ladies opposite undressing. Talbot Rothwell was one of those who did, adding, 'If my office had a view like that, I'd never go home.'

Frank said, 'Well, we do sometimes stay till half past seven on Late Closing days.'

The floor below us housed the Head Office of Atkinson Blankets. Going down in the lift with George Wadmore one day, we stopped there to admit a dignified older gentleman. After some pleasantries, he introduced himself as Lord Limerick. George shook his hand warmly. 'Great to meet you. I love calypso music.'

Throughout the years of its run, we always rounded up the 'warm up' for *Take It From Here* in the same way. After the cast had been introduced and each had said a few cheerful words of welcome to the studio audience, the red light would start flashing and they would hear the preparatory 'Ten seconds to go' from the control room. At which point, Jimmy Edwards would register sudden dismay and, clutching at his pockets, exclaim, 'My script! Where's my script? I must have left it in the reading room!'

Sitting in the front row, Frank would react immediately to this. Scrambling to his feet, he would dash out through the nearest side-exit door as Jimmy confided to the audience, 'Well, I always read in there.'

Within seconds, Frank would come rushing back through the swing doors, triumphantly brandishing a script. But before he could place it in Jimmy's outstretched hand, he would trip and go crashing to the floor, the pages of the script scattering all over the rostrum.

And it was exactly at that moment, with the audience gasping and

Frank flat on the floor, that the red light would steady and the first four notes of the show's signature tune would be heard. As the tune swelled to its finish, a calmly smiling Jimmy would remove his script from the back-pocket where it had been nestling all along.

Week after week Frank took that fall, never failing to win an audible response from the audience. By the end of each season he had collected so many bruises, we sometimes wondered whether a smart lawyer could present them as 'work related injuries', thus qualifying him for some kind of huge compensation claim.

The only times Frank and I got into real voice-raising, finger-wagging, door-slamming arguments was when we had to decide which name to give a character in the script. Later, when he was writing his autobiography, any time he hit a bad patch, I used to console him with, 'Well, at least you don't have to think up a name for the principal character.'

Sheldon Keller told me that in the thirties, there was a prolific writer of Hollywood B movies who sidestepped the problem by using the same six names for his characters in every film. Sheldon could reel off all of them but the only one I can remember is Kincaid, probably because I still hear it in the afternoon black-and-whites on ITV3.

A journalist friend of ours in Los Angeles provided us with a time-saving godsend he picked up after enrolling in a local 'How to Write Successful Magazine Fiction' course. One of the student-aids it supplied was an incalculable list of typical Christian names for twelve different nationalities. He copied it and sent it to us, as well as their guide to the psychological impact of certain Christian names. This included the useful tip that no bad guy should ever be called Jeff. (Jeffs can only be good guys.)

We had a fondness for Tozer as a character surname, can't remember why. And Pacefoot for the surname of period heroines. (How many twigged it was a nod to Steptoe?)

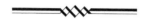

We were prompted to write *The Glums* partly as a reaction against the over-cosy situation comedy families of that time but mainly as a response to contemporary attitudes towards what might be called 'The Rules Of Engagement'. In that era, early fifties, engaged couples such as Ron and Eth still did not Do It. Ron and Eth yearned to Do It and they were aware they would eventually Do It but during the interim the proprieties of the time forbade their Doing It.

It was that conflict of impulses which attracted us to their situation. As Mr Glum variously described it to Ron, it was 'like trying to drive a car with one foot on the brake and the other on the accelerator', or 'like being given a present for Christmas that you're not allowed to open till Easter'.

It was, however, within Eth rather than Ron that the banked fires raged fiercest. And while, by reason of the prevailing broadcasting ordinances, those feelings could never be made explicit, how skilfully June Whitfield hinted at them.

If my parents were not home when I got back from Craven Park Elementary School, I would sometimes go up the road to my Auntie Winnie's for tea. Her teas differed from those I was accustomed to at home in that she always offered a choice of two dishes for dessert. (Or 'afters', as we then called them.)

Such lavishness was, however, not without its drawbacks. 'Which would you like?' she would ask. 'I've got stewed apples or rice pudding.'

'I'll have the stewed apples, please,' I would answer.

'Not the rice pudding?'

'No thanks. I'll have the stewed apples.'

'I thought you liked rice pudding.'

'I do, I'll have the rice pudding.'

'Have the stewed apples if you prefer.'

'All right, I'll have the stewed apples.'

'I cooked the rice pudding specially.'

'In that case, I'll have the rice pudding.'

A pause. 'Shame to let the stewed apples go begging.'

'I'll have the stewed apples.' For reasons I can no longer recall, 'I'll have a bit of both, please' was not an option.

Many years later, we transplanted this dialogue exchange, practically verbatim, into an episode of *The Glums* where Eth, having just cooked her first-ever meal for Ron, was trying to coax from him which of two alternative dishes he would prefer. The toing and froing of stewed apples and rice pudding worked out quite well in the studio, with the laughter building nicely throughout and even a spatter of applause at the end of the sequence.

The morning after the broadcast, I dropped in to see my parents and when my mother opened the door, she was shaking her head and her face was filled with reproach. 'You couldn't find anybody else to make a mockery of? You had to hold up your Auntie Winnie for the whole world to laugh at?'

I was dumbfounded. 'Mum, how could anybody know it was Auntie Winnie.'

'With the stewed apples and the rice pudding? Everybody will know!'

She was inconsolable. 'Didn't you for one moment take into consideration all the times she came round and sat with you when you had one of your throats?'

That afternoon I took Auntie Winnie a bunch of flowers, but I don't know if my mother ever forgave me.

There was a time when both television and radio made much more of Christmas than the current perfunctory nod to it. Most of the popular TV light entertainment programmes were called on to supply a specially written Christmas offering which, because of problems with studio space and crewing, as often as not were recorded much earlier in the year. This could occasionally be as early as August, which meant that members of the studio audience wearing open-neck shirts or summer frocks had to be kept well out of camera shot.

Prior to that, back in the days when *Take It From Here* began, BBC Radio's longest established and best-loved seasonal programme was *Christmas Night with the Stars*. It was a two-hour show, broadcast live from the big studio in Aeolian Hall in Bond Street, and featured everybody whose name warranted thick print in the *Radio Times*. After Frank and I had contributed bits and pieces to it for a couple of years, they decided Jimmy Edwards should host the next one and asked us to write the whole programme around him.

No one can say we didn't warn them. Going out live from 7 to 9 p.m. meant the host would have to be in the studio all day rehearsing. That is, all day Christmas Day, knowing that the only refreshments on offer would be tea, coffee and soft drinks. We suggested that, Jimmy being Jimmy, might alcohol not be advisable – perhaps in a small anteroom?

They drew our attention to the signs: 'No Alcohol Allowed in the Studio'. We were instructed to impress upon Jim the significance of the broadcast, the huge listening audience it attracted, the important place it occupied in the lives of the housebound and the lonely.

All this we obediently conveyed to our star and though we had to deal with a certain amount of grumbling and glowering around 5 p.m., when the red light went on at 7 he rose to the occasion magnificently. He bestrode it like a colossus, obeying his given timings, resisting any temptation to adlib and punctiliously sticking to every word of the script.

With the exception of the finale. Here I must explain that, by tradition, every *Christmas Night with the Stars* made its farewell with the same words. The host's closing speech would run: 'Well, listeners, that's about all we have time for. But our party will be continuing here in the studio as we hope yours will be out there. So please join us in a final chorus of "Auld Lang Syne" by imagining there is a hand stretching out from your wireless set and that hand belongs to the BBC. Hold it in yours and sing with us (SINGS), "Should auld acquaintance be forgot ,etc."' And the programme would fade out on the entire cast singing.

Jimmy so nearly made it. Word for word, he declaimed, 'Well, listeners, that's about all we have time for. But our party will be continuing here in the studio as we hope yours will be out there. So please join us in a final chorus of "Auld Lang Syne" by imagining there is a hand stretching out from your wireless set and that hand belongs to the BBC.'

Here he unexpectedly paused. Then, at full volume, he continued, 'Get an axe ...'

From that year on, every *Christmas Night with the Stars* was pre-recorded.

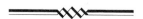

Although Frank's peerless autobiography, *A Kentish Lad*, has already revealed the phrase with which we probably inflicted the deepest dent in the BBC's corporate sensitivities, a little more in the way of background detail may not come amiss.

When *Take It From Here* began establishing itself and our voices were being heard on a couple of panel games, we were asked if we would take on the writing and presenting of a 'light-hearted' radio documentary built round the approaching Paris fashion shows.

We were reluctant. The BBC was persuasive. The word 'prestigious' was insinuated. 'We'll give you the very latest in portable recording machines and guarantee you ringside seats for every top fashion house.'

We said we didn't think it was us.

'You'll mingle with the most glittering names in haute couture, interview the seamstresses and chat with the big buyers. We'll get you into the models' changing rooms.'

'We'll do it.'

As was their custom, BBC Copyright Department sent us a cheque to cover the 'commissioning fee', a preliminary fifty per cent of the total fee, the balance to be paid when the programme was completed. Travel arrangements were discussed, hotels suggested, important contacts noted. Then, for a variety of reasons, chiefly to do with time-tables, the whole thing fell through. On the weeks we could make it, the BBC couldn't and vice versa. By the time we hit on mutually suitable arrangements, the Paris fashion show season was over.

The BBC bore no rancour, neither did we. We were well into the next season of *Take It From Here*, when a letter from Copyright Department arrived. It said, 'We see from our records that you were paid a preliminary fee in respect of a proposed programme about Paris fashions. As this programme was never made, we would be glad if you would please return the commissioning fee.'

On impulse we wrote back, 'Thank you for your letter. We regret that we have no machinery for returning money.'

Never heard another word.

'It looked so good on paper' is a frequently heard expression of regret after a show has failed to live up to its expectations. (Alfred Marks claimed he had even heard it used with reference to sex.) Charles Maxwell, *Take It From Here*'s producer, would sometimes quote it, when turning down pages we submitted, maintaining that although they had amused him while he was reading them, they would be less effective in performance.

He was often correct in this assessment, although we would rarely admit it at the time, sullenly claiming as we walked back to the office to start a rewrite that he had only turned the stuff down because we were tall. Charles was not much over five foot and Frank and I were six foot four and six foot two and three-quarters respectively. We would quote with relish Lenny's remark in *Of Mice and Men*, 'Curly's like a lot of little guys. He hates big guys.'

As I say, there were not many occasions on which his judgement proved wrong but there was one he always admitted to. It was a small sequence we wrote for a parody of *Julius Caesar*. While agreeing that it worked on the printed page, he suspected that saying it aloud would confuse the listener.

Placing our faith in the fact that so many of our audience had recently been only too familiar with military drill, we persuaded him to leave the lines in. They went as follows:

> Jimmy Edwards as Caesar addresses his troops:
> CAESAR: Roman soldiers – Number!
> FIRST SOLDIER: I.
> SECOND SOLDIER: I-I.
> THIRD SOLDIER: I-I-I.
> FOURTH SOLDIER: I-V.
> FIFTH SOLDIER: V.

Because *Breakfast with Braden* was a radio series designed to go out on Saturdays at 8 a.m., when it was originally offered to the Light Entertainment Department we called it 'Something for the Weekend', a title which, as we should have foreseen, stood no chance at all with the BBC of those days.

It was the first comedy show to be broadcast that early in the morning, and listeners took some time to get round to the fact that it had no serious intent. In an early episode, Bernie announced, 'I know some of you have trains to catch but instead of constantly interrupting the show to give you time-checks, we'll get them all out of the way in one go. So, at various points throughout this programme, it will be 8.07, 8.12, 8.17, 8.23, 8.26 and eventually 8.29.

We received shoals of aggrieved letters explaining why this move was of little use to commuters. By programme seven, however, when we employed a similar tactic, inviting listeners to let us help them time their breakfast boiled egg ('By now, your egg will be rock-hard'), there were hardly any protests. They'd caught on.

Rehearsals for the later series of Braden radio shows took place on Monday mornings, so the high point of the first tea-break was always Nat Temple recounting details of the function for which he and his band had provided the music the preceding Sunday night.

Frank and I particularly liked hearing about some of the 'requests' he would receive on these occasions. People would ask, 'Would you please play "She Gets Too Hungry"?' – their way of soliciting 'The Lady is a Tramp' – while a request for 'That's What You Are' masked a plea to hear 'Unforgettable'. Similarly, the older crowd would sometimes demand 'Lisa Brown' – an errant mnemonic for 'September in the Rain'. ('The Lisa Brown, Came tumbling down, remember, That September in the rain'.)

Another memorable request came from a Scottish lady, who asked if his band could oblige her with the title song from *No, No, Nanette*. When Nat had to confess that it was a tune most of his younger players were unlikely to have in their repertoire, the lady's expression became severe. 'Do they no' know "*No, No, Nanette*"?'

Ian, the Mayfair Hotel's resident pianist, always played at the birthday parties the Bradens held there. It was on one of these occasions that he told me about the Australian visitor who had leaned on the piano and asked, 'Can you play "Isle Of May"?'

Ian, the possessor of the West End's most extensive repertoire of vintage popular songs, was momentarily baffled. Then, in the way these things do, the melody came back to him. Pleased with his ability to recall this very minor Andre Kostelanetz tune, he played two choruses of it and then looked up expectantly.

The man smiled back and said, 'Thank you. Now can you play "Isle Of May"?'

Defeated, Ian said, 'I thought I'd just played it. Can you give me some idea how it goes?'

'Sure,' said the Australian and sang, 'Isle of May, Why not take Isle of May.'

Nobody had a better ear for the nuances of demotic speech than Al Read. I need only refer you to the implicit nods and mouth-tightenings in his 'Enough was said at our Edie's wedding.' For those labouring in the fields of comedy, an encounter with a remark like that can provide the same sudden exaltation as any line of poetry.

I remember experiencing a similar surge of emotion the first time I heard Chic Murray's 'If you hadn't got here before me, I'd have been here the same time as you.' It also happened with Jimmy James' sublime, 'Whenever she hangs out her bloomers, the people next door lose an hour of daylight.'

Jimmy Edwards, the gentleman for whom Frank and I most frequently performed services of a scriptwriting nature, always maintained that, out of all the acres of lines we put before him, his favourite was: 'His name was Winterbottom. A cold, stern man.'

Jim would insert it into all manner of contexts, maintaining that it brought together all the ingredients that appealed to the English sense of humour: a deflation of dignity, a pun, a reference to bottoms and a mention of the weather.

The major flaw in this analysis was that, more often than not, the line failed to get a laugh, being what is known in the trade as a 'slow burner'. By the time the audience had made the necessary connection, Jim was on to something else. This never ceased to irritate him.

BBC Radio, Aeolian Hall, early fifties. Jim Davidson was a somewhat forbidding and fiercely patriotic Australian who held an executive position for a while at the top of BBC Radio's Light Entertainment Department. At the time, the Department was going slightly overboard for 'Gala' programmes, with large orchestras and big-name guests from all walks of life, with correspondingly inflated script budgets. Jim was one of the prime initiators of this type of star-strangled entertainment, so when Sid Colin, Frank and I were summoned to attend him at his Aeolian Hall office one morning, we were there on the dot.

'The planners have just given the thumbs up to a special ninety-minute Gala one-off I put forward for 26 January,' he announced. 'And your three names are down on the list of suggested writers.'

We murmured our gratitude, attaching no particular significance to the date. 'I've been thinking about a suitably atmospheric opening for it,' he went on. 'Something that'll well and truly set the scene. And for what it's worth, here's my suggestion. We fade in on a steady fshhhhh, fshhh, fshhhh. Fshhh, fshhh ...' As he continued the fsshhhhing, Frank was the first to catch on. 'Surf?'

Jim nodded approvingly. 'That's the first sound we hear. The steady pounding of the surf. Then through it, very gradually, almost imperceptibly, music creeps in. Duh dah di-dah, duh dah di-dah.' He continued the melody in this fashion, the three of us looking at each other blankly. Then Sid had an inspiration. 'I Tawt I Taw a Puddy Tat!'

Jim broke off and, after a moment, said quietly, 'It's the Australian National Anthem.'

And, of course, 26 January is Australia Day. Needless to say and, I suppose, understandably, we were not chosen for that writing commission. I must confess, though, that, even today, I never hear those stirring opening strains of 'Arise, Australia Fair' without mentally confirming its resemblance to the inglorious Puddy Tat.

Sometimes the shortest distance between two points in a comedy script is, of necessity, a straight line. Jimmy Edwards, however, could not abide them. Whenever he found he had been allotted a straight line in a *Take It From Here* script, his brow would darken. 'What do you expect me to do with "How do you do that?"?' he would mutter. 'What's funny about "How do you do that?"?' In an effort to avert his wrath, we would sometimes try to disguise the line's straightness by prefacing it with an elaborate stage direction. Notably: JIMMY (Wryly, but with a touch of acerbity): 'How do you do that?'

It was the only one that disarmed him. In fact, he considered titling his autobiography, *Wryly, But With a Touch of Acerbity*.

In 1951, when Frank and I went to Australia to write the *Gently, Bentley* series for ABC, it was agreed that the scripts would be reworked versions of the shows we had written in England for Bernard Braden. We found suitable Australian equivalents of Benny Lee and Pearl Carr and the whole thing worked out well enough, except for a few moments when the Oz accent gave the dialogue an unexpected jolt.

This was particularly true of a passage where, in the original, Pearl Carr was complaining to Benny Lee about a sable coat her boyfriend had sent her.

'What was wrong with it?' asks Benny.

'On the label, it was sable,' Pearl answers. 'But in the box, it was fox.'

In the Australian show, the producer had asked the girl playing the Pearl part to assume a particularly down-market type of accent, of a type they referred to as 'drongo'. Consequently, and to no one's dismay but ours, her response was delivered as, 'On the lybel, it was syble. But in the bux, it was fux.'

In Sydney, we were given a mid-morning tour of the RCA Building, home to most of the city's many commercial radio stations. It included a stroll down a long corridor, on both sides of which doors opened into various small studios, each of them transmitting one

The Gaumont State Kilburn, 1937

THIS PAGE: The Trocadero, Elephant and
Castle and the auditorium

LAC D. Norden

Nick and Maggie on a foreign beach

BELOW: Post CBE ceremony –
Nick, Maggie, DN and Avril

Wilson, Keppel and Betty

The man who made
script writing respectable,
Ted Kavanagh

Frank Muir and DN with producer Charles Maxwell: end-of-season orgy

Take It From Here: Wallas Eaton, Dick Bentley, Alma Cogan, Jimmy Edwards and June Whitfield

Batting *Take It From Here* to and fro

From Breakfast to Bedtime with Braden

What's My Line: Frank, Lady Isobe
Barnett, Barbara Kelly and DN

Vera was later replaced by a
very young Shirley Bassey
in her first West End show

or other of the umpteen quarter-of-an-hour daily soaps that went out live every morning between nine o'clock and noon.

We were constantly obliged to give way to actors hurrying from one studio to another, glancing down at scripts and muttering. Budgets did not allow much, if any, time for rehearsal but, as we were soon to discover, Australian radio actors were superb sight-readers. They could slip into any assigned characterisation within a couple of syllables. Many of them would play the leading part in one daily serial, then hasten along the corridor for a two- or three- line supporting role in a couple of other productions.

Every now and again, our guide would open a studio door at random to let us hear a moment or so of whatever fifteen-minute drama was being enacted within. And brief though these snatches of overheard dialogue were, they were usually enough to provide an accurate outline of that soap's entire storylines. Here are some I've remembered and some I probably only think I've remembered:

'What's happening to us, John? Sometimes I have the feeling I don't know who you are any more.'

'Don't you understand, you are not the child's father.'

'And then, my friend, the voice of the Tong will once more be heard in the land.'

'We'd better not see each other again till after the trial.'

'Why are you doing all this for me, a stranger?'

'All right, it's true. I hated him. But I didn't kill him.'

'I don't belong in your world and you don't belong in mine.'

For us, *In All Directions* represented two quite separate but equally satisfying achievements. First, the preliminary lunch at the Caprice where Pat Dixon, the producer, Frank and I met Peter Ustinov to try and persuade him into taking on a radio series. It went on till half past four and racked up the largest expenses bill submitted thus far (1952) by any member of the BBC Light Entertainment Department.

Its second departure from the norm, one that worried the executive high-ups no end, was that it was the first ever BBC comedy series to be broadcast without a script.

During the exploratory lunch, we had found that Ustinov could improvise such extravagant and wondrously complex conceits on a minimum of prompting, we were all for putting this rare gift at the programme's centre. Pat, always the most radical of the Department's producers – across the wall behind his desk he had nailed the rebel flag of the US Civil War – saw virtue in this and promised to shield us from the inevitable wrath the execution of this format would provoke.

The series, which took its title from a favourite Stephen Leacock line, 'He jumped on his horse and galloped off madly in all directions', purported to be an ongoing car journey undertaken by Ustinov and Peter Jones – every bit his equal as an improviser – in search of a mythical Copthorne Avenue, with the two of them supplying the voices of all the characters they met on the way, as well as providing most of the sound effects. Ustinov was particularly hot on car noises and creaky doors opening.

The two Peters would come to our office at the beginning of each week and ad-lib various responses to the characters and situations we suggested they might encounter en route. ('Why don't we pull up and ask that debby-looking girl selling flags where we are?'; 'Look, outside that Boys' Club there's a poster announcing that Field Marshal

Montgomery will be opening their new table tennis room.')

We would record all their improvisations on such themes with a primitive tape machine Pat scrounged for us. Then, after they had left, listen to the various segments, choose the most apt, then rearrange them into some kind of coherent running order. This we would issue in note form to the two Peters, who would turn up on the day of transmission and recreate them, still sans any kind of script.

My one regret about *In All Directions* is that, somewhere down the years, the recorded bits of Ustinov and Jones we had not selected for the programme went missing. I'm quite sure that, even today, their wit and agility of comic invention would still be something to savour.

Peter Ustinov was an avid Fred Astaire fan. He told me the reason he opted for Westminster School instead of St Paul's was because in those days Westminster boys wore top hats.

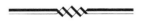

In the same way that the Victorians employed professional mourners to augment the grief at funerals, so studio audiences serve to augment the hilarity at radio and TV comedy shows. They used to be a hotly debated topic in post-war radio, both in the columns of *Radio Times* and among the practitioners. Was an audience an intrusive element or were they useful atmosphere setters?

Frank and I rather supported their presence in peak-time programmes, mainly because they tended to put the performers on their mettle. For Variety shows, they were indispensable, though the BBC did insist that all audience members received a set of detailed instructions as to how they should conduct themselves during the broadcast. These were usually issued in a jocular form by the producer during his preliminary warm-up speech. ('And, remember, our all-star artists only get paid according to the amount of laughter you give them. Roughly, this works out at tuppence a titter, sixpence a snigger and a bob a bellow.')

Other programmes handled the induction process more formally. Derek Roy was a former resident comedian on the venerable *Variety Bandbox* and when he put in an appearance on *Looks Familiar*, he brought along a copy of the printed card handed to every incoming member of that show's audience. It read:

> We welcome your laughter at any time, we hope for your applause, but at appropriate places only, that is, at the end of a scene or a musical number, or on the entrance of an artist who you think deserves it. But we do NOT want: (1). Clapping for individual gags or jokes during an act or scene. It holds up the programme and often spoils the show for listeners. (2). Catcalls, whistles and cheers. They make a horrible noise on the air.

They still do. Producers of TV Reality shows, please take note.

Frank, who remained to the end of his days one of Doctor Johnson's staunchest allies, would often enlist him in our defence when, as frequently happened, we were accused of being overly fond of puns: 'Sir, a good pun may be admitted among the small excellencies of lively conversation.'

One of the consequences of finding fewer opportunities for lively conversation these days is that I have been left with a quantity of small excellencies and no place to unload them. Until now. So let me put on record my immediate affinity with an American PBS radio station that put out an announcement inviting its listeners to fax in requests for a forthcoming programme of seventeenth-century classical music. The announcement concluded 'Remember – if it ain't Baroque, don't fax it.'

I have also been hoarding an incident in the early life of Erich Maria Remarque, the German-born author of *All Quiet on the Western Front*.

He was the youngest member of a large family, so poor they could not afford the bus fares to take the children the local school. Instead, they had to rely on the kindness of a group of more affluent neighbours who would stop by at the Remarque cottage every morning and give each of the children a lift to school in their cars.

One snowy November morning, however, little Erich Maria's lift failed to arrive. Seeing the shivering child waiting at the cottage gate, the man next door said to his wife, 'That last Remarque was uncalled-for.'

At a cocktail party the Automobile Association gave to launch *Drive*, a new magazine they were publishing, I ran into Alan Coren. He raised his glass and observed, 'I suppose you could call this drinking under the influence of *Drive*.'

Out of the many Frank and I were responsible for in our time, only once did we manage to construct a pun that stretched across five syllables. It was part of a *Take It From Here* sketch, where June Whitfield played the poor but honest north country working lass who is lured to his palatial mansion at midnight by the rascally mill-owner (Jimmy Edwards).

'May I offer you a soda scone, my dear?' he asks, his intentions plain for all to see.

'Nay,' she answers. 'I never eat a soda scone so late.'

'But why not?'

'It makes me so disconsolate.'

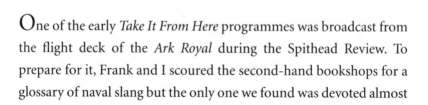

One of the early *Take It From Here* programmes was broadcast from the flight deck of the *Ark Royal* during the Spithead Review. To prepare for it, Frank and I scoured the second-hand bookshops for a glossary of naval slang but the only one we found was devoted almost entirely to synonyms for 'rum rations'.

When we sought the advice of the two young midshipmen who had been seconded to the programme, they could not have been more charming or more helpful. Practically dousing us in pink gins, they put forward various suggestions, one of which they recommended unreservedly. 'You absolutely must drop in a reference to the golden rivet,' they insisted, explaining that in the building of every naval vessel, the last rivet to be put in place was always a special one, made of gold.

We were a little doubtful. 'Interesting, but what's funny about it?' They became more confiding. 'Well, every rating in the audience will know that when visitors come aboard, someone will always ask one or other of the prettiest girls if she'd like to see the golden rivet. And after she's been told what it is, she'll be led to one of the lower-deck portholes and told that if she doesn't mind being lifted up so that her head and shoulders can go through it, she'll be able to view the golden rivet just to her left.'

Now we glimpsed the possibilities. 'And while she's hoisted up in that position?' Obeying the traditions of the Silent Service, the officers merely gestured. It was enough.

In the event we did not, as they say, make a meal of it. We merely had Joy Nichols, in the opening sequence, refer to how nicely her escorting officer had behaved as he showed her round the ship. And, as an afterthought, she added, 'He even offered to show me the golden rivet.'

A gratifying murmur of laughter rippled across the flight deck. It was only as we heard it grow steadily louder and more raucous that Frank and I began to feel apprehensive. Had we been double-crossed?

Indeed, we had. Later enquiries revealed that it is not in the context of pretty girls that the golden rivet subterfuge lingers in naval folklore. As readers of George Melly's *Rum, Bum and Concertinas* will have twigged, it's to do with cabinboys.

Following the success of a song entitled 'The Thing', in which loud thumps on the timpani were substituted for certain words ('Get out of here with your Boomp! Boomp! Boomp!/ And never come back no more'), we wrote a *Take It From Here* item exploring whether this method of economising on words might profitably have been extended to the lyrics of some other well-known tunes.

As an example, we wanted to instance a song of the day, 'It Only Happens When I Dance with You', rendering it as 'It Only Happens When I Boomp! with You'. Suspecting, however, that this might be a little on the racy side for Charles Maxwell, our producer, we decided to employ the 'bargaining chip' tactic. In other words, put forward as our example a totally different song, one where the timpani substitution would render the lyric so inexcusably outrageous, any milder alternative would seem acceptable by comparison.

Unfortunately, the sacrificial song we chose worked too well. It was another popular hit of the day entitled 'Be Careful, It's My Heart' ('It's not my glove you're holding,/ It's my heart'). We sang it to Charles, indicating where the 'Boomp!' replacements came by thumping the side of his desk. 'Be careful, it's my Thump!/ It's not my Thump! you're holding, it's my Thump!'

We got no further. He was so completely appalled by those two lines, he placed a complete veto on the whole idea. It took years, though, before either of us could rid ourselves of the habit of mentally running through the lyrics of any newly encountered popular song to estimate its Boomp! potential.

We crossed the border into censorship territory again with a *Take It From Here* parody of Terence Rattigan's successful play and film, *The Winslow Boy*, in which Dick Bentley played the timorous, cowering schoolboy accused of theft.

At the start of the trial, he is asked, 'How do you plead?' The lad is weeping so copiously, he finds difficulty in answering. Finally, he manages to get out the words 'Not guilty' before relapsing into further racking sobs.

Surveying him, the Judge (Jimmy Edwards) observes, 'Well, you're a miserable pleader.'

Even this approximation to what was still a forbidden word earned us a summons to Broadcasting House the next morning.

The year that Jimmy Edwards stood as a Tory candidate in a by-election, *Take It From Here* was taken off the air until the results were declared. The reasons given were that any words he uttered during the programme would not only have to be considered as contributing to the Conservative Party's allotted airtime, but – even more unlikely – their content might be construed as Tory propaganda.

We wrote to the Board of Governors suggesting that instead of depriving us of our earnings by resorting to this drastic foreclosure, the BBC should adhere to their time-honoured tradition, 'balance' – i.e., commission another half-hour comedy series to star the Labour Party candidate. To date, no reply has yet been received.

Arthur Schwartz was the composer of some of the greatest 'standards' in the American songbook canon – has there been a better one than 'Dancing in the Dark'? – and shortly before he made a guest appearance on *Looks Familiar*, I had been hearing about various censorship difficulties American radio networks had inflicted on certain popular songs.

For instance, the British wartime hit, 'I Didn't Say Thanks For That Lovely Weekend' ('Those two days in Heaven you helped me to spend') never received the US airplay it deserved because certain stations banned it on the grounds that neither the verse nor the chorus contained any indication that the couple concerned were married.

Other well-known songs only gained admittance to the play list providing certain modifications were made to the lyrics. 'Let's Put Out the Lights and Go to Bed' had to be rendered as 'Let's Put Out the Lights and Go to Sleep'; 'He Loved Me Till the All-Clear Came' required amending to 'He Hugged Me Till the All-Clear Came'; and in the popular 'Why Don't We Do This More Often?', singers were made to change the following line, 'Just what we're doing tonight', to 'Just what we're doing today.' Even Bob Hope sometimes had to adjust his signature tune, 'Thanks for the Memory', delivering his reference to 'That weekend at Niagara/ When we never saw the Falls' as 'That weekend at Niagara/ When we hardly saw the Falls.' (Which, to my mind, actually makes the point more effectively.)

Mentioning these to Arthur when we met before the show, I asked him whether he and his lyricist partner, Howard Dietz, had ever run into any problems of this kind. He could only think of one instance. For the 1941 film, *Kiss the Boys Goodbye*, starring Don Ameche and Mary Martin, they wrote a song called 'I Never Let a Day Go By'. Mr

Ameche asked them to alter the title-line to 'I Never Let a Day Pass By', just in case Italians in the audience took the former version as a concealed ethnic slur.

Another example of what could be called 'extra censorship perception' was furnished by Jack Benny. He told us that in one of his fifties radio shows he played a Great White Hunter, guiding his guest star, Deborah Kerr, through the jungle. When they were captured by chanting cannibals and tied up beside a cooking pot, Jack has an inspiration. 'I speak their language,' he says. 'If I can make them laugh, maybe they'll let us go.'

She agrees it's worth a try, so, 'I'll recite a funny limerick,' he says and launches forth into a passage of pure gibberish, along the lines of:

> 'There was a galoom from Nowarga
> Who oola magana tomarga.
> He aga noo wadd
> Nakowa kasadd
> And booga lanoya kararga.'

This is greeted with howls of cannibal laughter and prolonged cannibal applause and, sure enough, the two of them are freed. As Deborah is being untied, she says, 'That was wonderful, Jack. What did it mean?'

'Oh, I couldn't possibly tell you,' he says.

'Why not?'

'It's filthy.'

'And would you believe it,' Jack went on, 'they told me I had to cut out the limerick. Why? Because I'd said on the air it was filthy. Even though,' he added, 'they agreed the words were nothing but nonsense, in their world once you've told an audience something is filthy, that's what it becomes.'

He was probably the most likeable of all the great American comedians we met. Who can resist a man who, on receiving a Lifetime Award for Comedy, remarked, 'Wouldn't it be funny if my next show was lousy?'

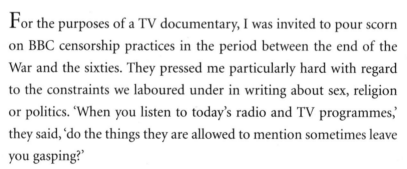

For the purposes of a TV documentary, I was invited to pour scorn on BBC censorship practices in the period between the end of the War and the sixties. They pressed me particularly hard with regard to the constraints we laboured under in writing about sex, religion or politics. 'When you listen to today's radio and TV programmes,' they said, 'do the things they are allowed to mention sometimes leave you gasping?'

I had to answer, 'Of course. But it's not the sex, religion or politics that does it. It's the brand names.'

During the period they had bracketed, nobody on-air was allowed to Hoover a carpet, they were obliged to vacuum clean it. We were similarly forbidden to make use of certain brand names which, heretofore, we had not even realised were brand names: Cellophane, Linoleum, Vaseline, Escalator, Menthol, Aspro – though you could get away with aspirin.

The strictures extended to some of the best-loved lyrics in the popular song canon: 'I Can't Give You Anything but Love' had to mutilate the line that mentioned 'Diamond bracelets Woolworths doesn't sell, baby', while singers of 'You're the Top' would be told to omit its reference to 'You're cellophane'. For his version of the Andrews Sisters' hit, 'Rum And Coca Cola', Edmundo Ros was instructed to content himself with 'Rum And Limonada', while Lonnie Donegan had to substitute the words 'chewing gum' for the brand name mentioned in Billy Rose's 'Does the Spearmint Lose Its Flavour on the Bedpost Overnight?'.

The ban extended into some fairly far-flung areas. Of the two reprimands Frank and I received for breaking the brand name regulations, one was for basing a sketch on a forthcoming Boy Scout 'Bob a Job' week. The mention was held to constitute 'advertising'. The same charge was levelled at some dialogue devoted to a national 'Save Water' campaign during a drought-ridden summer in the late fifties.

On BBC TV, they were equally punctilious about permitting brand names to appear in shot. If a particular product was essential to a scene, it was the duty of the prop man to disfigure its logo with a felt pen so that the name was no longer apparent. Hence, a treasured sitcom moment: a breakfast-table scene in which the foreground was occupied by a cereal box bearing the label, 'Ellogg's Orn Lakes'.

In a curious reversal of these prohibitions, out of the blue one week Frank and I were sent a case of VSOP brandy, accompanied by a letter from an advertising agency representing some kind of trade association of brandy distillers. It thanked us profusely for our help in publicising their client's latest campaign.

We could not imagine why they considered we had done this, until we recalled that, for the current season of *Take It From Here*, we had taken to beginning the final item every week with Jimmy Edwards in a gentleman's club, demanding, 'Waiter, two more brandies and soda, please', before launching into an introduction to the sketch that followed.

In a further letter, the agency explained that their present advertising strategy was to try to reposition their product as not just an after-dinner drink, but one which, like whisky, could also be drunk before a meal. To that extent, having Jimmy ask for a 'Brandy and soda' instead of a 'Whisky and soda' suited their purpose admirably.

What to do? We were by now about halfway through the series and to abruptly, not to say inexplicably, change the by now familiar 'Brandies and soda' to 'Whiskies and soda' would have provoked more questions than it answered. We decided, in everybody's interests, to leave things as they were.

We wrote to the agency, thanking them for the gift, but explaining that the brandy references had, in fact, been entirely fortuitous. They wrote a comforting letter back, confirming that they quite understood our position in the matter. And kept the cases coming.

MOSTLY
TELEVISION

Back in the cradle days of Television, its sprinkling of viewers entertained some eccentric notions about their new acquisition. According to the letters they wrote to the BBC, many believed their TV set weighed more when it was switched on than it did when the screen was unoccupied. Some claimed to have conducted tests proving this, others confirmed it by quoting the maker's instruction manual, which advised that the set should always be switched off before attempting to move it.

Another sizeable group of correspondents wanted it known that a TV set in the room served to keep away mice. According to some of them, this was due to the rays emitted by the cathode tube, while others put it down to the high frequencies Television operated on.

My local paper carried a letter advising new viewers that a length of cellophane hung in front of the set was a sovereign remedy for eye-strain. But by far the most prescient of such notions may have come in a letter the BBC received from a viewer some years later. It advocated that the BBC should take steps to prevent people from yawning while appearing on Television.

The writer's rationale for this prohibition was simple. A yawn is so infectious that anyone yawning on-screen was likely to set off a bout of yawning among everyone watching. And if millions of viewers all yawned at the same time, who knows what damage this simultaneous mass intake of oxygen could do to the Earth's atmosphere?

NB to eco-warriors: might it not be worth crunching some numbers on this?

Somewhere around 1950, Frank and I made our first TV appearance together. It was in a strange Variety programme, produced by Eric Fawcett. He had at one time been Jack Buchanan's understudy and in moments of quiet elation would still execute a creditable soft-shoe.

We certainly gave him no cause for one. Artists' Bookings Department had only offered us the show in the belief that the perpetually conjoined names of Muir & Norden indicated that we were some kind of Variety double act. But as we never turned down any kind of work in those days, we pitched up at Alexandra Palace with six minutes of hastily written cross-talk.

It went down quite well at rehearsal. At least, that was what Eric Robinson, the show's Musical Director, assured us when he wandered across. 'But what are you going to do for a finish?' he asked. 'I don't seem to have your band parts.'

Being more conversant with Variety than Frank, I blamed myself. I had completely forgotten that all double acts of that era concluded their performances with a musical number. Could we sing something? Frank, who had sussed out my singing abilities even at this early stage in our partnership, didn't even pause to consider the question.

Instead, he ventured one of his own. 'Think we could get away with the handbells?' It was something we had seen someone try out at the Windmill, where it had failed dismally. But only because, we had agreed, it had not received sufficient backup in the way of loud musical accompaniment. Here in the studio we would have a full sixteen-piece orchestra behind us. It was worth a try.

Hastily cutting two minutes out of our dialogue exchanges so as to conform to our allotted time, we threw ourselves on Eric Robinson's mercy. If he would just wangle us a table with a set of handbells on it? And could the band busk a very loud version of 'The Bells of St Mary's'?

Fortunately, the idea tickled him. So, at the end of our cross-talk, the band went into a full-out, no holds barred 'Bells of St Mary's', while the two of us rhythmically picked up and shook any bell that came to hand, desperately hoping that the fortissimo blasting behind us would drown out whatever discordances we were producing.

Apparently it did. Or put it this way: according to the Duty Officer's report, not one music lover rang up spluttering.

No subsequent TV programmes have matched the hold which the original *What's My Line* exerted on its viewers. It became an essential component of Sunday night for every family with a television. All of them, young and old, would sit round the set totally absorbed in playing the game along with the panel, most of them obediently shutting their eyes when Eamonn Andrews invited them to do so if they did not wish to see what the next contestant did for a living. (Was this the first example of audience interaction?)

T. Leslie Jackson, its producer, treated his Sunday night responsibilities with unremitting seriousness. When Frank and I joined the panel for a season, the admonitory briefing he gave us before our first programme would have daunted an astronaut. 'This is not a personality showcase,' he warned us. 'The game itself is what is all-important. Keep thinking. Keep concentrating. And always bear in mind,' he concluded, 'the worst crime you can commit on this programme is to ask a question that someone else has already asked. The viewers hate that more than anything.'

'But what's the best way to avoid that?' I said, knowing too well how askew my wits could go on occasions like this.

He was a patient man. 'On the desk in front of you, there's a notepad and a BBC pen. Listen to what the other panellists ask and keep a note of the answers they get.'

Lady Isobel Barnett began the questioning. 'Do you work outdoors?' she asked the first contestant.

'Yes,' he replied. I jotted it down.

'And do you wear a uniform?'

'Yes.' Down it went.

'Do you perform a service?'

A whispered conference with Eamonn. Then 'No' – which meant the questioning passed to Frank. 'Do you sell something?' He got a No immediately, so it moved to Barbara Kelly, a skilled practitioner. 'Do you need any kind of diploma or certificate for what you do?' she asked.

'Yes.' Now we were getting somewhere, but a couple of questions later Barbara received a No so it finally became my turn. Smiling confidently at the camera, I glanced down at my jotted notes. They read, 'Yes, Yes, No, No, Yes, Yes, No.'

Realising that everyone was waiting for me, I asked, 'Do you work outdoors?'

In 1951, Frank and I were conscripted to write *Here's Television*, the first TV programme expressly designed to send up Television itself. The target that came to mind most immediately was the BBC's almost nightly breakdown ritual.

In those days, the 'Normal service will be resumed as soon as possible' caption appeared on-screen so frequently that the Drama Department had established standard procedures for its showing. An off-screen presentation announcer, generally Macdonald Hobley, would tell viewers what had happened, then a record would be played. That first record would be something in keeping with the mood of the play, so it tended to be an orchestral work of a sedate or thoughtful nature. When the record finished, if things had shown no sign of improving, the announcer's microphone would be faded up again for, 'Well, I'm afraid we're still unable to continue with the play, so here's some more music' and in the hope that the mood could still be maintained, the music would continue in a similarly serious vein. If the fault still persisted, there would be another consoling announcement but now, fearing that more of the same might plunge viewers into gloom and hostility, the third record would be distinctly jollier. For any trouble that went on beyond that, viewers would be treated to one of the 'Interludes' ('The Potter's Wheel', etc.) or a short 'interest' film, generally about Sweden.

For *Here's Television*, we decided on a sketch showing what went on behind the cameras when a breakdown happened. We had it take place during the transmission of a tense period drama and began it shortly before a shirt-sleeved Floor Manager unexpectedly entered the scene, waving a script and shouting, 'All right, folks, ease up. Transmitter's packed in.' He then draws their attention to an easel a stagehand has hastily brought on, bearing the caption 'Normal service will be resumed as soon as possible.'

As he talks urgently into his neck mike, we hear the record playing in the background and see the actors relaxing, some mumbling their lines, others puffing on cigarettes, reading a newspaper, etc. Then another stagehand carries on a stand mike and the FM calls 'Macdonald Hobley! Where's Macdonald Hobley? Anybody seen MacHobley?' One of the actors replies, 'I heard him say he was going to try to get a quick shower.' The FM reacts and Mac Hobley enters hurriedly, clad only in a less than luxurious bath towel.

I've lost touch with how the sketch went on from there but it doesn't matter because it was at that point that the script ran into trouble. When it was submitted for approval, we had a shocked phone call from a stratospherically high-up BBC official.

'Out of the question,' he said. 'Under no circumstances can we allow Macdonald Hobley to appear in front of the public wearing only a bath towel.'

'Why not?' we asked.

'Because it is he who will be making the official announcement when the Queen Mother dies.'

Let me remind you, this was back in 1951, when the lady could not have been more robust. After a great deal of pleading, and with Ronnie Waldman, then Head of Light Entertainment, making strong representations on our behalf, the high-ups relented and the bath towel stayed in.

But we would have to admit to keeping an interested eye on Royal health bulletins for the next two or three decades.

Doctor Jacob ('Bruno') Bronowski was Sid Colin's brother-in-law and long before his soaring *The Ascent of Man* series, he made several programmes designed to help demystify science. Before embarking on the very first one, he asked whether we could offer him any useful presen-tation tips.

We both issued the same warning. 'Make sure that you rehearse the final run-through with the actual props you're going to be using on the programme. Familiarise yourself with them. On a live show, all sorts of unforeseen things can go wrong.'

He looked disappointed. 'Not in this case,' he said. 'Everything that I demonstrate will be illustrations of certain basic and inviolable physical laws. Gravity, boiling temperature, that kind of thing.'

On the night, of course, a number of things fell apart and others failed to behave as predicted. It wasn't disastrous but there were enough departures from the norm to provoke a rueful phone call from Bruno. 'I think we might now consider amending all known statements of scientific fact by adding the rider "except on Television". For instance, "Water will boil at a temperature of 212 degrees Fahrenheit. Except on Television." 'A falling body will accelerate at the rate of 32 feet per second per second. Except on Television.'

He reeled off another half a dozen such examples, none of which I can now recall, though I'm confident their truth goes marching on.

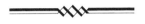

Patrick Campbell possessed an unfailing ability to reduce me to helpless giggles simply by catching my eye, then staring at me po-faced. Well aware he had this power, whenever we were together on one of David Frost's chat panels, he would continually angle his long, solemn face towards me in an effort to attract my gaze, while I would employ every possible stratagem to avoid meeting his eyes. Concentrating on this would occupy more of my attention than the subjects under discussion.

Although he was known for the well-judged use to which he put his stammer, I heard of one occasion when he was wrong-footed. It was at the beginning of a *Call My Bluff* series for which a new producer had been appointed. As Patrick was sitting alone in his dressing room before the show, there was a knock on the door and the young man rushed in. 'Only got a moment,' he said. 'So just wanted to remind you. Energy! Give it bags of energy! Don't let up. Lots of energy. Have fun.' And he was gone.

Gazing after him, Patrick said, 'C-c-c-come in.'

Back in the earliest days of TV, if an actor in a live drama forgot his lines, he, as well as everyone viewing, could rely on hearing a muttered 'prompt' from somewhere off-screen. The points at which their memory went bad on them were sometimes surprising and while nothing we saw matched theatre's most famous 'prompt' ('Or not to be'), both Frank and I witnessed one that ran it a respectable second.

It occurred during a sultry, Graham Greene-ish drama about an angst-ridden doctor in French colonial Africa who had recently left his wife in favour of someone else's and was now steaming up-river towards his new life.

Suddenly, however, the boat receives a radio message from his former hospital. A virulent plague has broken out locally and guess who has just been admitted to the isolation ward as one of its first victims? Even if you didn't manage to guess, the sudden jump into close-up on his anguished face would have given you the answer. It's his wife.

Cut now to the wife, who is lying on a narrow isolation ward bed under one of those ceiling fans. After the camera has registered a few rather decorative plague-spots on her face, the door opens and in comes the local priest.

He was played by a well-loved old, fifties character actor whose nimbus of white hair made him ideal casting for far-flung servants of the Church. Taking the girl's hand, he gazes down on her with concern and says, 'My child, they tell me you have lost the will to live.'

She answers, 'That is because nobody cares whether I live or die.'

The priest shakes his head reprovingly. 'My child, there is Someone who always cares.'

'Who?' she asks wearily.

And that's when it happened. Over his face came the familiar glazed look. As he stood there, in his cassock and dog-collar, clutching his battered prayer-book, you could actually watch his mind racing round in search of the elusive line. Glazed turned into double-glazed but nothing emerged. During that no more than ten seconds of silence, eternity happened.

Then, from somewhere unseen, all of us at home heard the hoarsely whispered monosyllable.

The priest brightened. 'God,' he said, with so much relief in his voice, it went up nearly an octave.

Whatever we thought of those black-and-white programmes Television put before us in the early fifties, viewers could rarely escape a feeling of being in touch with the miraculous. Whether we were looking at a game of ice-hockey or a behind the scenes tour of a paper-plate factory, there was always an awareness that although it was taking place there, we were sitting watching it here.

For all of us, though, there came a time when that awareness of the wondrous would fall away, sometimes gradually, sometimes abruptly. Where Frank and I were concerned, it happened soon after the arrival of Eurovision made it possible to transmit pictures all the way from France. In the flurry of planning that followed, we were among a group invited to submit ideas for programmes that would take advantage of this exciting new development.

For both of us, one of the most congenial pleasures France had to offer was just sitting at a pavement café table, watching the world go by. Accordingly, we argued the case for simply placing a concealed camera on a table outside one of the cafés in the Madeleine, preferably on a Sunday afternoon, and letting it rove the passing strollers, pausing at a face here, or an elegant fashion model there, while carefully placed microphones would provide the pleasing Parisian background track of taxi horns, chatter and street musicians. What better way for British viewers to savour Television's unique ability to deposit you in the middle of somewhere else without actually moving you from your armchair?

They tested the idea with a trial fifteen-minute programme and, as Frank and I were the first to admit, it proved to be beyond belief boring. Just a lot of unremarkable people dawdling along a street. Boring, boring, boring. Sadly, we had to acknowledge that Television viewing had gone beyond the stage where a miracle was enough.

C.A. Lejeune told Frank and me that an early edition of *Animal, Vegetable, Mineral* had Professor Julian Huxley and Sir Mortimer Wheeler on the panel. When they presented themselves to the make-up girl before the show, she looked at Huxley and said, 'I don't think there's much I can do for you, sir.'

Then, inspecting Sir Mortimer, she said, 'I simply must do something for you.'

Later on, the two eminent men of science would spend much time debating which of them had come out best from that encounter.

We helped out on a lavish 'Saturday Night TV Special' built round Jimmy Edwards and performed at the Shepherds Bush Empire. For its finale, we had Jimmy conducting a large orchestra in a full-blown version of 'The 1812 Overture'. It was a no-holds-barred orchestration, with full artillery effects and, on its final crashing notes, a flock of trained pigeons descending on his head.

The pigeons played their part admirably, except that when the show was over, they flew up into the ceiling and nothing would induce them down again. Envisaging them fluttering round the upper circle all night we asked their trainer, a stocky man with a strong Welsh accent, if there was anything we could do to help.

'Does that open?' he asked, pointing upwards.

As it happens, the domed ceiling of the Shepherds Bush Empire does open and shut at the touch of a button. When we told him this, he nodded his satisfaction. Reaching for his coat, he said, 'They'll be back in Cardiff before I will.'

In 1954, we wrote Dick Bentley's first British TV series, six live programmes entitled *And So To Bentley*. Brian Tesler, our producer, wanted him to be supported by two strong, dependable comedy actors, so we suggested Peter Sellers, with whom we had frequently worked in radio, and Bill Fraser, my former CO in the RAF.

Peter was on his usual fine form in the opening show but in the next couple of programmes some of the zest went out of his performance. In fact, he even began to show signs of strain during their final rehearsals.

Our friendship was close enough for us to tackle him about it.

After some hesitation, he confessed that he seemed to have suddenly become afflicted by an acute form of stage fright which, try as he may, he could not shake off. He was in such a bad way that I got his permission to ask Bill, the oldest, most experienced and probably wisest of us, if he knew of any remedy. Straightaway, he advised a medical hypnotist. What is more, he even came up with a name, a highly regarded Harley Street consultant I shall call Doctor P.

He was certainly in demand. The first appointment he could give Peter was the following week at four o'clock on the afternoon of the day our next show was due to be transmitted. We cut its final rehearsal short to give him time to get from Shepherds Bush Theatre to Harley Street, then we waited for his return with our fingers crossed.

When he got back, he was, quite literally, speechless. Peter was always one of the world's great gigglers but on this occasion he was so convulsed by giggles, he could hardly get a word out. Finally, we calmed him down and he recovered sufficiently to tell us what had happened.

Dr P had proved impressive, both in manner and appearance. Quiet, attentive, immaculately dressed, he was, as they say, perfect casting. He listened gravely to Peter's problem, then persuaded him to lie down on a couch where, after a few soothing words, Peter fell fast asleep.

He awakened abruptly but, as he soon became aware, a little before he was supposed to. Dr P was saying, 'In a few moments I will snap my fingers and you will wake up and open your eyes. All those sensations of nervousness will have gone and you will feel refreshed and totally confident. And one more thing. When you leave this office, you will pass my secretary, who is always too embarrassed to ask patients for money. You will therefore stop at her desk and say, "How much do I owe you?" So now –' and Peter heard the snap of fingers.

He performed exactly as directed on leaving the consultant's office and he sailed through the show that night with equal brio, remaining in high spirits for the rest of the series. We could never decide whether this was the result of hypnotic suggestion or premature resuscitation.

Shortly after eight o'clock on the night of 22 September 1955 – it was, of all unimpressive days, a Thursday – an estimated two million screens displayed a picture of a Gibbs SR toothpaste tube encased in a block of ice. Suddenly our Television world was filled with scented soaps, tinned beans, mature ladies in crossover bras and a smiling man who emerged from a small tent on a sunlit hillside to tell us, 'There's no pleasure like rolling your own.' Almost overnight we learned that margarine has a hard 'g', armpits are to be referred to as underarms and distinctions must be observed between fast relief, fast, fast relief and express relief.

Somewhere round 10 p.m. that night, Frank and I made an appearance in a commercial for, and how we blushed to acknowledge it a few years later, Capstan cigarettes. It was intended to be the first in a series whose whimsical catchphrase, they assured us, would soon be taking the pubs and clubs by storm.

It began with me proffering a packet of twenty to Frank, with the words, 'Have a Muir, Mr Capstan.'

'Thank you,' he replied and, offering me his own packet of twenty, 'You have a Norden, Mr Capstan.'

The commercial bore out all our long-held beliefs about pre-planned catchphrases. As far as research can establish, it was never shown again.

I arrived early for a *Take It From Here* rehearsal one Sunday afternoon in 1954 to find Johnny Johnston and the rest of the Keynotes grouped round the piano, running through a chorus of 'Cherry Ripe'. The song was far from the usual type of material they featured on the programme, so it must have been my look of surprise that impelled Johnny to take me into his confidence. The melody was one of the many non-copyright tunes he was checking out for future conversion to advertising jingles.

As Commercial Television was still over a year away, this was the kind of shrewdness that led to his later coronation as 'King of the Jingle'; alternatively, 'The thirty-second Mozart'. Among the more durable successes he had us humming were, 'Hands that do dishes/ Can be soft as your face', 'I'm going well, I'm going Shell', 'A Double Diamond works wonders', 'A Thousand And One Cleans a big, big carpet for less than half a crown', as well as my own favourite example of craftsmanship in fitting a melody to an unpromising lyric, 'Save, save, save with the Co-operative Permanent Building Society'.

As there wasn't much around in the way of tape for recording purposes in those days, when Johnny had to send off a jingle for the client's approval, he would put it down on vinyl and repeat it a half dozen times to save the client the trouble of continually lifting the record-arm off and on. 'Every now and again,' he told me, 'the client phones to let me know that after they played it through, the Board unanimously voted for the tune on track five.'

The tale Johnny most liked to repeat concerned the first of his jingles to get on the air. 'It was for Bournvita and the tune was very simple. It went, "Sleep sweeter, Bournvita", which was repeated, then there was a yawn and "Good-night". It was one where I did the sing-ing myself and, do you know, my mother, who was getting on a bit, would never go to bed until she'd heard me sing it. Didn't matter how tired she was, she'd never go upstairs till she heard me say "Good night".'

Even when Commercial Television went on air in September 1955, not everybody at its helm could be described as taking the long view of its possibilities. At the beginning of that year, Lew Grade called the comedy writers to a meeting where he outlined the golden future ITV envisaged for all of us. If we could use his channel to create some brand-new comedy stars, he explained, there was every chance he could then top theatre bills with them at Blackpool the following summer, where we would be able to share the riches by writing their sketches.

It was an inviting prospect but, in the light of Independent Television's subsequent history, hardly what you would call visionary.

While we were writing sketches for George and Alfred Black's Blackpool shows, the news came through that their company had been awarded one of the new TV franchises, specifically for the North-East region.

George was extremely chipper about it and when we congratulated him, very firm about his intentions for the new station. 'It's not going to be all dancing girls and comedy shows,' he said. 'We'll be doing serious stuff as well. Documentaries. Really serious documentaries. After all, we've got prostitutes in Newcastle as well, you know.'

Our first stab at writing anything in the way of a commercial came when a friendly advertising man who looked after the drink called Tia Maria asked us to have a go at writing the lyric for a Latin-American type of love-song with that title. He had already commissioned the melody for it and if the lyric fitted, Edmundo Ros was willing to feature it on one or more of his many broadcasts, thus insidiously bringing the drink's name to a wider audience.

We came up with a suitably fervent love-lyric – something along the lines of 'Tia Maria,/ My heart grows light,/ The world is bright,/ When you are neeyah' – and Edmundo not only played it on the radio several times, he recorded it.

It didn't seem to trouble anybody that 'Tia Maria', to whom the song's romantic sentiments are addressed, translates as 'Aunt Mary'.

In the mid-fifties Television was as embroiled in looking for new panel games as it was later to become in the search for reality shows. Frank and I were as caught up in the quest as anyone, so when Frank Tarloff suggested one bearing the promising title *Who's Whose?*, we persuaded the BBC to allow us to produce a pilot.

It was an idea very much of its time, based on the observation that when most people found themselves at a social gathering where the other guests were strangers, they were likely to indulge in a mental game of pairing them up. 'Which of those women is that man's wife?' 'Which man is married to that woman over there?' (Marriage, in that patch of time, still being the only acknowledged male/female partnership.)

In *Who's Whose?*, an unnamed husband, referred to as Mr X, sat with his back to three wives, Mrs A, Mrs B and Mrs C. Surveying them was a panel, made up of an eminent psychiatrist, a clergyman, a tabloid agony aunt and an off-the-shelf celebrity. Their purpose, to work out which of the three women behind him was actually Mrs X.

To this end, they all started off with an 'instinctive' guess, based solely on their first impressions of the four people. Then they were allowed to ask each of the quartet a limited number of non-specific questions and, from the answers to these, produce their 'reasoned' guess as to who was Mrs X.

After playing several rounds, some of them with the genders reversed – i.e., a wife in front and three possible husbands behind her – two interesting points emerged. The first was that the panel's 'instinctive' guesses tended to be correct more frequently than the answers they came up with as a result of shrewd questioning. Secondly, there was only one round in which the entire panel arrived at the same answer to both their 'instinctive' and 'reasoned' guesses, and that was also the only one where they all came to the same conclusion: namely, that Mr X was the husband of Mrs C.

In the event, he turned out to be married to Mrs A. But that, of itself, was not what put paid to the programme's chances. What scuppered it was that, after the show, while we were all having drinks in the Hospitality room, Mr X and Mrs C were observed moving wide-eyed towards each other and subsequently cosying up with noticeable enthusiasm.

It did not escape the eye of Tom Sloan, the Head of Light Entertainment. He made it known there and then that the BBC would not, dare not, run the risk of associating itself with a game that had the seeds of such possible consequences.

Nor did he take kindly to Frank Tarloff's later suggestion that we could always call it *Who Was Whose?*.

There is a postscript to the story. Many years after it had appeared in print elsewhere, I was phoned by an American independent production company. They told me they were seeking ideas for a proposed new cable outlet, to be known as the Divorce Channel. Were the format rights to *Who Was Whose?* still available? 'Couldn't be more available,' I replied.

Since when, not another word.

It must have been around the early fifties when Ronnie Waldman, then BBC Television's Head of Light Entertainment, called all the writers together for a special screening. 'What I'm going to show you,'

he said, 'is an example of Television entertainment that is doing fantastically well in the States. It's called a situation comedy.'

We then watched a grainy black-and-white kinescope of a half-hour episode of the top-rated US sitcom series, *Ozzie and Harriet*. When it was over, Ronnie brought the lights up and asked, 'Can we do something like that in this country?'

We looked at each other dubiously. Then almost as one, we sadly shook our heads. 'Out of the question.' The unsurmountable obstacle, we explained, was the English class system. To illustrate how that would immediately capsize any attempt to reproduce the success of the *Ozzie and Harriet* format over here, we instanced various moments in the storyline.

It was an episode where Ozzie and Harriet, representing your average loveable middle-class husband and wife, were seen at home in their comfortable house in the suburbs. Earlier that day, Ozzie had decided to surprise Harriet by leaving the office before his usual time and spending the afternoon with her and the kids. However, when he gets there, he finds it is the afternoon she has invited all her girlfriends round for lunch and a gossip. She orders him out again, with, as they used to say in *TV Times*, 'hilarious consequences'.

We pointed out the inherent drawbacks. Firstly, he decides on a purely personal whim to leave work at midday. Over here, who but the upperest of the upper classes could do that? And what percentage of our viewing audience would identify with them?

Back to Ozzie. After driving home (He owns a car! And, look, his own driveway!), he enters by the kitchen door, carrying one of those oversized paper bags with no handles that Americans affect, calls out the obligatory 'Honey, I'm home' and begins stuffing its contents in the refrigerator. (They've got a refrigerator! To English people back then, that was akin to owning a private jet.)

142

We drew Ronnie's attention to several more such anomalies. Lurking behind all of them, we pointed out, lay the sad fact that, unlike Americans, English viewers were not disposed to chuckle sympathetically at the domestic problems of people in an income bracket manifestly far above their own. In fifties England, the class divide still regulated our responses.

Whether our verdict had the effect of holding back the advent of situation comedy over here for any significant time I don't know. What may be relevant, though, is that the first English domestic sitcom to achieve viewing figures that encompassed all the demographics was *Life with the Lyons*. All the main characters in this were Americans and thus enjoyed the same degree of separation from every stratum of the English class structure.

Everyone in the laughter mongering trade has a show they would prefer to leave out of their CV. For Frank and me, it was a TV series called *How to be an Alien*, adapted from the successful book by the Hungarian humorist, George Mikes.

The project only came about because we happened on a stall in Rupert Street which was offering an enormous collection of vintage black-and-white stills from silent films. Each one captured a moment of high emotion in the film's story, enacted with burning-eyed intensity by leading actors of the period. The collection provoked so many giggles when we showed it around the office, we began casting about for a way of putting it to wider use.

It was Tony Hancock who provided a clue. Visiting us one day, he was so tickled by some of the stills, he began ad-libbing incongruous lines the leading characters might be declaiming, in much the same way as *Private Eye* covers add unsuitable speech bubbles to photographs of well-known faces in the news.

From that came the notion of converting the stills into slides with which we would illustrate a series of Television lantern lectures, presented by the two of us, standing at an old-fashioned magic lantern. We decided to use George's title as an excuse for airing some additional thoughts on the theme of alienation, enlisting the likes of June Whitfield and Ronnie Barker to voice the unexpected and, we hoped, amusing lines the people in the stills would be uttering.

It turned out to be an idea whose time had gone. From the very first minutes of the very first programme we knew we were on a loser. As a mechanism for Television comedy, it just plain did not work. We had condemned ourselves to what Sheldon Keller, a writing colleague on *Buona Sera, Mrs Campbell*, once summed up as 'The Three F Syndrome': 'Format Fatally Flawed'.

Unfortunately, Associated-Rediffusion retained their enthusiasm for it. They had been keen on the show's structure from the moment we first suggested it and now, unconvinced by our qualms and undaunted by the unanimously poor reviews the first programme received, they kept assuring us that we only had to persevere with it and the series would, in their phrase, 'catch on'.

It never did. And while Associated-Rediffusion valiantly pulled out every stop to promote it, their ever more glowing promos may well have narrowed its chances even further. It is an observable fact that if you tell an audience a programme is going to be exciting and it turns out not to be, they will exhibit little resentment. But tell them it's going to be funny and it turns out not to be, they react as though you've plundered their life savings.

We might have managed some kind of resigned acceptance of the show's excoriating notices, especially as we could put up no real arguments against such verdicts as 'desperately unamusing', 'mind-numbingly appalling' and 'thoroughly lame'. What did get under our skin was the sheer number of these onslaughts. To give just one instance: over the same period that the series was on-air, a leading London evening newspaper tried out a policy of featuring a different guest TV critic every week. The result was that instead of receiving one unfavourable critique from that paper, we ended up with six successive batterings from the same publication.

Moreover, the series was adopted by some of the critical fraternity as a sort of template against which other unsuccessful shows could be measured. Thus, for ages after it had disappeared from the schedules, we would pick up a newspaper or magazine and the TV column would present us with something along the lines of 'Last night's such-and-such a show was execrable. Not as execrable, of course, as *How to be an Alien* but ...'

The series ended in March and by June, with the press potshots still echoing round us, we decided to seek shelter. Frank and his family went off to Corsica and I took my lot to the South of France for a couple of weeks at a hotel in Beaulieu.

When I entered the lobby, the first person I saw standing by the reception desk was George Mikes.

'Denis?' he exclaimed in surprise. Then, clasping me with Hungarian fervour, 'Loved the show!'

For me, there was a springtime air to BBC TV's Light Entertainment Department when it was headed by Eric Maschwitz, and not solely because he had written such songs as 'These Foolish Things' and 'A Nightingale Sang in Berkeley Square'. He was an enchanting man, brimming with zest and energy, bright-eyed, long-legged, prowling his office in shirt-sleeves and braces, still convinced that romance lurked round the next corner and tireless in his efforts to imbue his exhausted young producers with the same belief.

When he invited us to sign on with his Light Entertainment Department for three years as, in his words, 'Consultants and Advisers on Comedy', Frank and I found it hard to refuse, even though we were a little doubtful about the job's nomenclature.

They were doubts Mel Brooks shared, as we found out a few weeks later, when we tried to explain to him what we did at the BBC. 'Consultants and Advisers on Comedy?' he repeated in disbelief. 'You mean – you know?'

When Eric needed to escape from telephone calls he would sometimes drift into our office where, often as not, he would find us sitting silently on opposite sides of our wide desk, both of us with our feet on top of it, gloomily staring at each other. Aware that this indicated we were stuck for the next line in a script, he would quietly move the visitor's chair forward and, without a word, lower himself into it and place his own long legs up on the desk.

Sometimes we would maintain this triangular communion of silence for as long as ten minutes before he broke it, generally with something quite irrelevant, but always cogent. 'What do you think is the opposite of a dry wit?' he asked once. Another time, he told us that an American music publisher had recently offered him an enormous sum of money to write an updated version of 'These Foolish

Things'. But he would be turning it down, he confided. After careful consideration he felt the original had used up all the best 'ings' rhymes.

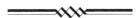

Despite the various corruption scandals which went on during the time Frank and I held executive positions at the BBC, neither of us was ever offered any kind of bribe. Afterwards, we could never decide whether this was because nobody believed we would take one, or because nobody thought we were worth one.

Frank and I joined BBC TV at a time when American comedy LPs were beginning to creep into this country and there was much dinner-party bandying of names such as Lenny Bruce, Bob Newhart, Nichols and May, Shelley Berman and Mort Sahl.

On our trip to America we met Sahl and Berman on the same day, a conjunction I was to recall when Melvin Frank and I were in Italy casting *Buona Sera, Mrs Campbell* and we lunched with Sophia Loren, then, four hours later, had tea with Gina Lollobrigida.

All the names on the comedy albums offered English listeners something that was different but Mort Sahl was the comedian who, for our money, did most to divert comedy from the traditional mainstream. There was no precedent for what he did. His extempore topical monologues added a touch of the intellectual to the standard standup, and his LP was the first ever live comedy album. There were many over here who could quote slabs of it by heart.

Although his sometimes frantic delivery earned him the title of 'Rebel without a pause' and despite claims that he was more of a humorist than a comedian, there's no doubting that he kicked the holes through which an entire generation of 'alternative' comedians clambered.

As there were no comedy clubs in those days, he worked in jazz clubs, in particular the 'hungry i' in San Francisco. Here, he would make his entrance, wearing a V-necked sweater over an open-necked shirt and carrying a rolled up copy of that day's newspaper, from which he would weave his tapestry of ruefully comic observations.

We found him an engaging character, very unshowbiz, and we were delighted when he agreed to do a 'Special' for the BBC. Our first move was to plan the engagement so that he arrived over here ten days before the programme, during which time we kept him well stocked up with all the British newspapers and magazines, so that he could apply his mordant edge to matters of local concern.

Came the night and before as glittering an audience as has ever been assembled for a comedy show, he entered in his trademark sweater and proceeded to repeat practically everything they had been listening to for months on his breakthrough American LP.

Fortunately, he proved so vital and appealing in person, he managed to carry them with him. Frank and I were disappointed, but forgave him much for his mention of a college friend who had majored in fourteenth-century Tibetan theology and was working as a bank clerk until he could find something appropriate in his field.

The Seven Faces of Jim was Ronnie Barker's first TV series and our first opportunity to get to know him. We found we shared a fondness for the same end-of-the-pier jokes, agreeing that the best of them began 'A man went into a chemist's shop.' (Favoured example: 'A man went into a chemist's shop and asked for a bar of soap. "Want it scented?" asked the chemist. "No, thanks, I'll take it with me."')

Ronnie also introduced us to the joke which, in his auto-biography, *Dancing in the Moonlight*, he cites as his all-time, flat-out favourite:

'I have two hundred more bones in my body than you have.'

'Why's that?'

'I had a kipper for breakfast.'

'Two words you can't go wrong with,' Eric Morecambe put on record during a *Looks Familiar* session, 'are kippers and Cockfosters.'

While we were working with him on *The Big Noise*, Bob Monk-house told me that one of his ambitions was 'to write the Ultimate Joke'. This would be a joke so funny, so satisfying, nobody who heard it would ever need to hear another one. Whenever he or she felt like laughing, they would only have to recall this joke and the laughter it would again provoke, unfailingly, time after time, would be sufficient to quench all desire for more.

Over the years that followed, I would occasionally ask Bob if he was making any progress with the Ultimate Joke. 'I think I may have got close to it last night,' he admitted once. 'Or at least, the opening line. I think it starts "A man went into a chemist's shop ..."'

During that patch of the early sixties when we had an office at TV Centre, a survey came out reporting that the majority of viewers tended to watch BBC Television rather than ITV at times of national disaster and on New Year's Eve.

The latter preference was due to a widely held belief that when the BBC told us it was 12 midnight, it was dead-on 12 midnight. There were still lingering suspicions that, should some commercial advantage accrue, the other lot might let it go a minute or so either way.

During a dinner with Henry Cecil, he told us about a recent County Court case in which he'd remarked to a defendant: 'You've been up in front of me before.'

'No, Your Honour.'

'I never forget a face. You've appeared in front of me before.'

'I have, Your Honour. But not in this court.'

It was only then Henry realised he was an actor who had played a part in one of the *Brothers in Law* episodes.

Something I feel I should be able to recall more vividly than I do is sitting next to Kenneth Tynan on the programme in which he uttered the first 'Fuck' ever transmitted on peak-time British Television. Harvey Orkin was the third guest in the discussion and Robert Robinson the chairman who guided the conversation into another direction so promptly and smoothly, there were many viewers who did not immediately comprehend the enormity they had just witnessed.

Though I felt sure that Ken had it in mind to employ the word from the beginning of the discussion – at the time, he was waging a prolonged public campaign for the abolition of the Lord Chamberlain's office and the offending monosyllable had come to symbolise the absurdity of its censorship powers ('Is the word "duck" seventy-five per cent obscene?') – nevertheless, he looked very strained and white around the nostrils as we left the studio.

When we arrived at the doors of the Hospitality room, one of the BBC's corps of disabled commissionaires came hobbling up. Waving a sheet of paper, he announced, 'Some telephone messages for you, Mr Tynan.' Ken inspected the paper and showed it to me.

One message was from George Melly, the other from Jonathan Miller, both offering their congratulations and support. Ken muttered, 'Now I know I'm in trouble.'

Although Frank and I lived miles away from each other, he in Surrey, me in North-West London, we were called for jury duty on the same day. According to Henry Cecil, with whom we were working at the time, 'The chances of that happening are about the same as your chances of winning the Pools.'

'Then why couldn't we have won the Pools,' Frank asked, reasonably enough I thought.

I was luckier than he was as regards the circumstances of our jury service. He spent two weeks at the Old Bailey on a fraud case of numbing complexity and tedium, while I had a week at the London Sessions on an assortment of minor cases, all of them rich in human drama.

The first was a lad charged with indecent behaviour in a cinema. He and his mate had been sitting behind two girls and during the intermission, he had suggested that his mate join one of the girls, while the other sat with him. They had agreed and when the lights went down, he put his arm round the shoulders of the girl who had joined him. Twenty minutes later she ran sobbing up the aisle, told the manager she had been the victim of an indecent act and the police were called.

'I asked the plaintiff for his version of the incident,' the policeman said in the witness box. 'And he said,' and here he consulted his notebook and quoted, 'He said, "She let me keep my hand on her tit for more than ten minutes so I thought it would be all right."'

The boy's defence counsel rose. He was a young man and even I could see by the way he plucked at his gown that his large moustache was an attempt to disguise his inexperience. 'I put it to you, constable,' he said, 'my client did not use the word "tit", he said "breast".'

'He said tit,' the PC replied.

'I am assured by my client that tit is not a word he is accustomed to using. He would have said breast.'

'He said tit.'

'Not breast?'

'He said tit.'

'Can you be one hundred per cent positive he did not use the word breast?'

'He said tit.'

Before counsel could get his next question out, the judge interrupted. 'You're not going to ask him that again, are you?'

'It goes to character, Your Honour. The sort of boy who customarily uses the word tit is altogether different in character and behaviour from one who refers to that part of the body as ...'

'Oh, do give over,' the judge said.

I could barely contain my pleasure. Despite all my doubts, people in courts did behave like characters in a Henry Cecil novel.

MOSTLY
MY WORD!,
MY MUSIC
AND THE GUILD

As the great majority of people currently walking the street are unlikely to have heard the radio programmes from which Frank and I compiled our six books of *My Word!* stories, let me fill in a little of their background. *My Word!* was devised by Tony Shryane and Edward J. Mason in 1956 as a literary quiz in which the contestants, instead of treating the subject with the reverential solemnity the BBC usually accorded it in those days, would be encouraged towards a certain amount of what Robert Frost called 'perhapsing around'.

For one of the questions on the first show, Frank and I were each given a quotation and asked to explain when, where and by whom the phrase was first used. The two quotations were 'Let not poor Nelly starve' and 'Dead, dead and never called me mother!'

As the first was too easy and the second a bit difficult as regards names and dates, we both chose to invent an alternative origin. These proposed that Quotation One was first uttered by the chef at the Savoy. Finding himself short of desserts late one night, he poured some stuff over a peach and, hastily christening it 'Peach Melba', sent it out to a famished Dame Nelly Melba. Quotation Two, it was suggested, was first said by a lad reeling away from a vandalised telephone box after finding that the damaged instrument had made it impossible to put in the nightly call to his silver-haired parent.

This round became a permanent finale to the show and, as the years rolled by, the short invented stories became longer, wilder and more circuitous, while the puns they led up to grew steadily more intricate and oblique, not to say desperate. After the first season we gave up ad-libbing them, partly because they didn't always work out successfully, but mostly because, with so little time to reflect, we had to go with the first idea that came into our heads and, sometimes, that would prove a little too salty for the current broadcasting palate.

I remember Frank being asked once which, among his abundant crop of *My Word!* stories, his favourite was. For many reasons, one of which I'll come to elsewhere, he nominated the tale he manufactured to explain the true origin of the phrase, 'Goodbye, Mr Chips'. To my mind it was also one that reflected so much of his individuality and style that I append it below.

Goodbye, Mr Chips

I am usually such a happy little chap, ever ready to dispel gloom with a merry quip or a saucy bon mot. I don't think that I would be breaking a confidence if I reveal that many years ago the lady with a mole who taught Sunday School at the Congregational Church referred to me as 'one of Nature's sunbeams'.

But a few months ago I changed. Instead of dashing about the house wreathed in smiles and throwing off jolly epigrams I took to leaning silently against the wallpaper, scowling and plucking at the hem of my jacket.

The change came over me one day when I was lunching at the BBC canteen. I looked down at my tray, veal-loaf fritters and a waffle, and the awful realisation dawned that the meal epitomised my career: frittering my time away and waffling on the radio. I had achieved nothing for which I could be remembered by posterity. But what to do about it? What mark does one have to make so that when one is dead and gone one will be remembered long after one is forgotten?

The answer came to me on a bench in Hyde Park, where I was sitting brooding. A Japanese tourist beside me was fanning his face with a folded copy of the *Evening Standard* and a headline caught my eye: 'Paul Getty pays £15,000 for National Gallery's *Washerwoman.*'

This seemed to me to be a stiff price to pay for recruiting domestic staff, even for a man reputedly not short of a bob. So my curiosity was aroused. I found that by getting on my knees in front of the tourist and synchronising my head with the oscillations of the newspaper I could read the whole piece. What emerged from the article was that Paul Getty had bought a terracotta portrait head from the National Gallery. It was a study by Rodin of his washerwoman, Mme Gautier. She was a friendly, excitable woman aged 34, with two daughters, etc. etc.

Of course! The way to go down to posterity is to be sculptured! If the biography of an unknown washerwoman could, a hundred years after her death, still cool the brow of a Japanese tourist, surely the same fame would attend me? I can see the newspapers now – 'A terracotta head changed hands for £15,000,000 today. It is reputedly the head of F. Muir, who lived a hundred years ago. Now famous, he was little known at the time being a trade fritterer and waffler. A lady with a mole once called him "one of Nature's sunbeams", and certainly his noble brow betokens ...' etc.

I set to at once to sculpt a terracotta head of myself to present to the National Gallery.

It seemed to me that the best way to ensure a likeness would be to work from photographs. So I persuaded the Egham Photographic Society to help. Eighty of them turned up one sunny Saturday. I formed them into a circle, stood in the middle, 'click', and a week later I had eighty photographs of my head, each taken from a slightly different angle.

The next problem was the terracotta. I always thought the

word referred to beefy nursemaids who hurled the baby into its cot. But it turned out to be a reddish clay. Happily our house is on a gravel soil. So I only had to dig down some five feet before striking clay. It was somewhat yellow so I mixed it with a tin of dark-brown boot-polish.

I had about enough terracotta to make two heads, each about the size of a grapefruit. So I decided to make a test run on one of the lumps first, just in case sculpting was more difficult than it looked.

I bashed the clay into shape with my fists and then pushed it about with a spoon and a toothpick until it began to look something like a human head. I was not attempting a likeness at this time, which was a good thing because I had managed to get both ears on the same side. And three nostrils to the one nose.

Then into the oven it went, one hour at Regulo Mark 4. When it came out – disaster. For some reason the whole head had slumped and spread. It still looked vaguely like a head but the head of a baboon.

'It's bound to sag when it's all in a lump,' said my wife. 'It's the same with pastry. What you want to do is treat it like we do a pie. Make it hollow, fill it with dried peas so that it keeps its shape, then lay the top on, pinching the edges together as you do with pastry.'

Which is what I did. It was a tricky operation with a tacky lump of clay-and-boot-polish, and it took nearly a pound of dried peas to fill it, but I managed it. Then I lined up my eighty photographs, took spoon to hand and started.

Who can explain the workings of fate? Was it a fluke? Was it the awakening of latent genius? All I can say for sure is that after ten minutes with spoon and toothpick I had produced a startling likeness of myself, an amazing little portrait head which the National or any other gallery would be proud to shove in a glass case next to the postcard counter in the foyer. I shouted for my wife to come and see it.

'Incredible!' she breathed. 'So lifelike, and exact. And sort of peaceful!'

'So it should be,' I replied. 'It's full of peas.' (I was quite my old self again.)

With infinite care we carried the head through to the kitchen and slid it into the cooker. As my wife closed the oven door I drew a chair up to the oven and prepared for a long vigil.

'No you don't!' said my wife. 'There's nothing more you can do until the clay is baked. Let's go to the pictures.'

It was a Saturday, and on Saturdays my son often dropped in. He had finished at university and was working in the City. Down a hole in the City, digging up Roman remains before the office blocks cemented them away for ever. It was his practice to nip home sometime over the weekend with his pockets full of clothes to be washed, stand up in the bath and scrape Thames mud and mediaeval effluent off his salient features, eat whatever he could find in the house as long as it was hot and preferably smothered in chips, and disappear leaving a laconic note on the kitchen table.

We arrived home from the pictures. I made straight for the oven. As I had my hand on the oven door I heard my wife saying, 'Hello, Jamie's been home. Funny. I don't remember leaving out a –'

At that moment I opened the oven door to look at my masterpiece. And the oven was empty.

I knew instinctively what had happened, of course. 'Farewell posterity,' I whispered to myself as I held my hand out for Jamie's note.

Yes. There it was in black and white. Just five words: 'Good pie. Missed the chips.'

Listeners would write in suggesting punnable lines we could use to top-and-tail the stories we told at the end of each programme. Unfortunately, we could not take advantage of such contributions, having been advised by those in the know at the BBC that to do so could land us in all kinds of copyright trouble. Among the lines we, sometimes regretfully, had to discard were:

Into each reign some life must fall
An Englishman's comb is his hassle
Don't hatchet your Counts until they are chicken. (Proposed as a
    cautionary tale of the French Revolution.)
There's no police like Holmes
Putting Descartes before the whores
Tara Raboom, DA
Au pair answers are deceptive
Nice Finnish guys last
The old woman who shivved in a loo. (No, I couldn't at
    first, either.)
Bike up the Strand
Honey saw key Mali ponds

One of the later *My Word!* programmes contained a 'Famous Last Words' round, during which we learned that Mr Gladstone's final utterance was reputed to be, 'I'm feeling a lot better.' When it came to my turn, I was asked, 'Whose last words were, "Will peace never come"?'

I had no idea so, obeying our brief – 'When you don't know the answer, say something facetious' – I volunteered the first thing that came into my head, 'Mrs Peace?'

There was a moment's shocked silence, then came an audience laugh that grew louder and louder as they took in my realisation that I had said something whose double edge had not immediately occurred to me.

After the show I sought out Tony Shryane, the producer, and apologised. 'So sorry, Tony. Just didn't realise it at the time. But you can easily cut it out, can't you.'

'Cut what out?' he said.

'That Mrs Peace line.'

'Oh, that was a good laugh,' he said. 'We definitely want that in.'

'But "come",' I persisted. 'Will peace never "come"? Mrs Peace. Come.'

He looked at me blankly. Then realisation dawned. 'Oh, for Heaven's sake,' he said. 'You'd have to have a really filthy mind to make that connection.'

The line stayed as it was. Nobody wrote in to object. Perhaps Tony was right.

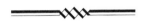

Driving home one rainy night, I noticed when I pulled up at the traffic lights that the driver of the adjoining car was repeatedly jabbing a forefinger at me to attract my attention. When he saw me looking his way, he began vigorously thrusting his finger down-wards, the universal gesture for 'You've got something wrong with your engine.'

I nodded my thanks and as soon as the lights changed, drove on at a snail's pace till I found somewhere to pull up. I got out and, sum-moning up my meagre knowledge of mechanical matters, I opened the bonnet and looked inside. Nothing appeared to be missing or out of place, so I closed it and walked round to the back. The exhaust pipe still seemed to be where it was supposed to be. By now the rain was pelting down, so I got back in the car and cautiously drove on.

Arrived at another red light, I glanced at the car next to me. To my dismay, the driver was making the same urgently pointing downward gestures at me as the first. Acknowledging him, I inched forward till I found another parking place, opened the door and subjected the car to the same rigorous inspection as before. Again, I discovered nothing amiss. Thoroughly soaked by now, I got back inside and drove on, resolved to chance it and try to get home.

In an effort to lull my lurking fears of an engine fire or an exhaust explosion, I switched on the radio. To my surprise, I heard an unexpected repeat of *My Word!* It was only after listening to it for a couple of minutes that I realised what that mime had been trying to tell me: 'You're on the car radio.'

On the tedious car journeys to the Midlands when *My Word!* began, journalist Nancy Spain and I would pass the time by singing choruses of lesser-known thirties popular songs, the obscurer the better. Nancy not only had total recall of all their words, she could even remember most of their verses.

Trouble was, neither of us had much of a knack for staying in tune. So Frank, who did not share our musical tastes, tended to find these duets something of an endurance test. In fact, they probably sharpened the edge of the public comments he went on to make about my singing efforts on the subsequent *My Music* series.

For these programmes, the final round required each of the contestants to sing a song, with Steve Race providing the piano accompaniment. In a typical week, Frank would be first on, generally with a slightly faded ballad, the more sentimental the better. He would be followed by John Amis lending his pleasing light tenor to an unfamiliar (to me, anyway) folk song, often embellished by some virtuoso whistling. To ensure a properly enthusiastic audience response to the show's finale, the closing song was always allotted to the experienced larynx of Ian Wallace, whose robust arias never failed to do the trick.

This running order left me sandwiched between John and Ian, a position which made it all the more apparent that whereas they possessed what musicians call perfect pitch, mine is what cricketers call bumpy pitch. It was a disparity to which Frank rarely failed to draw attention.

His comments ranged from the allegation that I was receiving 'unplug' money from music publishers – i.e., cash sums paid in return for not singing their songs – to the sudden lyrical outburst of 'Oh, what is so rare as a day in June? A song that Denis sings in tune.'

They included 'He not only left his heart in San Francisco, he left his voice there as well', 'Sounds like a wounded reindeer recorded at the wrong speed' and 'You know that line on the sheet music that says "Refrain"? Well, you really should, you know.'

It was in an effort to deflect these darts that I began casting about for some way of making my melodic shortfall less obvious. Then it occurred to me that one solution might be to lay hands on songs whose lyrics were sufficiently entertaining in their own right to make up for any discrepancies in their musical rendition.

And that was how I came to acquire my collection of twenties and thirties comic songs. Hunting down their yellowing sheet-music copies meant that I spent most of my spare time between seasons of *My Music* grubbing around all manner of out of the way and frequently seedy second-hand bookshops. Another agreeable source of supply turned out to be furniture warehouses, some of whose dustier corners harboured discarded piano stools. Extraordinary the variety of things people used to stuff inside a piano stool before getting rid of it. You're as likely to find an ornamental ceramic key-fob as a cover-missing 1922 sheet-music copy of 'I'm The Only Yiddishe Scotsman in the Irish Fusiliers'.

More on these finds anon.

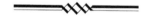

In the course of one of the *My Music* programmes, John Amis told the audience about an interview he had once had with the ninety-two year-old Artur Rubinstein. 'Ninety-two!' John emphasised. 'And he was still giving recitals. Don't you find that remarkable?'

'Not necessarily,' I found myself thinking. 'He was probably on the same pension plan I chose.'

All those sheet-music copies of twenties and thirties comic songs I dug up to justify my place in the *My Music* singing round have now either crumbled to scraps, wandered off somewhere when I moved offices or been sent to listeners who organise entertainments for defenceless people in care homes.

Odd lines from some of the songs still drift across my mind occasionally and, even though it was written to be sung by a female, memory has somehow retained all the words of the one that prompted by far the largest number of stamped, addressed envelopes, 'More Like a Friend'. Give or take a word here and there, it went:

> He was more like a friend
> Than a husband to me
> More like a real good pal.
> Never swore when the dinner was late,
> Never threw his plate in the grate.
> At times I forgot we were married,
> So happy our ways seemed to blend
> And no one would think I was only his wife,
> 'Cos he treated me more like a friend.

It was surprising how many of the songs were originally intended for female delivery, particularly those that inclined towards the gently libidinous, items such as 'Oh, Charlie, Take It Away', which turns out to be a reference to 'The little bit of hair you wear/ Upon your upper lip./ It tickles me, Charlie,/ Take it away!'; or the somewhat bolder 'You'll Have to Show It to Mother, Before You Can Show It to Me', where only the last line told us that the 'It' this time referred to an engagement ring.

One that had the more experienced woman in mind was called 'I Might Learn to Love Him Later On' and featured the pleasing rhyme:

> Though he's gouty and cantankerous
> He's just bought up half St Pancras
> So I might learn to love him later on.

Most of the songs, however, expressed the sentiments and habits common to your average seaside postcard male and ranged from the brash 'Have You Anything on Tonight, Matilda, Darling?' and 'I've Seen Isabel in Her Deshabille' to the rollicking 'I Love to Go Swimmin' with Women':

> I get these crazy notions
> When I see floating queens,
> I dive right in the ocean
> And I play submarines.

On another tack, there were the admonitory 'Never Let Your Braces Dangle' and 'Like the Big Pots Do':

> Never put both elbows on the table when you eat,
> Leave a bit of room for other folk to plant their feet.

Or the more wistful 'You Taught Me Lots of Things I Never Knew', with its pensive final question:

> Please tell me do,
> Who taught you
> All the things that you taught me?

Of some of the songs, only the odd punchline lingers – 'But what's the good of a kilt to me, When I'm a window cleaner?' and 'So I'm going back to Imazas, Imazas the pub next door' – though occasionally it's the scraps of a domestic detail:

> On a Sunday afternoon, on a Sunday afternoon
> Oh, what a luxur-ee,
> Muffins and crumpets for tea.
> The organette upstairs
> Is playing a lively tune
> And we always send the kids outside
> On a Sunday afternoon.

Out of all of them, the one that caused the most ructions was a parody of 'Are You Lonesome Tonight?', a song that actually pre-dated Elvis by quite a few decades. It was sent to me by an ex-member of the Women's Auxiliary Air Force, with a note explaining that it had been one of their wartime favourites and they still sang it at WAAF reunions. However, when I gave it an airing on *My Music*, it provoked such a torrent of disapproving letters from feminist listeners, I hesitated about including it here. Not for long, though.

> Are you lonesome tonight?
> Is your bra far too tight?

Are your corsets all falling apart?
Does the size of your chest
Wear big holes in your vest,
Does your spare tyre reach up to your heart?
Are your stockings all wrinkled,
Your shoes wearing thin?
Are your knickers held up
With a big safety-pin?
Are your dentures so worn
They drop down when you yawn?
Then no wonder you're lonesome tonight.

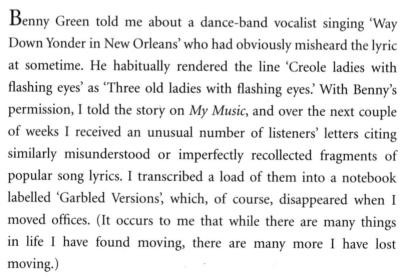

Benny Green told me about a dance-band vocalist singing 'Way Down Yonder in New Orleans' who had obviously misheard the lyric at sometime. He habitually rendered the line 'Creole ladies with flashing eyes' as 'Three old ladies with flashing eyes.' With Benny's permission, I told the story on *My Music*, and over the next couple of weeks I received an unusual number of listeners' letters citing similarly misunderstood or imperfectly recollected fragments of popular song lyrics. I transcribed a load of them into a notebook labelled 'Garbled Versions', which, of course, disappeared when I moved offices. (It occurs to me that while there are many things in life I have found moving, there are many more I have lost moving.)

Among the few that memory retained were:

The painfully diffident Jimmy Edwards in *Whack-o!*
The opposing team on *My Word!* – Frank and Dilys Powell

SIXPENNY EDITION.

IT'S BETTER
TO HAVE LOVED A
SHORT LITTLE GIRLIE
(THAN NEVER TO HAVE LOVED
A TALL!)

WORDS BY
WM EWART

MUSIC BY
R. CONNOR
LEIGH

Sung by
LESLIE, STANELLI AND EDGAR

Price 6º NET

THE ECLIPSE MUSIC PUBLISHING CO LTD.
36, ST MARTINS LANE
LONDON.
W.

I never see Maggie
Alone

SONG FOX-TROT

Words by
Harry Tilsley

Music by
Everett Lynton
(Composer of "High Street, Africa")

Featured with Tremendous Success by
JACK
HYLTON
And his Band

Cecil Lennox Ltd   134 Charing Cross Road
London ——— W.C.2   6 D.

I'VE SEEN ISABEL
IN HER DESHABILLE

FOX-TROT SONG   WITH
UKULELE OR
BANJULELE
BANJO
ACCOMPANIMENT

Written and
Composed by
R.P. WESTON
& BERT LEE.

Played and Sung
by
SYDNEY
NESBITT
with his UKULELE.

Copyright 1926, by Francis, Day & Hunter Ltd.
FRANCIS, DAY & HUNTER LTD.
138-140, CHARING CROSS ROAD, LONDON, W.C. 2.
NEW YORK. LEO FEIST Inc. 231-5 WEST 40TH STREET
SYDNEY: J. ALBERT & SON, 137-139 KING STREET

6D.
NET.

PRINTED IN ENGLAND

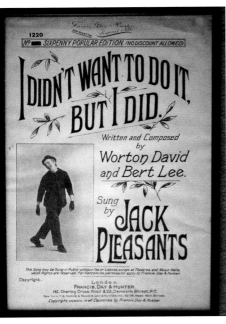

Selection from DN's
My Music repertoire

The rest of *My Music* team in 1982:
Steve Race, Frank, Ian Wallace and John Amis

FROM 5 JAN

BRITAIN'S BIGGEST LAUGH-RAISERS

THAMES LIGHT ENTERTAINMENTS

306 EUSTON ROAD NW1

PRESENT A SEASON OF GOLDEN NOSTALGIA

LOOKS FAMILIAR

BY POPULAR DEMAND SWITCHED-FROM MATINEE TO AFTER NEWS AT TEN!
EVERY MONDAY THROUGH THE WINTER

YOUR ENIGMATIC M.C. & CHAIRMAN
THE CROWN PRINCE OF GENTLE WIT

DENIS NORDEN

INTRODUCES A COMBINED CHAT SHOW
AND PANEL GAME WHICH TAKES A
NOSTALGIC LOOK AT THE MUSIC, FILMS,
PERSONALITIES AND ASSORTED
EPHEMERA OF THE '30s AND '40s

MESSRS.

PETER & VINCENT CUSHING PRICE

HEROES OF HAMMER HORROR

SONGS AND PARODIES
FOR ALL OCCASIONS—
FROM AMERICA,

SAMMY CAHN

'HIGH HOPES'
'ALL THE WAY'
'THREE COINS
IN A FOUNTAIN'
'LOVE & MARRIAGE'
'CALL ME
IRRESPONSIBLE'

THE 'SHORT FAT HAIRY' HALF:

EFFERVESCENT

ERNIE WISE

THE ZANIEST BRAIN
IN BRITAIN

MICHAEL BENTINE

PETER SELLERS

PERFORMS HIS UNFORGETTABLE
DICK BARTON IMPERSONATION

THE INIMITABLE

MR ERIC MORECAMBE

STAR OF STAGE, SCREEN &
LUTON TOWN F.C.

WE'LL KEEP A
WELCOME FOR

HARRY SECOMBE

THE 'SMALL
WELSH ZEPPELIN'

GORDON

JACKSON

THE VOICE THAT LAUNCHED
A MILLION CHUCKLES

HERMIONE GINGOLD

LIVE ON YOUR SCREEN, THE SCINTILLATING STARS OF SHOWBIZ!

PROPRIETOR MR PHILIP JONES   PRODUCER MR DAVID CLARK
Printed at The Curwen Press

Some *Looks Familiar* guests: Dickie Henderson, Diana Dors and Danny La Rue

Alec McCowen, DN, Pat Phoenix and Eric Sykes

Alice Faye

David Niven

Another *Looks Familiar* moment with Sammy Davis Jr

'Night and day, you are a one'

(From 'They Wouldn't Believe Me') 'Your eyes, your lips, /Your
smile, your hair are in a class beyond repair'

(From 'Winter Wonderland') 'Later on, we'll perspire, /As we sit by
the fire'

(From 'Just One of Those Things') 'If we'd sawed a bit off the end
of it /When we started painting the town'

(From 'With a Song In My Heart') 'At the sound of your voice, /
Heaven opens its portholes to me'

'For it was Mary, Mary/Long before the Fascists came'

(From 'Can't Help Lovin' That Man of Mine') 'Birds gotta swim,
Fish gotta fly'

In one edition of *My Music*, Steve Race played part of Harry
Secombe's recording of 'If I Ruled the World'. Then he asked each of
us in turn, 'If you ruled the world, what would be the first reform
you'd initiate?'

In the order of answering I was always the fourth, so I had a few
moments to prepare. Having recently been made late for an appointment by a jeweller's outdoor clock that was ten minutes slow, I
decided to vent my grievance by saying, 'If I ruled the world, I would
bring back capital punishment for any shopkeeper whose outdoor
clock shows the wrong time.'

In the event, I got as far as, 'If I ruled the world, I would bring back
capital punishment' and the audience's instant storm of applause
drowned out the rest.

A musical moment I was able to shoehorn into a *My Music* programme happened during a telephone call to one of the big electricity companies. I dialled the number and after a few rings one of those infuriatingly soothing voices clicked in and said, 'I regret that all our operators are busy. However, we value your call, so please hold on and you will be answered as soon as is possible.'

This was immediately followed by the strains of 'It Ain't Necessarily So'.

Ian Wallace liked to recount the story of a recording session he attended where the orchestra included the distinguished harpist, Marie Goossens. While they were tuning up, the young guitar player called across to her, 'Hey, Grandma, give us an A.'

During the next break, he was severely taken to task by the orchestra leader. 'How dare you! Marie is a senior member of one of the most highly respected musical families in this country, a family that has given us such virtuosi as Eugène Goossens, Sidonie Goossens and many others. How dare you go calling her Grandma?'

'Because she is my Grandma.'

The BBC arranged an informal farewell dinner at the Garrick Club for all the cast, production people and sound engineers to follow the recording of the final *My Music*. We suggested they should also invite Jeff, a cheerful stagehand who'd been helping on the show for years.

We were disappointed when he didn't turn up. But the BBC high-up who had organised the dinner assured us he'd given him a personal invitation to join us.

It was not till months later that we discovered what had happened. Jeff's personal invitation had informed him 'We're having a little farewell dinner at the Garrick' with no mention of the word 'Club'. Consequently, he had eaten, and presumably paid for, a solitary meal further up Garrick Street in the little Garrick Café.

In 1960 fifteen of us got together in a basement room below 7 Harley Street to form The Writers' Guild of Great Britain. The group, which included Ted Willis and Bryan Forbes, had as its main purpose the negotiation of some kind of agreed minimum payments for Television writers. At the time, there were TV companies who were paying as little as £15 for a sixty-minute drama.

There had also been some odd anomalies. Before the introduction of techniques for recording programmes, the only way they could repeat a live Sunday night TV play on the following Thursday was to have the actors reassemble and re-enact the whole thing. However, as they and the production crew were now that much more familiar with the material, the play tended to go at a much faster lick. The result was that the second performance was often significantly shorter than the first, sometimes by as much as five minutes. As certain companies were wont to pay for scripts on the basis of so much per minute, this meant that the writer's payment for the Thursday transmission would be noticeably less than he had received for the same play four days previously.

It didn't take long to persuade the TV companies of the quaintness of such practices, Associated-Rediffusion taking a little more time than the others. Soon enough they were agreeing to terms that distributed the wealth a little more fairly.

When Marks & Spencer first began selling avocados, they were accompanied by an illustrated leaflet explaining how they should be eaten. As I recall, the preferred method was to remove the stone and fill the holes in the two halves with dry sherry.

It was an era when we were being introduced to all manner of foods we had never sampled before. One such played a significant part in what Frank and I came to refer to as 'The Scampi Parable'.

It centred round Fred Robinson, the writer of a successful ITV sitcom of the early sixties, *The Larkins*. Starring Peggy Mount, David Kossoff, Shaun O'Riordan and Ronan O'Casey, the show's origins had become something of a media fairy tale.

Fred had originally written its first six scripts for a series of concerts put on by his local Boy Scout troop, while he was working as a ticket clerk at East Croydon railway station. A leading London agent had seen one of the concerts and was so taken with it, he had borrowed the scripts and, in the face of much opposition, persuaded ATV to commission Fred to adapt them for Television.

The series was a success from the start. At the time, I was fairly deeply involved with The Writers' Guild, and it was there that we began to hear a slightly different account of the show's origins. In this version, after the Scout show had been seen by the agent – I'll call him Jimmy G, though that's nothing like his real name – he had indeed collected the scripts and after reading them that same night made an appointment to show them to ATV the following morning. The company had immediately appreciated the quality of the writing, so much so that they had there and then given the green light for a series, at an agreed writer's fee of £125 for each script.

That evening, Jimmy G went back to Fred and delivered himself of something along these lines: 'Well, son, I've now spent all day poring over your scripts and there's something about them I like. In fact, as a gambling man, I'd be prepared to make you a proposition. I will give you the sum of £75 per script in return for your permission to try and persuade one or other of the Television companies to put them on as a series. If I manage to talk somebody into buying them I'll keep whatever sum they go for. If I can't sell them – well, as I say, I'm a gambler, I'll take the loss.'

This, remember, after he had already sold the six scripts at £50 more for each one than the £75 he was offering. Fred, however, was so overwhelmed by this unexpected stroke of good fortune, he accepted immediately. At the Guild, after we had confirmed that this was how the series had really come about, we decided that, in all fairness, Fred should be told that he was being taken for a ride.

When I rang him to suggest a meeting, he asked if he could come to our Conduit Street office so that he could meet Frank as well. After we had shaken hands and had a coffee, we congratulated him on *The Larkins* and then, as gently as possible, explained the royal screwing he was getting as regards his fee entitlement.

Although slightly taken aback at the news, his response was unhesitating. Almost apologetically he said, 'I really don't mind how much Jimmy G is getting out of it. I've never earned anything near £75 a week in my life. As it is I don't know how to spend all of it. If I was to get any more, I wouldn't know what to do with it. So he's welcome to the extra £50.'

We were unable to budge him. What's more, his feelings about it were so obviously heartfelt, we didn't really try to. Even though he let slip that on top of everything, Jimmy G was also subtracting 10 per cent from the £75 as agent's commission.

So the matter rested. That first series of *The Larkins* finished in a blaze of glory and the show was well over halfway through its second series when we received a phone call from Fred. Could he come up to the office and talk to us about something? Buy us lunch, possibly? We had both liked him enormously at that first meeting, so we agreed immediately. When he turned up, we could not help but notice the change in his appearance. As well as a different style of haircut, he was wearing a smartly cut camelhair overcoat. Moreover, his manner of speech was more direct. Coming straight to the point, he said, 'Can the Guild still do something about my arrangement with Jimmy G?'

'Of course,' we said. 'Be no problem at all.'

His relief was evident. 'I need the extra,' he said. 'Just can't seem to make do on that money any more. It's like everything's got more expensive.'

'Don't worry about it,' we said. 'He'll cough up.'

'Great,' he said. 'I've booked a table at Verrey's.' And, as we were going down in the lift, 'I already know what I'm going to have.'

'What's that?'

'Scampi,' he said.

They had only recently begun to feature scampi on restaurant menus and Fred was vehement in his enthusiasm. 'I have them all the time,' he said. 'With everything.'

Now it was plain what had happened. Fred had crossed what Frank and I came to think of as the Scampi Line. We could redress the financial balance in his favour, but now that he had tasted scampi, the damage had been done. Back there in the sixties, the scoffing of the scampi brought about the same consequences as the eating of the forbidden fruit.

It was during the period when, with Hazel Adair, I was co-chairman, that The Writers' Guild became affiliated to the TUC and has been represented at every annual Congress ever since. Despite this, I have never yet plucked up suffi-cient courage to enter a discussion with, 'Well, speaking as a former trade union leader ...'

The least enjoyable period of my Writers' Guild chairmanship began when, much to our surprise, the Duke of Edinburgh consented to be guest of honour at our first awards dinner. A few days later a Palace equerry briefed me on the protocol I would be expected to follow on the night. Pre-dinner, we must arrange for a private room with bar, and that would be where I introduced the members of the Guild's Executive Committee to the Duke. The drill here would be that I would present each member individually, HRH would have a few words with him or her, then, when he shifted his gaze, that member would move away and I would present the next in line.

I should have foreseen what would happen when I relayed these instructions to the Committee at our next meeting. That year's Committee harboured a more than usually high quotient of socially committed firebrands, whose eyebrows went skyward at the very mention of 'moving on when his gaze shifts'. All of them holding strong views on such matters, there was an immediate rumble of dissent. How could I have agreed to such a feudal procedure? One by one, they proclaimed their intention of using the occasion to button-hole His Highness regarding various social concerns on which he needed enlightening.

To this day, I'm not sure whether they were winding me up. All I know for certain is that nothing I said would deter them and I spent the next few meetings veering between appalled and desperate. Then, to my enormous relief, the King of Greece died. The Court was immediately plunged into official mourning and all Royal engagements were cancelled.

I received a charmingly regretful letter from the Duke's secretary and the Committee promptly replaced him at the top table with the totally undemanding Richard Marsh, MP.

The most enjoyable, not to say thought-provoking, of The Writers' Guild negotiations I attended was the first time we came up against Lew Grade. Receiving us in his office, he handed round his daunting cigars, then assumed his role as ATV's one-man Industrial Relations Committee. He listened courteously to our carefully rehearsed arguments and when we concluded, he thought for a moment, in silence.

Then, 'Here's how I see it,' he said. 'Bring me a ninety-minute play by a Clive Exton or an Alun Owen or a John Hopkins, I'll pay them whatever they want for it. What we're here to negotiate today is how much per minute do you want me to pay for crap?'

He put the question in all seriousness and, thanks be, we had the sense to address it the same way. We left his office with a satisfyingly generous minimum terms agreement and I suspect that, to this day, Lew's query lies at the heart of most negotiations relating to Television output.

MOSTLY
LOOKS FAMILIAR,
MELVIN FRANK AND
ALRIGHT ON THE
NIGHT

Looks Familiar dealt in thirties and forties nostalgia, so when Kingsley Amis turned up as a guest, it seemed appropriate to question him about his almost perfect pastiche of a thirties English detective mystery, *The Riverside Villa Murders*. There is a scene in the book when the schoolboy's parents are at the local Conservative Club, dancing to the strains of 'Saddle Your Blues to a Wild Mustang'. The song was so instantly redolent of that time and that place, I asked Kingsley how many other third-rate tunes of the thirties he had considered and discarded before deciding on that one.

He seemed surprised. 'None,' he said. 'That's the one that would have been playing.'

It was not his only notable contribution. Later on, when Max Wall joined us for a drink, we got on to the subject of comedians. I mentioned that whenever we had any of the greats on *Looks Familiar*, their conversation would always be larded with references to the days before they had become successful, particularly the occasions when an audience had barracked them, or given them the bird. 'I suppose,' Kingsley said, 'you could call it nostalgie de la boo.'

From the very first *Looks Familiar* programme, I wrote my notes and questions on colour coded cards, held together by a rubber band. During the opening titles, I would pull off the rubber band and slip it round my wrist.

Regularly every week I'd get letters asking, 'Why do you always wear a rubber band round your wrist?'

It was only after fourteen years of receiving this enquiry that I began replying, 'What would you prefer me to wear it round?'

A regular question on *Looks Familiar* invited guests to recall the favourite tuckshop sweets of their childhood. They tended to make similar choices each time – Montpellier drops, sherbet dabs, cinnamon balls, mint lumps, gobstoppers. One week, however, someone mentioned Tiger Nuts.

This struck an immediate chord with me and because others on the panel seemed unfamiliar with them, I explained that they were little wizened brown lumps, very similar in appearance to ancient rabbit droppings but tasting strongly of coconut. 'You could chew one mouthful of them for hours,' I remembered, 'and there was a whole stretch of my boyhood when I was practically addicted to them. What a shame you can't get them any more.'

While we were all having a drink after the show, producer David Clark, much younger than the rest of us, revealed he had never even heard of Tiger Nuts before, so I enthused further. 'Not only did you get a whole bag of them for a penny but when I brought it home, I never had to share it. My mother and sister couldn't stand them and every time I offered my father some, he'd shake his head regretfully and say, "I like them but they don't like me. They give me really violent indigestion." I'd think "Poor old bugger" and get on with the rest of the bag.'

The Thursday following that programme's transmission, a courier brought a large package from David. The accompanying note said, 'You were wrong about Tiger Nuts not being available any more. Apparently, a lot of health shops still sell them and, as you'll see by the enclosed, viewers have been inundating us with packets of them. Enjoy.'

I took out one of the packets, opened it, put a couple of Tiger Nuts in my mouth, gave a tentative chew and, straightaway, was transported back some fifty-odd years. It was so good, I sampled the whole packet.

An hour later, I was doubled over with really violent indigestion.

On one of his many *Looks Familiar* discussions about 'getting the bird', Ted Ray told the story of a contralto in a provincial theatre who was having a particularly rough time with the raucous audience. Then a voice from the gallery shouted, 'Give the poor old cow a chance.'

The contralto stepped forward and said, 'Thank you, sir. I'm glad there is one gentleman in the house tonight.'

I believe it was on that programme that Michael Bentine suggested that Ted should publish a book of his 'getting the bird' anecdotes. A suitable title, he added, might be *Done to a Turn*.

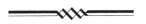

Frank and I received two copies of Val Guest's screenplay for the 1935 Will Hay comedy, *Boys Will Be Boys*, from a producer who wanted us to rewrite it as a vehicle for Jimmy Edwards. Individually, we read it that night and when we arrived at the office next morning had come to exactly the same conclusion. It was such a perfectly constructed and characterised piece of comedy, neither of us wanted to be party to altering a word of it.

In our estimation, Val also deserved some kind of award for writing the funniest three-word line of dialogue in any film comedy. In his *Oh, Mr Porter!*, a remake of *The Ghost Train*, Will Hay, accompanied by Graham Moffatt, arrives at a totally deserted and rundown country station to take over as station master. Finding no staff or passengers on either of the dilapidated platforms, he knocks on a closed ticket window. A moment's pause, then the shutter shoots up to frame the grinning face of Moore Marriott ('Harbottle'), a wizened old man with one single tooth in his upper jaw.

'Next train's gorn,' he announces. And slams the shutter down.

During one of Ray Galton and Alan Simpson's *Looks Familiar* appearances, I was delighted to discover that they, too, would nominate that line as their favourite. Later in the evening, we spent a lot of time discussing the admirable concision of 'Next train's gorn' and then, later still, decided that it also sums up the existential dilemma of modern man.

When Gloria Swanson appeared on *Looks Familiar*, she told me that in 1924 she'd been in a movie that had been made title-first. It was called *Manhandled* and was the result of someone at Paramount saying, 'Find me a story zippy enough to live up to that title without outraging the guardians of public morality.'

Whenever Arthur Askey appeared on *Looks Familiar*, his fondest reminiscences were of the days he spent touring with Eddie Gray. Rarely would he let the evening go by without recalling the occasions when they would be strolling down a busy street and Eddie would suddenly station himself in front of a letter box. Placing his ear to the slot, he would stand listening gravely. When a sufficient number of curious passers-by had gathered to stare, he would turn his head and ask the slot, 'But how did you get in there in the first place?'

Variety was continually printing stories about Joe Frisco, who seems to have been as folkloric a figure in the world of American comedians as Eddie Gray was among the British fraternity.

Researching for *Looks Familiar*, I found a short bit of film footage that showed him to be, if nothing else, a wonderfully funny, eccentric dancer, indulging in some ingenious business with a bowler hat.

When Eddie Bracken appeared on the programme, he told me that Frisco was famously less than adept at managing his finances. One day, he was called to the Internal Revenue Service to discuss a tax bill running into thousands and, on his way out, he met an old friend, a fellow comedian, waiting to go in.

'Hi, how are things going?'

'Not too good,' his friend said. 'I haven't worked in months, my rent's overdue, my agent's dropped me and now the IRS say I owe them $97.'

'Don't worry,' said Joe and, reopening the door to the tax office, he pushed his friend in and called, 'Put this on my tab.'

Also attributed to Joe Frisco is the advice I first heard from Melvin Frank: 'Make one small bet every day. Otherwise, you could be walking around lucky and never know it.'

There was a strange, almost inaudible, little sound, part sigh of recognition, part murmur of pleasure, which we would only hear from our grey-haired *Looks Familiar* audiences when somebody in the vintage film clips we showed them touched a really sensitive nostalgia nerve. It greeted no more than a handful of thirties and forties performers, chief among them Jack Buchanan, Bud Flanagan and Alice Faye.

Although you rarely hear of her today, Alice Faye was the biggest name in movie musicals during the war years, a favourite forces pin-up who starred in such films as *Alexander's Ragtime Band, Hollywood Cavalcade, The Great American Broadcast* and *You're a Sweetheart*, in the process almost single-handedly saving the fortunes of Twentieth Century Fox.

A well-proportioned blonde, she had a pleasing touch of huski-ness in her singing voice and a wryness to her expression which was in no small measure due to a customarily out-thrust and often slightly moist lower lip. 'For all the world,' someone once remarked, 'as though she's just had a trombone wrenched from her mouth.' I make no secret of the fact that, during the peak years of my ado-lescence, she was someone who caused me acute wriggling about.

Aware of my lifelong predilection for the lady, Thames Television were at first a little reluctant when I asked if they would bring her over from Hollywood, so that I could do an entire programme in which she would be the sole guest. But when I showed them evidence of the quite exceptionally warm response her clips always received from viewers and studio audience alike, they relented.

A suite was booked for her at the Connaught Hotel and arrange-ments were made for me to have tea with her there the afternoon before the recording. I arrived promptly and waited, as agreed, in the foyer, feeling ridiculously nervous. After fifteen minutes, there was no sign of her and, just as I was wondering whether I should ring her room, I met the gaze of a regal old lady sitting in a tall armchair facing the entrance. 'Are you looking for me?' she asked.

There was no mistaking the smile. After we had introduced our-selves and were chatting with growing ease over a notably scrump-tious tea, she confessed to some reservations about the following day's recording. 'I would rather not sing anything,' she said. 'I have a slight cold and, anyway, my voice isn't what it was.'

It was an enormous disappointment and I tried as hard as I could to change her mind. Explaining that 'You'll Never Know', the ballad she had introduced in *Hello, Frisco, Hello*, was for most of us not only the best-loved song of the War, her version of it was still 'our tune' for countless British ex-servicemen and women. I recalled how I had watched the movie sitting on the ground with hundreds of other RAF personnel when the Army Kinematograph Service rigged up an outdoor cinema outside our encampment in Eindhoven and how still they had all been during her singing of 'You'll Never Know', not one of them stirring, even to light a cigarette. 'If that studio audience tomorrow doesn't hear at least a moment of it,' I pleaded, 'even if it's just "A million or more times", I doubt if they'll let me leave there alive.'

After hesitating, she smiled and said, 'Well, we'll see.' She was beginning to look younger.

In fact, over the course of the programme next day, the years fell away. When I introduced her to the crowded audience ('The lady who upgraded the fantasies of an entire generation'), her reception was rapturous. From then on, despite the misgivings she had expressed, she willingly performed excerpts from some eight or nine of her numbers, her voice exactly as we remembered it. When we came to the end of the show and I thanked her, her eyes were shining.

Then, as our closing signature tune struck up, she rose to her feet and taking my hand, she said, 'Dance with me.' So, to the strains of 'Seems Like Old Times', there I was dancing with Alice Faye.

But here's the odd part. Holding my youthful ideal in my arms, I was suddenly conscious of a strange chafing sensation at the back of my neck. It took me a moment or so to identify it as the rough, coarse collar of my RAF tunic.

Among females of maturer years, David Niven was regarded with a warmth of affection that amounted almost to adoration. So when the canteen ladies of Thames Television heard he was appearing on *Looks Familiar*, they quite literally clamoured for tickets. David Clark, our producer, not only made these available, he suggested the ladies join us for refreshments in the hospitality room before and after the show.

All of them did so, some bearing wonderful home-made cakes, and Niven was introduced to and chatted with each of them. Then it was down to the studio for the recording, which ran over an hour as Niven was in fine story-telling fettle. One story I remember told of his meeting with another expat British actor, Basil Rathbone, one of Hollywood's finest purveyors of suave villainy.

Asked how he was, Rathbone confided, 'I appear to be developing a cold sore on my upper lip.'

'Does it hurt?'

'Only when I sneer.'

Afterwards, we came back to the hospitality room for drinks, where Niven remained chatting amiably till the limo arrived to take him back to town. After bidding us goodbye, he made for the canteen ladies and said a personal farewell to every one of them individually – 'Goodbye, Jean', 'Goodbye, Alice', 'Goodbye, Edna' – addressing each of the ten or so of them by name, without getting one name wrong.

In many ways, it was more than just a feat of memory.

Rosemary Clooney's appearance on *Looks Familiar* was notable for some colourful recollections of her early days travelling round America in a coach with the band. In a memorable phrase, she admitted 'They were on everything but roller-skates.'

All my life, I have been a victim of 'Witzelsucht', a disability defined in *Stedman's Medical Dictionary* as a morbid tendency to make puns. I have it on the authority of Stephen Fry that it is also known as 'paronomasia'.

Whatever its title, the condition rarely works in one's favour. When we had Buddy Rich on *Looks Familiar*, it led me to introduce him as 'someone whose name could be defined as 'the opposite of "a friend in need"'. So deeply did this furrow his brow, we abandoned it.

I was driven up a similar blind alley after another season of *Looks Familiar* had seen Melvin Frank, Sammy Cahn and Jule Styne appear in separate episodes. My affliction led me to propose that if we were now to book the three of them for one special programme, we could bill it as *Looks Familiar – The Monster Edition*.

'Why "monster"', asked my patient producer, David Clark.

'Frank, Cahn, Styne.'

David put his head in his hands.

Melvin Frank's wife, Ann, used to complain that the conversation of long-married couples consisted solely of 'maintenance talk'. It was a phrase he didn't fail to borrow for the first draft of *Buona Sera, Mrs Campbell.*

I brought the idea for that film to Melvin after reading a local newspaper item about a girl who had been receiving monthly payments for her child's support from three different men. We collaborated on the screenplay, an interesting experience for both of us because it was the first major project Melvin had written without his long-time writing partner, Norman Panama, and the first I had written without Frank.

We came to the conclusion that one of the main advantages of collaboration is the reassurance it offers. If two of you agree that a line is funny, then chances are that a fair proportion of other people will find it so. On the other hand when you are writing on your own and you put down a line you think is funny, it is by no means impossible that there is no one else in this whole wide world who will laugh at it.

Having both agreed that ours was a craft where reassurance is all, we also decided that for such as us there is nothing in life more dispiriting than watching your secretary yawn as she types one of your comedy scripts.

As a result of some kind of set-to he had had with the lady in the distant past, Melvin Frank always referred to Olivia de Havilland as

Ohavia de Livalland. It invariably sent my mind back to my apprenticeship at the Gaumont State, Kilburn, where, as part of my Front of House training, I was assigned to the late Saturday night ceremony known as 'changing the marquee'.

To perform this task, I had to climb up a ladder that stood on the canopy that projected over the front doors, remove the outsize metal letters which spelled out the title of the current film and carry them down to the letter store, a cramped space in a corridor off the foyer. I would then sort out the letters that made up the title and stars of the film showing on Sunday or the following week and, after conveying them up the ladder, slot them carefully into their rightful places on the giant display frame.

Apart from the difficulties that could be presented by heavy rain, blustery winds and having to walk past groups of girls while carrying an oddly shaped giant apostrophe, I was constantly being warned to make sure I checked my spelling before leaving the canopy. To illustrate the necessity for this precaution, they would cite a predecessor who had hoisted aloft an S instead of a Z the week the big picture was *The Great Waltz* and, even more telling, though possibly apocryphal, the appalling omission made by a cinema in Leicester Square premiering *The Count of Monte Cristo*.

Although my own record as a title changer remained unblemished, there was a ten-minute patch which can still bring on night sweats. The film for that week was *The Adventures of Robin Hood*, one of the longest titles in the golden age of Hollywood cinema, starring Errol Flynn and Olivia de Havilland, one of the longest names in the golden age of Hollywood stardom. In all, it entailed lugging fifty-one letters up that ladder.

On the plus side, the film also brought us one of the most cherishable romantic exchanges in the golden age of Hollywood dialogue:

'I have loved you all my life.'
'But we only met yesterday.'
'That was when my life began.'

On that wet Saturday night, though, it was only when I was back in the warmth of the letter store that a dreadful memory flashed into my mind. Could it be true? Could I possibly have? To make sure I hadn't, I dashed across the foyer, out of the cinema, and across the rain-soaked Kilburn High Road. Standing on the opposite pavement gazing upward, I saw immediately that I had.

Up there, floodlit and emblazoned on the night for all Kilburn to see were the words, *The Avdentures of Robin Hood.*

It took no more than minutes to get it corrected and, thanks to the night's storminess, there had been few people abroad to register it.

When I told Melvin about it, he comforted me with the thought that I had created one of the few titles that could have accommodated Ohavia de Livalland.

During his boyhood, Melvin Frank's family ran a saloon in one of the rougher neighbourhoods of Chicago. As the youngest in the family, he was cast from birth as the one destined for higher things than saloon-keeping. Consequently, while his older brothers spent their evenings dealing with beer barrels and drunks, Melvin would be in the upstairs room with his grandfather, diligently reading his books or doing his homework.

One evening, his grandfather persuaded him to run down to the corner store and fetch him some tobacco. On his way back, a brother intercepted him with it and the whole family joined in noisily berating the old man for interrupting Melvin's studies.

The grandfather shrugged. 'Okay, okay. So he'll be a doctor ten minutes later.'

After the series finally came to an end, I was asked by a TV reporter, 'When you began *It'll Be Alright on the Night*, did you ever think it would last twenty-nine years?'

I had to be truthful. 'When we began *It'll Be Alright on the Night*, I didn't think Television would last twenty-nine years.'

'According to Sigmund Freud, there are only four categories of joke: the concealment of knowledge later revealed; the substitution of one concept for another; the unexpected conclusion to a hitherto logical progression; and out-takes.'

(From the introductory link to an early *It'll Be Alright on the Night*.)

The series could not have had a more comfortable or speedier birth. I was having a cup of tea in the London Weekend Television canteen with Paul Smith, one of their brightest young producers. We were chatting about the famous *Blue Peter* episode featuring Valerie Singleton and the incontinent baby elephant when one of us – and, for the life of me, I can't recall which – mused, 'Wonder if it would be possible to string together a whole programme of out-takes?' (Although, strictly speaking, that one wasn't an 'out-take' because it had been transmitted, which made it what we later categorised as a 'blooper'.)

After mulling the notion over for what must have been all of five minutes, Paul said, 'Let's put it to Michael.' Using the canteen telephone, we called Michael Grade, then Head of Entertainment for London Weekend Television, told him we had what might be a programme idea and asked if we could set up an appointment to talk about it. 'Come up now,' Michael said.

He received us, red-braced and shirt-sleeved, waved us into chairs and said, 'Tell me about it.' I can recall the next two lines of dialogue verbatim.

'What do you think about an entire programme of out-takes?'

'How soon can you let me have it?'

We left his office half an hour later with a recording date and a budget. Michael had even suggested a title which, Paul and I agreed on the way down, wasn't that hot, but seeing he had been so accommodating, it might be best to go with it. We went with it for twenty-nine years.

From the very first *It'll Be Alright on the Night*, we paid a fee to every performer on view in an out-take. If the out-take was sold abroad, he would receive an additional sum. As the number of out-take shows around the world increased, so did the amount the performer would earn. Thus, we arrived at a position where someone could receive twice as much money for doing a thing wrongly than if he had managed to do it correctly.

Outside of running a railway or managing a pension fund, it is hard to think of another activity where those who make a mistake can get paid extra for it. I once likened it to owning a farm where you earn more from the manure than from the cattle.

It was suggested to me that the reason why the blunders and screw-ups we showed on *It'll Be Alright on the Night* were so well received was because the English nourish a deep-grained fondness for well-intentioned failure. After all, what is the one historical date no Englishman ever forgets? 1066 – the year King Harold neglected to get out of the way of an arrow.

And who is the only other obscure monarch to etch his name in the collective memory? King Alfred, whose sole contribution to our island story was to burn some cakes.

Similarly, what does England's best-known poem celebrate? That well-loved military disaster, the Charge of the Light Brigade. Finally, in all our history, who is the only Englishman to be honoured by having a day named after him? Guy Fawkes, who signally failed to blow up the Houses of Parliament.

And this is without even mentioning Dunkirk or the Eurovision Song Contest.

In order to select the hundred-plus clips that went into each *It'll Be Alright On The Night*, I looked at every one of the thousand-or-so our researchers would dig out of edit-suite dustbins round the world.

Some of their treasure trove presented a considerable challenge. You don't know what wandering attention is until you're obliged to sit through a two-hour reel of minor mishaps from a daily Korean soap opera, all of them verbal.

On the whole, though, the experience was agreeable. As the programmes consisted largely of what I once saw a management training manual describe as 'unplanned deviations from criteria-based standards of competence', it was not unpleasing to watch so many highly respected film and TV personages in their moments of alarm and unease. While other programmes set out to portray the ups and downs of show-business, we can safely claim that in twenty-nine years we did not portray one up.

Mr Williams, the English master for whom I willingly learned the entire text of *Hamlet* by heart, once confessed that, for him, the most beautiful combination of sounds in the English language was the word, 'cellar-door'. Though privately wondering whether this should not really be counted as two hyphenated words, I loyally wrote it down in my commonplace book and, over the ensuing decades, never failed to quote it whenever the opportunity arose.

Incurably urban, my knowledge of flowers and trees and so on has always been on the far side of minimal, but it was not until I was well into my fifties that the full extent of my townee ignorance emerged. I was working with Paul Smith at the time and he happened to mention that he'd decided to call his new production company 'Cellar Door' – 'because it's such a beautiful word'.

Delighted, I told him about Mr Williams and my own lifelong affection for it. 'Though I suppose,' I added, 'we should really count it as two words.'

'Why?' he asked and spelled it for me, 'C-E-L-A-D-O-R.'

I have since discovered that the word is a North Country variant of 'celandine' and though I must have frequently come across that small flower during the preceding half-century, this was the first time I made the connection.

According to Dorothy Parker, the two most beautiful words in the English language are 'Cheque enclosed.'

The three most beautiful words, Les Dawson said, are 'No Assembly Required.'

And, to quote Dickie Henderson, the three scariest words in the language are, 'That's him, officer.'

I have since read that James Joyce thought that 'cuspidor' was the most beautiful word in the English language.

When one of the *It'll Be Alright on the Night* programmes was put out against a BBC showing of *Gone With the Wind,* I was phoned by a brisk young lady from one of the tabloids.

'What are your reactions to being pitted against *Gone With The Wind*?' she asked

What could I reply but, 'Frankly, my dear, I don't give a damn.'

After what could be described as an icy pause, she said, 'Isn't that a little arrogant?'

It was further proof that, as you grow older, not only do you lose your illusions, you lose your allusions. These days, for instance, I have practically nobody left to share my recent discovery that Orville Wright was Robert Cummings' godfather.

Sometimes, during breaks in the recording of *It'll Be Alright on the Night*, I would invite questions about the programme from the studio audience. The one most frequently asked was, 'Why are you always clutching a clipboard?'

Just as regularly I would reply with the truth. 'It's because I never know what to do with my hands.'

On one occasion, someone at the back shouted, 'Ever thought of putting them over your mouth?'

Surprisingly few viewers wrote letters complaining about the programme's content, but among those who did, the majority, including Kingsley Amis and Willis Hall, took me to task for eliding the words 'All Right' to 'Alright'.

I was reduced to replying that if it was good enough for the Almighty, it was good enough for me. Always.

Over the years of *It'll Be Alright on the Night*, I must have inspected and passed judgement on, without exaggeration, umpteen thousands of out-takes. Maybe even more. It soon became apparent that, in order to avoid the programmes becoming repetitious, our first requirement was to separate the cock-ups into various themes, or categories. That way, we could ensure that the twelve or so different packages of them into which we divided each show could be varied from programme to programme.

This meant, in effect, defining and cataloguing as many different varieties of error as we could devise names for. There being no limit to the number of ways people can get things wrong, by the end of the show's run, these categories, or 'Files' as we called them, amounted to a fairly comprehensive survey of human fallibility. From the hundred or so we ended up with, I offer a few sample titles:

> 'Information Underload'
> 'A Talent for Self Damage'
> 'Unscheduled Exits'
> 'Unseemly Larkiness and Horsing Around'
> 'What Did I Do to Deserve This?'

'Malfunction Junction'
'Keep Going at All Costs'
'Career Limiting Moves'
'We Know Something You Don't Know'
'Slipping on the Soaps'
'Run That Past Me Again'
'Skills Deficits'
'Doomed Endeavours'
'Things That Appear But Shouldn't'
'Things That Don't Appear But Should'
'Stupidity Happens'
'Many a True Word Spoken in Out-take'

If *It'll Be Alright on the Night* did nothing else, it succeeded in reanimating the term 'cock-up', a carry-over from my RAF days. (Previously, Frank and I had managed, via Jimmy Edwards, to breathe fresh life into another grand old RAF staple, 'Clumsy clot!')

I was told, though I make no claims for the truth of it, that when the pioneer of in vitro fertilisation, Professor Patrick Steptoe, exhibited the first 'test tube baby' to the world, he received a telegram from his American colleagues. It said, 'Congratulations. First thing you Brits have managed to do without a cock-up.'

The phrase 'It'll Be Alright on the Night' joined that select group of incantations people use for disarming disaster. Others include 'Some you win, some you lose', 'That's the name of the game', 'A week is a long time in politics', and the one I picked up in the fifth form and have mentally clung on to all my life, 'Et haec olim meminisse iuvabit.' I have always translated it as 'And even these things we shall someday look back on and laugh.' In fact, I thought of titling these recollections, *It's Someday and I'm Not Laughing*.

In the eighties, *TV Times* ran a competition asking readers to send in details of their 'real life' out-takes. It attracted an unexpectedly large response, most of the letters offering further evidence that truth is not only stranger than fiction, it is frequently more embarrassing.

In addition to learning about the apparently nationwide predilection for confusing Durex with Dulux, we heard from a gentleman who fell over backwards while putting in eye-drops, another who pulled a wishbone and dislocated his little finger, to say nothing of a lady who tugged round a revolving greetings-card rack, bringing into view a gentleman from the other side whose tie had got caught in it.

Other readers left with skid marks on their psyche included a businessman who was showing a party of prospective Japanese clients round his small factory and when he opened the door to the room marked 'Quality Control', the handle fell off; another unfortunate, due to deliver an address to his trade association, took a last-minute look at his speech and discovered he had highlighted the important points with a black magic marker.

Some of the entries were dismissed by the editorial staff as too unlikely to be true, which I considered a pity, because if there was one thing *It'll Be Alright on the Night* had taught me, it was that the unlikely cock-ups are the ones most likely to happen. Consequently, I saw no reason to disbelieve the wartime incident submitted by a Leicestershire lady.

An amateur singer as a girl, her first big solo engagement had been at a crowded local concert for the troops. Being a Deanna Durbin fan she had chosen one of her songs for the occasion and sang it Durbin style, holding out her full-skirted blue dress. Such were her nerves, however, that throughout the song, she unconsciously scrunched it up in front, gradually and all unknowingly revealing more and more leg.

At the end of the song, she went off to a reception from the troops that was as vociferous as it was sustained. Almost deafened by the whistling and shouting, she was startled to find her mother in the wings, wringing her hands. 'When she told me what had happened,' our correspondent wrote, 'I almost died from shock and shame. The title of the song was "This Is Worth Fighting For".'

Throughout its long run, there was a small treasure trove of out-takes our *It'll Be Alright on the Night* team kept hearing about but never managed to track down. Some of these reports smacked of folklore, such as the one referring us to a seventeenth-century costume drama in which the heroine gave a disdainful toss of her curls and dislocated her neck. Others that got away were of more trustworthy provenance, including the game-show host who promised a winner 'Tea tickets for Tahooti', a blithe off-screen voice announcing, 'It's Crossmass at Crissroads' and, most sorely missed of all, the moment in another black-and-white historical piece when a nobleman barked at his servant, 'Go, varlet, and horness my harse.'

EARLY DAYS AND AFTERTHOUGHTS

A book that brought a glow of pleasure to my childhood was *The Coral Island*, by R. M. Ballantyne, mainly because I read it under ideal circumstances. What better way to relive a tropical tale of palm-treed adventures under a blazing sun than lying in bed with a slight temperature but not really ill?

I didn't pick up *The Coral Island* again until the 1960s, when Jean Lovell Davis invited me on to an agreeable half-hour book series she had devised for Radio 4. Every week she asked guests to reread a book that had cast a particular spell over them in childhood, then discuss with her how much of the magic still lingered.

When I arrived at the studio, I found Jean about to interview her other guest for that week, Lord Arnold Goodman.

'Hope you don't mind if I go first,' he said. 'I have a plane to catch.'

'Of course you do,' I agreed, because at that time there were few persons in the land more important than Lord Arnold Goodman, confidant of Prime Ministers, adviser to international statesmen, his name rarely out of the headlines.

His childhood choice was a novel by Angela Brazil. Surprising, but he spoke up for it with an eloquence that was as amusing as it was affectionate.

Even as he answered Jean's final questions, he was preparing to make his exit, bound for who knows what matters of pith and moment. On his departure, I took his place in the interviewee's chair and unfolded my notes. 'Hang on a minute, Denis,' came the producer's voice in my headphones. 'Afraid that segment overran a wee bit. Jean can we get Lord G back for a short re-record?'

'No chance,' said Jean. 'He's probably halfway to South Africa by now. But tell you what we can try. Suppose I just re-record my questions to him, but make all of them a bit briefer?'

'Yes, that'll get it right for time,' said the producer. 'Let's try.' The red light went on again and while I sat silent, Jean asked her series of rephrased questions. The red light blinked off and we waited. After a troubling pause, we heard from the producer again. 'Yes, it's spot-on for length,' he said. 'But, sorry about this, Jean, it doesn't work. We need the breathing.'

We both understood immediately. The other element of Lord Goodman's singularity was that he was by far the widest and bulkiest figure on the political scene and, as a result of carrying this weight, he was what is known in the trade as an 'audible breather'. All of Jean's exchanges with him had been accompanied by that gentle stir of sound.

Jean and I are old friends. 'It'll be a pleasure,' I said. So, while she once more went through her reworded questions, I sat at the opposite mike, mouth wide open, audibly inhaling and exhaling.

It worked a treat, leaving me wondering whether I should now embellish my CV with the modest claim: 'I breathed for Lord Goodman.'

Thanks to my thrice-weekly excursions to the public library, several of my aunts (Gertie, Winnie, Muriel) entrusted me with the responsibility of taking their books back and choosing new ones for them. Their preferences inclined towards what they called 'something meaty', which included any novels by Louis Golding, Louis Bromfield, Vicki Baum and the 'Peter Jackson, Cigar Merchant'

books by Gilbert Frankau. Fairly frequently they would put in a request for what I first took to be 'any eye book about doctors'. I soon discovered that, far from indicating a fondness for the oph- thalmological, it referred to any medical novel written in the first person.

Back in my boyhood days when I started spending all my pocket money on reading matter, I was constantly being warned, 'You shouldn't buy second-hand books and magazines. They get them from the Fever Hospital.'

Although this imparted an extra frisson to the reading process, it was only one of the many medical injunctions children had to bear in mind back then. If you drink cold water directly after hot soup, it gives you colic. If you cut that bit of gristle between your thumb and forefinger, you'll get lockjaw. If you swallow a piece of chewing-gum, your insides will stick together. If you sit on the classroom radiator, you'll get piles. ('Please, Miss, what's piles?')

My journey to City of London School took me by Underground from Manor House to Strand station. Here I would get out and walk through the Law Court gardens to the Embankment, always a delightful experience, except on the days when, after the age of fourteen, I had to wear my ill-fitting Officer Training Corps uniform. This uni-form, old-fashioned even in those days, included puttees, long itchy strips of rough khaki which I never acquired the knack of winding correctly round my spindly calves.

Often as not, they came unwrapped in the train, falling in coils round my oversized boots and once earning me the rebuke, 'Watch it, soldier, if your Regimental Sergeant Major gets to hear about this, you could be facing fifty lines.'

Mr Williams, my English teacher at City of London School, used every opportunity to encourage us to be 'verbally venturesome'. They said of him that if he had his way, Fire Drill would have been a written test.

Round the age of fifteen, I used to spend my Wednesday afternoons as an interpreter at the Salvation Army Home in Clapton which was acting as a shelter for refugee children from the Spanish Civil War.

The Wednesday that stands out in my memory from that time was the one when I learned on arrival that the town of Valladolid had fallen to Franco's forces. Many of the kids had parents and relatives there, so the Salvation Army people had taken pains to write as reassuring an announcement of the news as was possible, with special emphasis on the help that could be provided.

The kids' ages ranged from about six to twelve but when I read my translated version of the announcement to them, it was met with only a few stifled sobs.

As I was about to move away, one of the Salvation Army ladies came to my side and murmured, 'Would you please say to them, "Let us pray."'

Obediently, I returned to the lectern and, bowing my head, said, '*Oramos.*'

There was a moment's uncertainty. Then, all round the room, the left arms of these little ones shot up in the clenched-fist communist salute.

Among others at City of London school with me were Kingsley Amis, Derek Roy and Robert ('Monster Fun Book') Moreton.

Derek Roy was the first comedian to appear on ITV's first Light Entertainment show, opening proceedings with the words, 'Hello, deserters.'

'Did you always want to write comedy?' someone asked me the other day. Mulling the question over, it occurred to me that 'writing comedy' is in itself a comparatively modern locution. In my boyhood, the equivalent would have been 'writing humorous pieces' and a comedy writer would have been described as a 'humorist'. Indeed, the main rival to *Punch* at the time was a magazine called *The Humorist*. Odd, how far out of fashion that word is now.

My first published stab at the genre was an essay in the school magazine. I was about twelve or thirteen at the time and the essay was written to order on the subject of 'Honesty Is the Best Policy'. It reflected the powerful influence G. K. Chesterton was currently exerting on me, arguing that anyone who regards honesty as a policy, rather than a moral obligation, is essentially dishonest.

It won me the John Carpenter prize, any book of my own choosing. I opted for *The Collected Short Stories of Guy de Maupassant*, a volume whose raciness the Headmaster made apparent to all by the elevation of his eyebrows when he presented it to me.

Craven Park was what was then called an 'elementary school', sited in a fairly down-at-heel area. In fact, I remember two brothers in ragged blue jerseys who had to share one pair of boots. When there was snow on the ground, each of them would only come to school on alternate days.

Against this background, it has always struck me as more than odd that our favourite reading matter was *The Magnet,* a weekly magazine devoted to life at Greyfriars, an English public boarding school. We followed its characters and devoured its stories hungrily, even though we frequently had not the faintest idea what they were talking about. What was 'Prep'? Or 'Fagging'? 'The Remove'?

Not for a moment, did our ignorance diminish our enthusiasm for Harry Wharton and his associates. ('Hello, hello, hello,' said Bob Cherry cheerily.) Simultaneously, the cinemas were offering us an abundance of films about American college life. These we lapped up with equal enjoyment, despite their similarly incomprehensible allusions. What was a 'frat pin'? Or a 'Junior Prom'? And how did you 'Hold the mayo'? Again, we were perfectly content to remain baffled.

Such a grounding could explain why, along with many of my generation, the things that bring me most pleasure still seem to be those I don't quite understand.

My first night-time visit to the theatre happened when we were living in Hove. As a special eleventh birthday treat, my father booked seats at the Brighton Hippodrome for a new kind of show starring six comedians who had never appeared together before and were calling themselves the Crazy Gang. This was their pre-Palladium opening week and nobody quite knew what to expect.

It was my first experience of such a grand evening occasion and standing around in the foyer with the other early arrivals, I was conscious of an excitement in the air, something I had not sensed at the pantomimes and *Where the Rainbow Ends* matinees I had known up till then. This sense of occasion was heightened by a bewigged and richly costumed usher who moved across and bowed before looking at our tickets. Examining them, he tut-tutted, then, with a 'M'sieur, Madame', beckoned us to follow him up the big stairs that led to the Circle. I thought my father was looking puzzled, a puzzlement that deepened when the usher led us past the Circle and through a side-door up some stone stairs to the Upper Circle.

When my father ventured 'I booked seats in the Front Stalls', the usher put a finger to his lips, 'That was before the Revolution,' he said. He pushed a door that opened to reveal the rear of the Upper Circle. And we obediently followed him behind the back row across to the exit door on the opposite side. Pushing it open he politely indicated more stone steps, this time leading us downward. My father could contain himself no longer. 'I would like to see the manager,' he said, as we descended. The usher shook his head. 'Sorry, there are no more managers.'

After more doors, more steps, more crossings to and fro and my father's jaw tightening visibly, we suddenly found ourselves back in the foyer again. 'Follow me,' the usher said and, this time, led us through the Stalls door and down the aisle to three seats right in the centre of row A. From within his ornate coat, he produced a large box of chocolates and, with a bow, handed it to my mother, 'With the compliments of the Revolution.' Then before leaving, no doubt to return to the foyer and conduct some other customers all round the theatre, he shook my father's hand and said, 'Enjoy the show. My name's Bud Flanagan.'

I was entranced by him and remained so when I came to know and work with him. I wish I retained some memories of the show itself, but they have all fled, save for the moment in the interval when all six members of the Gang appeared in one of the boxes and tossed Barnett's sausages down into the audience. And that has probably only stayed in my mind because my next evening visit to a theatre was a school trip to see *Othello*. I remained in my seat throughout the interval in the unfulfilled hope of more sausages.

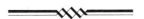

I count as the most totally hilarious period of my working life the days Frank and I spent at the Victoria Palace writing sketches and lines for a forthcoming Crazy Gang show. All of them were knocking on seventy by now but there was hardly a day when one or other of the elderly group didn't sidle up and confide, 'I'm working on a polone. Any chance she could have a walk-across in one of the sketches?'

After weeks of sporadic rehearsal, with Bud Flanagan as the moon-faced planet round whom the rest of the Gang revolved, the new material had become laden with so many 'bits' various of the members had recollected from previous shows that all agreed 'would just fit in nicely here', most of our new stuff had to be cut out to make room. The resulting amalgam, though, proved so enjoyable and we'd had so much fun in the Gang's company, we didn't grieve about it.

The surprise came after the show had been running for a couple of months. We received an unexpected call to the Hylton office, where Jack informed us, 'The Gang have now put back so much of the stuff you wrote for them, I think you deserve a little bit extra.

I can give it to you in cash or, if you'd rather, a few shares in one of these new TV companies I'll be doing some shows for when Commercial Television starts. Whichever you prefer.'

Displaying the kind of business acumen that never deserted us, we both opted immediately for the cash. He called 'Hughie!' and in came Hugh Charles who, in addition to writing songs like 'There'll Always Be an England' and Bud's 'Strollin', was Hylton's principal aide at that time. He was carrying a thick bundle of white fivers from which, unprompted, he counted out forty. Jack smiled benevolently.

Such an uncharacteristic gesture from this notoriously hard-headed impresario became a memory to be cherished and probably would have remained so if I hadn't mentioned it to Ted Willis.

It was several years later, while I was having a drink with him after a Guild meeting, and I had only brought the Hylton incident up as an example of those 'You never can tell' moments in a writer's life. Ted's response was, 'I had exactly the same thing happen.'

'With Jack Hylton?'

'With Jack Hylton.' He went on to explain that during what must have been more or less the same time that Frank and I were working with the Gang, Hylton had contracted one of Ted's plays, I think it was *No Trees in the Street*, for a long tour of the provinces. After it had been on the road a few weeks, Ted had received a similar summons to the Jack Hylton office.

Here he was told that the tour was proving so much more profitable than had been anticipated, Jack had decided he merited some kind of extra recompense. As with us, he was asked whether he preferred some cash or a few shares in one of the new Television companies.

Ted chose the shares. 'And a couple of months ago,' he said, 'I sold them for £11,000.'

The Crazy Gang were past masters at the game of 'Outwitting the Censor', in their case the Lord Chamberlain. One of their most ingenious successes, if only because its effect was achieved by pausing rather than speaking, was part of a North-West Frontier sketch, with Teddy Knox playing the very pukka Lieutenant Far-kew-harson ('Sir, they've blasted the dam!').

With the orchestra softly playing a Cole Porter tune, he described the huge idol before which the rebellious natives prostrated themselves. 'Sir, it's got two heads. Four arms. Six legs. BUT –' He fell silent as the orchestra arrived at the tune's title phrase: 'Just One of Those Things'.

The street cries of old London could still be heard around the suburbs in the thirties. Tradesmen of all kinds would wander up and down our street shouting their wares vociferously to cajole house-holders into coming out and buying. What I remember most vividly about their traditional cries is that they were, without exception, totally incomprehensible.

Leon Cortez, a popular Cockney comedian of the fifties, summed it up best when he was reminiscing about his boyhood days. He used to like nothing better than lying in bed listening to a man with a horse and cart, who would regularly plod along his street shouting, 'Uhdjagoo-meh! Uhdjagoo-meh!'

'Then along came the War,' Leon would conclude. 'Then all the cars and the buses and traffic and all the old street cries disappeared. Nowadays – well, you can hardly buy an uhdjagoo-meh anywhere.'

It was a recommended practice among the ungilded youth of my generation to put one's trousers under the mattress at night to produce a sharp crease in the morning. For me, it invariably produced a series of four creases, in diamond patterns.

When we had our office in Conduit Street, there was a branch of the Inland Revenue further down towards the Westbury Hotel. I never really noticed it till one day, caught in a sudden summer shower, I saw a man and a woman taking refuge from the rain in its doorway. It seemed a good idea, so I joined them and we stood together gazing comfortably at the soaked and scurrying passers-by.

After a while, to break the silence, I indicated the Inland Revenue brass nameplate and said, 'This must be one of those tax shelters you read about.'

They stared at me uncomprehendingly, then the man muttered something to the woman in a foreign language and they hurried away.

A similarly ill-fated punning expedition took place when I pre-sented myself at my GP's with a hacking cough and a voice so husky, it was practically inaudible. After a careful examination, he made that 'Mmmm' sound they go in for, then announced, 'You have an infec-tion of the upper respiratory tract.'

At my uncomprehending nod, he explained, 'It's what you might call a high chest cold.'

'As in High Chest Cold to Say I Love You?' I croaked.

It was met with the same blank stare as the couple in the tax shelter.

Several of the East End characters I came across during my researches for Dick Bentley's series of radio interviews offered an agreeable whiff of the spurious. I was having a cup of tea at a market stall with one of my contacts when he pointed out a man with a uniform cap who was hurrying past carrying an unusually large suitcase. 'There's someone you might be able to use,' he said. 'Name of Simmy, only works fifteen minutes a day.'

Having provoked my curiosity, he was persuaded by a further cup of tea and a bagel to enlighten me. Simmy was en route to Tower Bridge, whose two halves, one must bear in mind, were raised back then at 2 p.m. precisely every day. At a quarter to, Simmy would station himself on a site overlooking the bridge and, opening the suitcase, draw out two small folding stools. One of these he would sit, the other he put in front of him and placed on top of it a grey board, also from the suitcase, in the middle of which was a large red button set within the London coat of arms. Then he would produce a pair of binoculars, lift them to his eyes and gaze intently at the bridge.

Inevitably one of the crowd of sightseers milling around to view this traditional London spectacle would ask if he had anything to do with it. Simmy would explain that it was his official responsibility to make sure all was well before pressing the button that relayed the appropriate radio signal to the bridge's opening mechanism.

It was a poor day if at least one of the onlookers didn't ask if he, or more usually his child, could have a go at pressing the button. Simmy would go through an elaborate 'more than my job's worth' show of reluctance before yielding to the temptation of proffered high-denomination banknotes. 'Not till I tell you,' he would warn. Then, with one eye on his wristwatch, 'Now!' As the two halves of the bridge began to move upwards and the awe-struck button-presser gawped in wonderment at the majestic spectacle he had initiated, Simmy would pack his props back in the suitcase and slip away.

'Do you think Simmy would agree to be interviewed on the Bentley programme?' I asked.

'Unlikely,' he replied. 'I mean, a lot of those sightseers are visiting Australians. And if the programme's going to go out down there …' He paused. 'Still, there might be ways of persuading him.' He gave me a meaningful look.

After accepting two guineas as what was known as a 'finder's fee', he hurried off in search of his friend. I never saw either of them again.

After a lifetime spent wandering the foothills of comedy, the only thing I know for certain about it is that it can never be anything but a risk venture. Nothing can ever be guaranteed and there are rarely any insurance policies.

It was sometimes difficult to convince other people of this, particularly during a period of the late seventies, when I was writing sketches, lyrics and speeches for various elaborate sales conferences and product launches. Most of them were for fairly high-powered multinational companies, at a time when the vogue was for what they liked to call 'Industrial Theatre'. These were big budget stage productions that employed West End performers, choreographers, dancers, singers, composers and directors to put across the company's message in spectacular style to audiences of sales staff or customers.

Soon enough, such mini-musicals were abandoned in favour of computerised audio-visual presentations, but they were fun while they lasted. Several of mine were staged abroad, taking me to such desirable venues as the South of France, Vienna and Rio de Janeiro.

When it came to writing the material, I was constantly struck by how similar the task was to writing for troop shows during the War. As in the forties, it entailed sending up the officers sitting in the front rows, but never to the extent of inciting to mutiny. Of course, one first had to master the brief, the Unique Selling Points, the Target Sales Figures and so on, which was not always that much of a doddle. For one annual conference, a well-known High Street food brand set me the task of informing their assembled sales force that, in the year ahead, their sales commissions were going to be lowered, while their sales targets were to be raised. 'We were wondering,' the Sales Director said hopefully, 'whether you could put this across to them in such a way as to make it seem like an achievement.'

Often as not, the executive superintending the stage presentation would be someone who was convinced his entire future with the company hung on whether it was a success or failure. I remember an overseas IBM event where the man in charge was so worried about the script, he sent for me the night before the show. When I got to his room, he thrust the pages at me and asked, with more than a touch of desperation, 'Are you absolutely sure this is going to be funny?'

I felt the need to remind him of comedy's 'risk venture' component. 'If I could be absolutely sure something was going to be funny,' I said, 'IBM would be working for me.'

The cinema manager was expected to be on hand in the foyer at the start of each programme to welcome patrons coming in out of the weather. It was a part of the job I rather enjoyed, not least because I liked listening to the perennial squabbles among the incoming couples about whether or not they should leave their coats in the cloakroom.

Perhaps because people were more given to wearing overcoats in those days, the cinema cloakroom was in use more or less all year round. The disputes, often heated, always centred on whether the benefits of not having to sit through the whole programme with a heavy and sometimes damp coat across the knees outweighed the inconvenience of queuing up to retrieve the coats when they came out. I would linger to see just how long it took before one or other of them invoked the universal axiom that whenever you put your coat in the cloakroom, the seat beside you invariably turned out to be empty.

Another observable phenomenon was how frequently couples making for the back row would choose to sit with a heavy coat across their laps.

Horse Feathers, written by S. J. Perelman, is the film in which Groucho Marx, semaphoring energetically with his eyebrows, utters the entirely non-apropos line, 'Come, Kappelmeister, let the violas throb. My regiment leaves at dawn.'

I shared a TV talk show panel with Perelman and, as is usual when I meet people for whom my admiration is boundless, had some difficulty in finding anything non-gushing to say to him. Alan Coren had warned me that the Marx Brothers were his least favourite topic, so I steered clear of them and confined myself to recollections of exchanging cut-down wartime copies of the *New Yorker* with other uniformed devotees.

However, it was SJ himself (I could never bring myself to call him 'Sid') who introduced the subject with an anecdote about a seance Groucho had been reluctantly persuaded to attend. Towards the end of it, the medium announced, 'My spirit guide is tiring. We have time for only one more question, please.' Groucho immediately offered, 'What's the capital of North Dakota?'

My only attempt at writing something full-length for the theatre was in the seventies, when I was asked to adapt a New York comedy success, *Norman ... Is That You?*, for the West End. However, it was impressed on me that I must rewrite it in such a way that audiences would never suspect that it had come from America. Apparently recent Broadway hits had not gone down well in London so no trace of its origins must ever become apparent.

To that extent, my task was more of a translation than an adaptation. The producers had Harry Worth in mind for the lead, so we decided to set the story in the Midlands. I was in constant touch with the original authors, Ron Clark and Sam Bobrick – or as constant as touch could be before e-mail – and I made sure they understood and approved the reasons for every alteration.

It soon became clear that these changes could not be confined to variations in vocabulary, I also had to accommodate alien allusions and speech pattern. Ron and Sam became as fascinated by these mutations as I was, but it did not slow up the process until I came to a scene where the leading character described his adolescent love life. In the American version, he recalled how, as a secret trysting place, 'we used to use my Dad's garage'.

As played by Harry, this character had been brought up in humble circumstances in a town near Birmingham. For his father to have owned a car, let alone a garage, would have been entirely out of keeping. I racked my brains for a suitable English equivalent, somewhere similarly folksy and domestic where a lad from a lower-middle-class family of that era could have conducted his clandestine youthful gropings. Finally, with a faint feeling of triumph, I came up with, 'We used to use my Dad's allotment shed.'

When I sent the line to my American friends, they immediately replied with a cable, 'What in hell is an allotment shed?'

I ask you to believe that the process of explaining that small detail to Ron and Sam's satisfaction involved me in an airmail letter of no less than six closely typed pages, outlining salient events in English social history and conducting them, via the Allotments Act 1922, all the way back to the Industrial Revolution.

Norman … Is That You? enjoyed but the briefest of stays in the West End, though I drew some small pleasure from the fact that no one twigged it was an American import. Its other abiding memory for me is its pre-London opening at the Theatre Royal, Brighton. My daughter, Maggie, was at Sussex University at the time, so I invited her and as many of her mates as cared to come along to the dress rehearsal on Sunday night.

As has often been observed, students will go anywhere where it's warm and it's free, so quite a sizeable bunch turned up. They proved an appreciative audience and while I was taking them off to the pub afterwards, I asked if they had any comments about the play.

One of the males had a question. 'You know the scene where the girl comes in and when she takes her coat off it turns out she's only got her underclothes on underneath?'

I nodded. 'Yes, I know that scene.'

'Well, what she was wearing – was that meant to make her look sexy?'

She was wearing a black bra, black stockings and suspenders. 'Of course,' I said. 'Didn't you think it was sexy?'

He grimaced. 'Not really.'

'Well, what would you have found sexy?'

'I dunno. Nice pair of tights, body stocking …'

He left me brooding. Could it be that the term 'generation gap' simply referred to that gap between the top of the stocking and the edge of the knicker? If so, the distance separating the generations was no more than about four inches.

Comedy is the only form of entertainment whose success is evaluated by the frequency and volume of an audience's audible response. You never hear acrobats, for instance, claiming they received thirty-two per cent more gasps last night.

On the other hand, Miriam Karlin told me that when she and Topol starred in *Fiddler On the Roof*, every time they sang their poignant duet, 'Sunrise, Sunset', they would calculate the amount of eye-moistening it provoked by counting the number of little white patches of handkerchief they would see blossoming in the audience.

When an unexpectedly large crowd of sopranos lined up outside the theatre to audition for a part in a new operetta, the producer's assistant was seen walking up and down the queue, bellowing: 'All those with glasses and "Bird of Love Divine" need not wait.'

Among them was Joan Young, mother of April, my lifelong agent, and she treasured the line for the rest of her hard-working life.

I was only once faced with the task of auditioning a nimiety of sopranos. (It's a word I've been trying to pluck up the courage to use ever since I first came across it at the age of sixteen: 'nimiety' equals 'a too muchness'.) They descended upon me in excessive numbers during the post-war period, when we advertised for artists to appear in the Peter Waring show the Kavanagh office was putting together to entertain the troops in Germany.

By that time, 'Bird of Love Divine' had ceased to be the audition-piece of choice among sopranos, the current favourite being 'All Thru' the Night I Can Hear a Brown Bird Singing'. A melodious enough ballad, but I have to confess that round about the sixteenth time of listening to it, my concentration began to waver. I found myself wondering, as I do to this day, how she had worked out the colour of the bird in the pitch darkness.

In the early fifties, pre-ITV, Brylcreem was running an extensive press and poster campaign featuring the glistening black hair of Denis Compton. It was also around that time that *Take It From Here*'s listener figures began to climb, so Frank and I found ourselves mentioned in the newspapers fairly frequently.

Out of nowhere, I received a letter from an advertising agency asking whether, in return for a substantial, not to say mouth-watering, sum of money, Brylcreem could exhibit my own glistening black hair for advertising purposes?

Talking the offer over with Frank, we worked ourselves up into a fine old frenzy of moral dudgeon about it. Have my face plastered all over the Underground? Touting a men's toiletry product? As though

I was some kind of male model? Out of the question! I wrote them a stiffly formal reply, explaining why, as a serious professional writer, I could not accede to their request.

It was not until many years later that I came across a poem, author forgotten, based on the Biblical story of Joseph and the wife of Potiphar, his employer. The poem was in two stanzas, the first, written by Joseph as a young man, recounting how she summoned him to her chamber, where she attempted to seduce him. After describing how he successfully repelled her advances, he ends with the line, 'Lord, what a whore she was!'

The second stanza is written by Joseph as a much older man. And this time, as he looks back on their encounter, his concluding words are, 'Lord, what a fool I was!'

To this day, whenever I smooth the occasional modicum of Brylcreem over my thinning grey hair, it never fails to bring to mind the wife of that ancient Egyptian.

I was left in no doubt about the status of the accordion in the musical hierarchy of those days by Phil Baker, an American comedian who used one in his act. He told me that when he had his own radio series in the States, he was approached by a firm of accordion manufacturers to endorse their instrument.

'Why me?' he asked. 'There's lots of better accordion players around.'

'We know. But you're the only one who's working steady.'

When we arrived in Australia for our stint with the Australian Broadcasting Commission, we found they had arranged a press conference for us at the airport immediately after landing. In those days, the flight took five days, so we were more than a little tired, not to say grumpy. After an hour or so of questioning, lightheadedness was also setting in. So when somebody asked, 'How can two people write a comedy script together?' one of us – I forget which – answered, 'We use a very large pencil' and the other mimed the two-handed wielding of an oversize writing instrument.

A week or so later, we were shown a cutting from a New South Wales magazine in which the information appeared under the heading, 'Fifteen Fascinating Facts About Muir and Norden'.

One of the sketches in the revue *Take It From Us* was a courtroom scene in which Jimmy Edwards played a judge. On the wall behind his judicial chair was a large heraldic shield for which George Black asked us to provide a suitably legal-sounding Latin inscription. As we frequently parked our cars in the Lex Garage on Brewer Street, we suggested a scroll on which were written the words, 'Auto In Lex'.

Not only did it provoke the required little murmur when the curtain rose on the scene, it furnished us with free parking for the run of the production.

We were faced with a trickier task of scene-setting for the opening titles of *Whack-o!* These began with an establishing shot of the school gates, lingering on the sign that said, 'Chiselbury School, For the sons of gentlefolk, Headmaster, Professor J. Edwards.'

Douglas Moodie, our producer, noted there was room at the bottom of the sign for a school motto, preferably one that embodied Chiselbury's dubious record of scholastic achievement.

After turning down several of our suggestions, he settled for 'They Shall Not Pass'.

All things considered, it was relatively rarely that we had listeners writing in to complain about something in a *Take It From Here* script. In fact, there was only one occasion when the number of letters protesting that we had grossly overstepped the bounds of good taste reached triple figures. They were triggered by a line we had given Jimmy Edwards in an episode of *The Glums*. Far from being any kind of reference to sexual or religious matters, it came during an emotional outburst in which Mr Glum was bewailing Ron's treatment of his mother.

'When I think of the things Mrs Glum did for that boy! Never once gave him a cup of hot tea she hadn't already saucered and blowed. Always cut up his soldiers before opening his boiled egg. Never put his stewed apples in front of him without making sure she'd taken out the toenail bits.'

It was the 'toenail bits' that set off a wave of revulsion which stretched from Scotland to Land's End.

Tony Hawes was a brilliant if sometimes erratic comedy writer who regularly hired a bus for his birthday parties and went on to marry the daughter of his idol, Stan Laurel. But before he departed for America, back in the days when punning was in flower, he introduced me to the Don Ameche game. To play this, the punned name of a, preferably faded, popular star had to be inserted into the lyric of an equally faded popular song: as in 'I'll be Don Ameche in a taxi, honey', the first line of 'The Darktown Strutters' Ball'. (Anybody still with me?)

The game enjoyed quite a vogue among writers for a while and I can recall hearing contributions from Sid Colin, John Junkin, Benny Green, Marty Feldman, Dick Vosburgh and Bob Monkhouse among others. Their efforts included:

The John Wayne song: 'John Wayne on My Parade'
The Gunga Din song: 'Gunga Din Springtime Are You'
The Faye Dunaway song: 'Old Soldiers Never Die, They only Faye Dunaway'

Similarly:
'I'd like to be in a Mary Quant, Okay by me in a Mary Quant'
'On a Keir Dullea you can see forever'
'I'm always Jason Robards'
'Liv Ullman, you've had a busy day'
'Fats Waller like about the south'
'Sandra Dee night is the loneliest night of the week'
'The night they invented John Payne'
'Joshua Fit de Battle of Jericho, Andy Warhol came tumbling down'

The BBC converted the Paris, Lower Regent Street, into a broadcasting studio and for many years most of radio's comedy shows were recorded there. I could remember it from pre-war days, when it was a luxurious little cinema with comfortable red plush seats, showing the latest X-certificate, Adults Only films from France and Italy. (In those days, an X certificate was reserved for content of a sexual nature; anything in the horror or violence line received an H.)

During my early teens, I spent many happy afternoons tormenting myself there. Being six foot two at the age of thirteen, I had no difficulty disguising myself as an adult, especially with the aid of my father's trilby and an uncle's long, thick overcoat. From the kaleidoscope of images the Paris introduced me to, two have remained vivid.

One that sent me well-nigh dizzy with cravings was a sun-drenched scene in a film called *Naples au Baiser du Feu* that had the succulent Viviane Romance, in a low-necked peasant blouse, seated opposite her fisherman lover at the table of an outdoor café. As she leaned forward, the camera cut to an under-the-table shot showing her slipping off her shoe and slowly rubbing the underside of her bare foot up and down his instep. I almost fainted.

The second memory is one I recalled on a radio programme with the self-explanatory title, *The Last Night of the Paris*, the final show to be broadcast from the former cinema. The incident came from the same period of my life and was prompted by the same sort of film, very daring, very French.

In this case, the scene took place in a Parisian flat where a man and woman on a couch were locked in a fervent embrace. Their lovemaking grew more and more heated, reaching a point where the picture tactfully faded to black. When it faded in again, we were in the same room, but now it was daylight and the couch was empty.

Melvin Frank

Buona Sera,
Mrs Campbell

My treasured Thurber original

The Brylcreem touch

Origin of the 'Ah yee oh go' recognition signal

Oh, Mr Porter!: 'Next train's gorn' – Moore Marriott

Countdown: Richard Whiteley, Carol Vorderman and DN

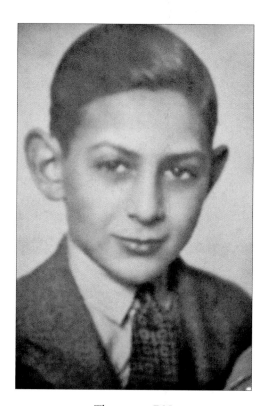

The young DN

Behind it, though – and, yes, I know this shot is a cliché today, but back then it was startling in its audacity – there, on the carpet behind it, stretched a trail of discarded clothing leading to a closed (obviously bedroom) door.

Still hardly able to believe such explicitness, I heard one of those clear Edinburgh voices behind me say, 'Isn't that typical! All over the floor for somebody else to pick up.'

Another of the London characters I interviewed for those early Bentley programmes was Mai Harris, who provided the English subtitles for most of the French and Italian films of that era.

A wise and cultivated lady, she proved an excellent subject, particularly interesting when she began talking about the way she sometimes had to completely reverse the sense of a line of foreign dialogue in order to render its appropriate English equivalent. When I asked her for an example, she thought for a moment, then cited a situation where someone has been knocked down by a car. As he lies in the road, a passer-by hastens over and kneels down beside him. 'In the original French or Italian,' she went on, 'the anxious passer-by's first question would be, "Are you hurt?" or "Are you injured?"' She shook her head, 'But that's not what an Englishman would ask. He would say, "Are you all right?"'

I still warm to the distinction. While both enquiries indicate an admirable concern for a total stranger, the latter signals our ingrained reluctance to get involved any further.

True story: in the early fifties, someone Frank and I knew bought an enormous quantity of war-surplus Bibles and advertised them in the *Daily Mirror* as 'The Book Every Married Couple Should Possess! Dispatched to you in a plain brown envelope. Send 7/6d.'

The following morning, he had to climb over the mailbags to get into his office.

Mutterings from Melvin Frank: 'I can't relax. Relaxation makes me tense.'

'If I can find my glasses when I wake up in the morning, that's enough happiness for one day.'

One of the few members of my trade who deserves to have a public park named after him is Spike Milligan, the man responsible for such eternal verities as 'Anyone can be 52, but only a bus can be 52B' or 'Some people are always late, like the late King George.' It is also to him that we owe the proposition that Tring was named after the inventor of the bicycle bell.

When three of us turned up together on the special programme BBC Radio put on to celebrate his eightieth birthday, he greeted us with the announcement, 'It's Sykes, Speight and Norden, back from the dead for one night only.'

One of my more searing memories of him goes back to 1964, when he was appearing in the West End in the play that became known as *Son of Oblomov*. They had given him free rein to ad-lib all he wanted, with the result that no two performances were ever the same.

On the night I saw it, I had the misfortune to be in a seat where he could spot me from the stage. Consequently, about fifteen minutes into the first act, he waved the proceedings to a halt, advanced to the footlights and, motioning me to stand up, introduced me to the audience. Then, addressing me, he confided, 'This next bit, it's a little dull. You're a scriptwriter, can you suggest anything I can do to cheer it up?'

When I stammered something desperately wide of the mark, he smiled encouragingly. 'Just some funny little line,' he said. 'Doesn't have to be a whole new scene. Work on it and if anything occurs, shout it out. God bless you, guv.'

He nodded me to sit down again and resumed the play. But during the rest of the evening, on at least half a dozen occasions – all of them, I must now admit, beautifully judged – he would halt the play and get me up again with such remarks as, 'Still nothing?' and 'I'm perfectly prepared to pay Writers' Guild rates' and, finally, 'You're not much without that fellow in the pink bow-tie, are you?'

When we went round to see him in his dressing room afterwards, he was in high spirits. 'I think that worked out very well, don't you?'

I could only gesture weakly at the whisky bottle.

Several decades back, an advertising agency enlisted me for a series of TV commercials they were preparing for one of the top-name detergents. At this remove, I cannot for the life of me remember which detergent it was, but I do recall how wildly excited the agency people were about the new advertising theme they had thought up for it: 'So white, even a man notices!'

It encompassed, they explained, everything the client could ask for in the way of impact and memorability, to say nothing of a certain sly humour. 'What we'd like you to write,' they went on, 'are a few sharp little scenes illustrating and supporting the proposition. Say, nine or ten? By the end of the week?'

I can now confess that I was nowhere near as bowled over by the concept as they were but this was the what-the-hell sixties and the money was good, so I set to. Of the six suggestions I managed to come up with, the only two that still remain in mind were somewhat similar in approach.

One was your stereotypical 'Come out of there, Lefty, we've got the house surrounded' scene, focused on a shabby front door, spotlit by police car headlights. As half a dozen SWAT team members, with guns in hand, move into shot, the door opens and out pokes a pole bearing a white flag. As it waves, 'Drop the gun, Lefty,' calls an advancing armed policeman. Then his attention shifts to the flag, 'Hey! How'd you get this so white?'

The second offering centred on an equally well-worn scene, this time a prison break. From a cell-window high on a grey wall dangles a rope of knotted white sheets, down which a convict is climbing. As he reaches the ground, a warder steps from concealment and claps a hand on his shoulder. Then, pausing, his other hand takes hold of the sheet and he gazes at it appreciatively ...

The agency's reactions were surprisingly enthusiastic, their back-slapping concluding with an invitation, 'Why don't you join us when we present to the client?'

Never having participated in this particular ritual before, I said, 'Glad to.'

The presentation took place a few days later in a specially booked private conference room at the Russell Hotel in Russell Square. It turned out to be a memorable illustration of the contradictory attitudes prevailing in those mixed-up sixties

I'd been told to get there at 9.30 a.m., half an hour before the client was due, and be prepared to spend the rest of the day there. In the event, I arrived first and was shown into a magnificent panelled room, with a dark, highly polished table down its middle, bearing eight thick notepads, each flanked by a variety of pens and pencils. Round the room, massive sideboards were laden with all manner of appetising buffet foods, drinks, beverages, game pies, joints of cold meats, an entire roast turkey, a huge side of sliced smoked salmon, different varieties of bread and silver bowls filled with seasonal and exotic fruits. Two uniformed waiters stood by in silent readiness.

The agency four turned up a few minutes later, all in what would now be called 'smart casual'. The one I later discovered to be the Creative Director said, 'We've decided you should pitch it.'

'Pitch it?'

'Read it to the client. Just read them the scripts, like you did with us. Doing the voices.'

Sharp at ten 'the client' arrived, three middle-aged men in sober suits who refused coffee and sat down facing us. After welcoming them, the Creative Director introduced me and the agency people all turned their faces expectantly in my direction.

Aiming to keep the occasion smart casual, I read the scripts out from a sitting position, with a minimum of pause between each one. When I finished, there were appreciative chuckles from the agency side of the table, but an expressionless silence from the side opposite.

The Creative Director picked up on it immediately. 'You don't find them amusing?'

'They're amusing all right,' said one of the client. 'That's the trouble.'

'We're not in the business of making washday a source of amusement,' said the man next to him. 'For your average housewife, it's a part of her role in life that helps define her identity.'

'Laughing at it could be tantamount to belittling it,' said the third.

Again, the agency faces turned hopefully in my direction. But the best I could manage was, 'Well, I suppose you know your own business best.'

We were out of there by 10.20 a.m. And throughout the rest of that long, empty day, all I could think about was those two waiters, alone in the empty room, feet up on the long, polished table, drinks in hand and occasionally nibbling at a turkey leg.

While we were filming *The Best House in London*, we used the Piccadilly Arcade for one of our Victorian locations, 'dressing' it with a period postbox. When shooting was over for the day and they were re-loading the box on the van, I noticed its door had swung open. I looked inside it and found twenty or so letters and postcards, all bearing modern uncancelled stamps.

Our Arcade had been closed to the public, so these could only have been posted at whatever film location the postbox had previously graced. Inspecting the postcards, we realised they were all photographs of that target for top-end tourists, the beautiful Wiltshire village of Castle Combe. 'That's where they shot *Doctor Dolittle*,' somebody remembered.

Some further discussion established that the filming of that had taken place about thirteen or fourteen months ago. So the letters and cards, all of them addressed to various places in America, had been lying inside the box gathering dust for more than a year. By common consent, we gathered them all up and reposted them in the nearest modern postbox.

I have often wondered since what tales the recipients now recount about the British postal system.

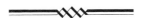

One of Bob Monkhouse's favourites among the lesser known American comedians was Milt Kamen, who claimed to have been such an emotional child that when his teacher told him that parallel lines never meet, he felt bad for a week.

It was also Kamen who stated his belief that all foreign languages were merely an affectation. Wake up any foreigner in the middle of the night by shouting 'Fire!' he'll immediately struggle up and say, 'What? Where, where?'

The great majority of Variety performers – the acrobats, dancers, jugglers, tap-dancers, knockabout teams, dog acts – never harboured any false hopes of attaining top-of-the-bill status. Indeed, for most of them, even the middle or across-the-bottom position on a poster was never even a possibility. To my mind, such limited expectations only made the diligence with which most of them would still work at perfecting every minor detail of their twice-nightly performances all the more admirable.

Although it was a world where your billing determined your salary, it was also a time when hardly a town in Britain was without at least one Variety theatre, so there was work in plenty for even the lowliest name on the programme.

On the night of the moon landing in 1969, David Frost hosted an all-night programme in Associated-Rediffusion's Wembley Studios, with all manner of people participating, especially during the run-up period when the world was waiting for the astronauts to touch down on the moon's surface.

David had asked me to contribute a solo three minutes, but in the presence of so many technological heavyweights I was at a loss to know what line to take. Then I remembered that Rediffusion had recently been taken to task for failing to make a sufficient number of serious documentary programmes. Furthermore, I had noticed that next door to the studio in which we were working, there was another larger studio, which was presently closed, padlocked and guarded by uniformed Security.

When it came to my turn, I drew the audience's attention to these two facts. Then I put forward the proposition that inside that locked studio could be found a skilfully detailed mock-up of the moon's surface, on which the TV company would shortly be making up for its documentary shortfall by staging a no-expense-spared production of a space landing. And it would be the pictures from in there that would be beamed round the world.

I was able to adduce a few other scraps of what seemed like supporting evidence for my theory and the idea just about held up for the required three minutes, though at no point did it become what Arthur Askey used to call 'a thigh-slapper'.

The interesting development arrived later. In 1978, a film came out called *Capricorn One*, a Hollywood adventure thriller in which an American reporter discovers that the first manned space flight was actually a hoax, a manufactured representation of the event staged inside a huge Television studio.

John Le Mesurier had a story about Collins' Music Hall, a notoriously 'Number 3' date ('They start here and they finish here') in what was then one of the least desirable areas of London. Asked one week why the theatre was doing such bad business, the manager replied, 'Oh, it's always the same when there's polo at Hurlingham.'

It brought back an occasion when Frank and I were taken to lunch by an old-time theatrical impresario, Jack Waller. He enthralled us with tales of touring shows around the African 'dorps' in the early part of the century, including an occasion in a remote township when the musical he had brought there played to minimal audiences for the entire seven days. On the Saturday night, the manager came round to apologise. 'I'm sorry,' he said. 'I'm afraid it's always the same when the elephants are on heat.'

That was the one we added to our private repertoire of excuses.

In the 1984 Royal Variety Show, I introduced a group of French artists performing the 'bell-ringing monks' routine I had first seen in a Robert Dhéry revue and later recommended to the Crazy Gang.

The rehearsal began early in the morning. When we broke for lunch, I found myself at a table with Paul Daniels, whom I had never met. We began chatting and almost immediately he asked me whether, as a writer, I enjoyed doing crossword puzzles. When I confessed I was no great shakes at them, he warmed to the subject and began extolling the skill and ingenuity required of crossword compilers, recommending that I really should try my hand at it.

We stayed with the subject, on which he proved very knowledgeable, throughout the meal and as we got up to leave, he said, 'Shall I tell you the best crossword clue I ever came across? It was "Tired postman."'

'How many letters?' I asked.

He gave a little sigh of satisfaction. 'Thousands of 'em!' he said triumphantly.

As we walked back to the Victoria Palace, I realised he had been preparing me for this for the past forty minutes or so. Once again I marvelled at the lengths comedians will go to in setting up a joke.

While I was writing a monthly column for *SHE* magazine they asked me to review one of those 'How to Do It' sex manuals that were proliferating around that time. This one was even bulkier than most, running to something around 400 pages.

Having reached the age when books of that kind are more or less in the nature of revision notes, the first sentence of my review ran, 'Judging by the size of this volume, sexual activities nowadays would appear to require as much in the way of preliminary instruction as operating a hydraulic forklift truck.'

I thought the criticism harmless enough, but the magazine hadn't been on the bookstalls more than a couple of days when I received a reproachful letter. It was from a director of one of this country's best known hydraulic forklift truck manufacturers. Did I not realise, the gentleman asked, that what I had written could well lead the hydraulic forklift truck-buying public to believe that learning how to handle a hydraulic forklift truck could be as stressful as learning how to handle sex. 'And to prove to you just how easy learning how to handle a hydraulic forklift truck can be,' the letter concluded, 'I have pleasure in enclosing the Standard Instruction Manual for our most popular model.'

And when I looked for the name of that model, it was, true as I'm sitting here, the Coventry Climax.

I made frequent use of this incident when I was doing the rounds of the after-dinner speaking circuit, always validating it by exhibiting the letter and the accompanying Instruction Manual. Unfortunately, in 1991, following a Junior Chamber of Commerce dinner in Leeds, they both went missing, believed snaffled.

The only other book review I was ever asked to write was on what some might describe as a related subject. In the late sixties, when Gershon Legman's monumental *The Rationale of the Dirty Joke: An Analysis of Sexual Humour* became available in this country, the *Evening Standard*'s literary editor rang up, suggesting I contribute a critique of it for the paper.

Immensely flattered at being offered a place among their distinguished coterie of reviewers, I did nothing for the next ten days but read and reread the book, writing pages of notes and tearing up any number of drafts. The book itself was enormous, well over 1,200 pages, and I discovered it was every bit as unfunny as Freud's *Jokes and Their Relation to the Unconscious*, though equally as illuminating.

Resisting the temptation to speculate on how far Legman's surname influenced the direction of his research, I concentrated on the part of his thesis which maintained that it is your jokes which define your character; leading to the conclusion that the only jokes you can tell successfully are you.

When the article appeared, I was delighted to find the *Standard* had made it its lead review, giving the whole first page of its literary section over to it. Quite inordinately proud of myself, I picked up a dozen copies and stopped on the way home to deliver a few to my parents. My mother was busy in the kitchen, so she merely glanced at the heading to make sure my name was in bold enough type and, assuring me she would read the rest of it later, went back to her cooking.

My father, who never gave up hope that I would one day abandon the precarious career path I had chosen and become a partner in his bridalwear business (his brand name was 'Nordenis'), sat down with the paper and carefully read every word of the review through to the end. Then he went back to the top of the page, shook his head and, indicating the book's title, sighed, 'So this is what you're now the big expert on?'

I switched on *Midweek* one morning just as someone was informing Libby Purves that the first tin-opener had been invented by a Frenchman in the year 1812. In the background I heard a familiar voice mutter, 'Ah, "The 1812 Ouverture".' Until then, I hadn't even known Frank was on the programme.

A line he would use to outrageous effect was reserved for the stuffiest of broadcasting's social occasions: a Chairman's dinner, or the presentation of a special award. Meeting one of the lady executives dressed in unaccustomed finery, he would take her hand and compliment her on how exquisite her dress looked. Then, leaning forward and dropping his voice to the most confiding of tones, 'Why pay more?'

On reaching the age of seventy-five, I received an official letter informing me that if I presented myself at the post office with birth documents proving that I was indeed the seventy-five I claimed to be, I could obtain my next TV licence free. I did as they asked and, sure enough, had the minor pleasure of receiving a licence without parting with a penny.

The following year, the same officials sent me another letter, stating that they would give me another free licence if I could once again furnish proof that I was over seventy-five. Puzzled, I wrote back, 'Are you asking me to prove that I am still over seventy-five? If so, is that because certain people have been found to be getting younger?'

In post-war Variety theatres, managers who were dissatisfied with your performance after seeing it first house Monday had the power to cancel you straightaway. Consequently, many dressing rooms bore a notice: 'Do not send out your laundry until the manager has seen your act.'

The demise of cinema double bills deprived us of the B movie, sometimes known as the 'second feature', 'the supporting film' or to many of us including my family, the 'Also'. While I regretted their passing, what I found myself missing even more were the cut-price trailers that promoted them. These occupied such a warm place in my cinema-going memories, in 1992 I persuaded LWT to let me make an entire one-hour 'special' about them. They entitled it *Denis Norden's Trailer Cinema*, having turned down the more accurate *Denis Norden's Trashy Trailers for Mediocre Movies*.

To place those trailers in their context: while the opulent first-feature films of those days enjoyed the promotional advantages of press coverage, posters, reviews and big stars, the only thing a humble 'Also' had going for it was its trailer.

As a consequence those trailers became the treasure house of Hollywood hype. In their efforts to divert attention from a B movie's basic shoestringitis, they would muster an alliterative armoury of overheated superlatives, breathless voiceovers and huge, slanting exclamation marks, often employing marvels of ingenuity, guile and falsehood to embellish their low budget products. To this day some of those empty promises still come back to me as I toss and turn:

'The story behind the story that stunned the nation!'
'The film that makes dimples to catch the tears!'
'Cold steel in his hands and a beautiful woman in his arms!'
'Jungle Africa as you have never seen it before!'
'Tartar terror sweeps across the Russian steppes!'
'The blood of a killer behind every kiss!'
'They've seventy-two hours in which to cram in a lifetime of living!'
'Here is a motion picture your conscience will not let you forget!'

When trailer-makers wished to elevate a B movie above its station in life, they would refer to it as a 'motion picture'. Another well-tried technique was to preface the name of some unknown and unlikely to be known starlet with the phrase 'And introducing'.

Like the smell of circuses and obscene phone calls, these proclamations invariably failed to match any expectations they aroused. In fact, few of us in the audience gave any credence to their transparently inflated claims. We knew – and the trailer producers knew we knew – that such cheapjack movies could never live up to such lofty promises.

But far from resenting them, we enjoyed them. We found them entertaining in their own right, completely disassociating them from the rubbish films they were trumpeting. If anything we relished the enormous chasm between what the trailer promised and what we knew next week's B movie would be delivering.

'A chronicle of emotion you'll never forget!'

'The dance sensation that's shaking the nation!'

'He stumbled out of the jungle, drained dry of man's essence!'

'A romantic experience that will live with you for ever!'

'A melodious mixture of wild gaiety and madcap merrymaking!'

'A probing testament of teen torment!'

'The laughter riot of the decade!'

'The world has a name for her! But don't say the word until you've seen this picture!'

'Only Republic Studios had the courage to bring this story to the screen!'

What is more there were few of us who would have denied an affinity with certain of the improbabilities they were wheedling us to sample. While acknowledging them as part of the trash culture of that time, most of us would admit to a favourite among the various genres of B movies. For some it was films about submarines, for others it was jungle princesses and volcanoes, while there was a healthy (or unhealthy) proportion who went for stories about women's prisons.

My own preference was for minor science fiction movies, especially those of the late fifties and early sixties which tended to dwell on voyages into the future, intruding aliens from Outer Space, 'Man was not meant to tamper with the Unknown', or unscheduled landings on the planet Cheapo. And I am willing to place it on record that, in those days, if there was anything that gave more pleasure than the underfinanced science fiction B movie, it was the trailer they put out for it:

'Radiation crazed crustaceans roam the city!'
'Your eyes will see wonders of a world no eyes in this world have
    ever seen before!'
'A story that may yet be true!'
'Tension tightens like a steel band!'
'A frenzy of screaming terror!'
'Whispered about but never before revealed!'

And my favourite among the favourites:

'The biggest thing since Creation!'

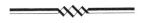

One of many of Frank's remarks worthy of preservation was addressed to Rudolf Cartier, the flamboyantly extravagant drama producer, noted for his predilection for large-scale production. His disregard of live Television's limitations was such that 'I'll need a hundred extras,' was his customary and immediate response to any new project.

When they met in the lift one morning, Frank greeted him with, 'Ah, Rudy. I understand your next play is *A Month in the Studio*.'

TV's most respected producer in those fledgling days was Michael Mills, known around the building as 'dark, satanic Mills', in acknowledgement of his Mephistophelean beard and deep-set eyes. He also owned the car with the longest bonnet in the BBC car park.

When I met Nunnally Johnson at Frank Tarloff's, I was tongue-tied with veneration. A close friend of F. Scott Fitzgerald and Ernest Hemingway, this was the man who'd been Hollywood's most consistently successful screenwriter, producer and director since the thirties. His films ranged from *Jesse James*, *Roxie Hart* and the magnificent *Grapes of Wrath* to *Rose of Washington Square, How to Marry a Millionaire* and *The Dirty Dozen*.

In an attempt to stop myself gushing into an idiotic outflow of adulation, I asked him about an article of his I'd read several years ago in an anniversary edition of *Variety*. It had listed the lines of dialogue in various genres of film which, in his estimation, had now descended into the category of movie clichés.

'But, Inspector, there's one thing I still don't understand ...'

'Come, senor, nobody works when it is fiesta.'

'How dare you, a servant, speak thus to the Caliph's daughter!'

'Lock this door and don't open it to anyone.'

And many others. Such lists have now themselves become clichés. But when I suggested to Nunnally that at the time he compiled his, it was probably a first – even allowing for S. J. Perelman's forays into the territory – he acquiesced.

'I can make that claim,' he added, 'because I was head of a studio at the time and my spies told me that the day the article came out, all the writers in the Writers' Building went through their scripts to make sure none of the lines I'd mentioned appeared in anything they were working on. Even more to the point,' he went on, 'I had to go through everything on my own desk and eliminate them from the screenplays I was writing.'

An assiduously promoted part of the Harry Houdini legend was that whenever he was about to perform a feat of escapology he considered particularly dangerous, he would give his wife a farewell kiss. Just in case …

This touch of showmanship was confirmed for me by Bobby Pagan, whose father had seen it happen. It was at a performance where Houdini, handcuffed, manacled and wrapped in a canvas sheet, was about to be buried in a deep pit. After a rigorous body search by the local police, he kissed his wife, then allowed himself to be lowered into the pit, with two other muscular locals shovelling spadefuls of earth on top of him.

Less than two minutes after the men stepped back, his scrabbling hands appeared at the edge of the pit and, a few seconds later, he hoisted himself out and stood panting and acknowledging the applause.

Obviously, he had somehow managed to unlock the handcuffs and manacles, but the mystery was, where had the key come from?

'It took me years to work that out,' Bobby's father told him. 'In fact, it wasn't till sometime in 1941, while I was watching a film called *You're in the Army Now*, the one where Regis Toomey gives Jane Wyman the famous three-minute kiss. It was halfway through that scene that the answer hit me. I found myself thinking, "With that amount of kissing-time, Mrs Houdini could have slipped Harry an entire bunch of keys."'

When Cinemascope came in Nunnally Johnson was asked how he had adapted his writing technique to allow for the requirements of the widescreen. He replied, 'I put the paper in the typewriter sideways.'

One of the most immediately impressive men I ever met was Paul Robeson. He appeared for a week at the State, Kilburn, while I was doing my training as a stagehand and they gave me the task of standing in the prompt corner and handing him a small glass of sherry when he came off at the end of his performance. He would take two sips, hand back the glass, nod to me courteously, then go back on-stage to sing what invariably turned out to be at least two encores.

For many of us, he will always be associated with an incantation which has come to be something of a recognition signal among those of my generation. To this day, if I happen to intone 'Ah yee oh go' and somebody nearby involuntarily responds 'Yigga dah', I can feel assured we are of an age.

Practically everyone else around will, of course, regard the sounds as pure gibberish, thus offering further proof that it is not only the young who find themselves in possession of their own private language. 'Ah yee oh go', followed by the answering chant of 'Yigga dah', were the mysteriously indelible opening words of the 'Canoe Song'

Paul Robeson, at the prow of an African canoe, sang so magnificently in the 1935 film, *Sanders of the River*.

Once they had heard the comedian's patter first house Monday, for the rest of the week the members of the pit orchestra would read a newspaper or do a crossword puzzle during his performance. When Sidney Caplan moved from the Holborn Empire to the Town Hall Music Hall, Watford, as Musical Director, he resumed his deplorable habit of sitting down facing the audience during a comedian's act and staring at them with an expression of sour boredom. (Think Walter Matthau.)

When I mentioned this to Tommy Trinder, on one of his many *Looks Familiar* visits, he recalled the occasion when a second-spot comedian remonstrated with Caplan about it. Caplan replied, 'Look, son, to them you may be a star in the making. To me, you're just a chord in G.'

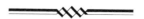

During my days in cinema service, it used to be taken as axiomatic that women didn't laugh at The Three Stooges. Consequently, their short comedies were less 'bookable' than those of, say, Laurel and Hardy.

So it was gratifying to read that at an American auction in November 1993, a signed group photo of Larry, Curly and Moe went for $1,820, while a signed group photo of Presidents Nixon, Ford and Carter fetched $275.

Working on *Countdown* was always a pleasant experience. Everyone connected with the programme was unfailingly friendly and I had the good fortune to hit on an idea for the guest monologues which sustained me over some fifty-odd appearances.

I wanted to base these two-minute Dictionary Corner solo offerings on something to do with words and while I was casting about for an idea I noticed an item in the local paper advertising 'Chest Freezers'. I began idly wondering why anyone would want to freeze their chest, then realised that this was something I constantly found myself doing: assigning literal meanings to phrases other people accepted at their face value. I remembered the alarming picture I conjured up when I first saw a sign on Morden Underground station that announced, 'Passengers Alight Both Ends'. Similarly the question that had come to mind on first encountering a bottle of 'Coconut Shampoo' was, 'What sort of person shampoos a coconut?' (Ditto for 'Lemon Rinse', 'Turtle Wax', 'Microchip Toaster' and 'Executive Shredder'.)

Out of this came the notion of 'Literalism', a medical condition which I defined as 'the congenital inability to interpret words or phrases other than in their literal sense'. Thus, a Literalism victim whose new portable TV bears the notice, 'Built-in Antenna' will find himself fruitlessly scanning his atlas for a country called Antenna; alternatively, he may be thrown into complete confusion by a headline that reads, 'New Bridge Held Up By Red Tape'.

After concocting a few of these on the first batch of programmes, I began receiving an unexpected number of letters from *Countdown* viewers confessing their own encounters with the Literalism syndrome. In fact, so many housewives and students sent me examples of their true-life experiences with it, I no longer needed to invent any. I simply quoted from their case histories.

There was the lady from the home counties, for instance, who admitted the befuddlement she felt on first sighting a road sign reading 'Heavy Plant Crossing', envisaging a massive African violet making its way across the A4. A philosophy graduate recounted his mixed feelings on reading the heading, 'March Planned for August' and an Oxford lady driver was similarly misled by the notice, 'Men on the Verge'.

This strange semantic handicap seemed to manifest itself most frequently in the way Literalism sufferers perceived such everyday commercial notifications as 'Gigantic Wedding Dress Sale' or 'Floral Arrangements to Match Your Interior'. Both brought Literalists up short, while that restaurant in the Covent Garden piazza which permanently adorns its open air tables with the notice, 'Customers May Not Eat Their Own Food' leaves them speculating whether they are expected to lean across and remove dishes from neighbouring tables.

That these short-lived lapses in concentration could also be deeply humiliating was evidenced by two further viewers' letters. A student at Northampton University told me how he had made an utter prat of himself trying to carry out the instructions printed on a packet of soup: 'Empty the contents of envelope and add two pints of water.' In case I had missed the literal point, he asked, 'You ever tried getting two pints of water into that little envelope?'

If you bear that misunderstanding in mind, I need only quote you the first sentence of the second letter, which came from a Literalism-afflicted pensioner in Bournemouth. 'On the fire extinguisher they installed in the hall of my flat last week, it said, "Turn upside down before using."'

It was Dick Vosburgh who drew my attention to one of the earliest examples of Literalism at work. It cropped up in a W. C. Fields movie of the thirties, where a customer enters Fields' grocery shop and asks 'Have you anything in the way of steaks?'

'Nothing in the way at all,' Fields answers. 'Can get right at them.'

There used to be a weekly magazine called *Time and Tide*. A few of its contributors got together and put a sign outside its front door, 'No Waiting'.

Riding the same train of thought: when I was pursuing the 'Literalism' theme on *Countdown*, a lady wrote in to tell me that during the course of some roadworks on the A272, the workmen took out the cats' eyes prior to re-surfacing and put up a warning sign reading 'Cats eyes removed'.

At dead of night, her son and some friends purloined the sign, drove to the nearest town and deposited it outside the surgery of the local vet.

Encounters with the public:

Coming out of stage doors and being asked: 'Are you anybody?'
Being told:

'You're taller than you sound on the radio.'
Letters from the public:

'Please send me a brief biological sketch of your career.'

'Could my friend and I please have a singed photo?'

'Could I please have a signed autograph?'

One of childhood's biggest disappointments is the discovery that the ice cream doesn't go all the way to the bottom of the cornet. As the years pass, this can be true of many other pleasures.

Some people pass their entire lives without being witness to the golden age of anything. I consider myself fortunate in my generation because we not only lived through the golden age of so many forms of popular entertainment, we were present at the birth of many of them, enjoyed their heyday and we were there to mourn their passing.

Among such golden ages I would particularly instance the vanished pleasures of:

MGM musicals

Short story magazines

Super cinemas

Variety theatres

Greyfriars

B movies

West End revues

Swing

Wall's Snofrute

Children's Hour

B movie trailers

Dance bands

The slow foxtrot

News theatres

John O'London's Weekly

Seaside concert parties

Westerns

Broadway stage musicals

Variety acts

Man and woman double acts

Lavish seaside summer shows

Radio Variety

Immaculate band leaders

Popular songs and songwriters

Tap-dancing

Tea dances

Radio stars

Cinema organ interludes

For the benefit of those unfamiliar with the term, a prop, short for property, is any movable object inside a set, with the exception of the clothing worn by the actors. Everything else on display within the fixed scenery – furniture, carpets, table lamps, pictures, books, food – they are all supplied by the props department.

For an early Television play set in Napoleonic times, the set designer called for a writing desk of the period, furnished with some quill pens and a few French letters. A note came back from the props department, stating that if the last item on the list meant correspondence, they could supply it. If not, it was the responsibility of the costume department.

Melvin Frank, who started by writing monologues for Bob Hope, told me that if Hope ever asked the writing team for a one-liner on a particular topic, they had to furnish him with a hundred. Sometimes he didn't like any of them, in which case, he called in freelance writers who would supply dozens more.

On one occasion they spent a whole day without submitting one that met with Hope's approval. Finally, late at night, Hope himself came up with a line. After showing it to the writers, he said, 'That's it. We'll go with this one.'

The line was so obviously no better and no worse than any of the previous possibilities, the writers felt obliged to ask him why it was the one he had decided to use. 'Because I like it,' he said.

As anyone who has ever earned a crust putting words in comedians' mouths can testify, there could have been no better argument for the line's retention. It was, on all counts, a perfectly valid answer.

A member of the Bob Hope Show's writing team told me about a fellow writer who was invited to submit some comedy material for one of Jimmy Carter's Presidential speeches. He turned the offer down, on the grounds that 'I have to see him work first.'

Frank Tarloff and I used to play tennis at Queen's and one Sunday morning we showed a group of the Hope Show writers round the club. They were particularly interested in a game being played on the special courts given over to the ancient game of Real Tennis. After watching in fascination for well over an hour, one of them said, half to himself, 'Hey, how come we don't do this no more?'

They were an indomitable bunch, the Hope Show writers. When one of them was in hospital dying of terminal cancer, his new night nurse turned out to be a lady of Hattie Jacques proportions. After tending him with the utmost care and tenderness, she asked him before leaving the room, 'Is there anything else I can do for you?'

'Yes,' he replied. 'Don't sing.'

As Frank has already indicated in *A Kentish Lad*, the line 'Oh, infamy, infamy! They've all got it infamy' was one we had written for a *Take It From Here* film parody. It was several years later that Talbot Rothwell, who had occupied a cubicle next door to ours in the Kavanagh Associates offices, rang up and asked whether he could use it for a 'Carry On' film. As we had more or less forgotten about it by then, we agreed readily.

Of the two deliveries, I would judge Kenneth Williams' cry the more heart-stricken; Jimmy Edwards' declamation the more thunderous.

Mike Craig, one of the North of England's top radio producers, came up with a highly satisfying place name. He claims to have discovered a resort on England's south coast named 'Hove Actually', on the grounds that whenever he asks certain Southerners whether they live in Brighton, that is invariably what they reply.

Mike took to travelling the high seas, entertaining luxury cruise line passengers with reminiscences of the great Northern comedians (Frank Randle, Norman Evans, Albert Modley, etc.). Aided by an encyclopaedic recall of their routines, he always drew attention to the skill with which they would summon up an entire way of life with a minimum of words. The example I cherish is the small boy who enters the local everything shop carrying a toilet-roll. He asks the proprietor, 'Would you change this for five Woodbines? Company didn't turn up.'

We were in at the birth of *This Is Your Life*. The BBC had just leased the rights and, prior to putting the English version into production, Ronnie Waldman showed us a sample episode from the original American series.

The subject was a concentration camp survivor who had become a cantor in a Mid-West synagogue. It was a harrowing half-hour, culminating in a sequence where they brought on his two older sisters, both of whom he believed had perished in another camp.

The two of them, arms outstretched, tottered towards him and as the cameras zoomed into enormous close-ups of their tear-stained faces, Ronnie turned to us. 'At moments like this,' he said, 'the BBC will, of course, cut away.'

During the time Frank and I spent at BBC TV Centre in the early sixties, the *This Is Your Life* office was only a few doors along the corridor from ours. It became an agreeable executive perk to saunter along there and find out, well before the rest of the world, which person the programme was about to alight on.

One afternoon, I strolled in there and found a couple of researchers studying the salient biographical details of Jessie Matthews, at that time the reigning queen of the airwaves as the keeper of *Mrs Dale's Diary*. ('I'm worried about Jim.')

'She goes back to your time,' one of the researchers remarked. 'Can you remember anything about her we could use?'

In fact, there was something that came to mind. But whether it was something they could use …? I was recalling a Sunday night at the Trocadero, Elephant & Castle, in the early forties. In those days, cinemas used to show 'For This Sunday Only' performances of a vintage movie and on this occasion we were reviving a notable British musical of 1934, *Evergreen*. It starred a radiantly youthful Jessie, long of leg and toothsome in every sense, singing and dancing her way through such Rodgers and Hart classics as 'Dancing on the Ceiling'. (Irrevocably imprinted as 'He dawnces overhead on the ceiling by my bed.')

The last performance of the night was underway and I was in the office 'cashing up', when one of the commissionaires, a ramrod straight former Irish guardsman, entered and said, 'Thought you should be told, sir. There's a patron committing an indecency in the upper circle gents. The police have been sent for.'

I hurried up there with him and, sure enough, there he was: a bespectacled man, bang in the centre of the tiled floor, energetically pulling at himself. He did not stop when we entered but simply gasped, 'Sorry, guv. I can't help it. It's her.' And, inclining his head in the direction of the auditorium, 'She's done it again.'

'Done what?' I said.

'I was seventeen first time I saw that dancing in the long black stockings. It drove me wild for days. And tonight, there she was again.'

Two policemen appeared and I left him with them. Now, in the *This Is Your Life* office, twenty-odd years later, I wondered if I should mention the incident to the researchers. I decided against it but not without regret. After all, it was unlikely their searches would uncover a tribute more spontaneous or more fervently expressed.

A pun that has lingered with me was the heading of an article by David McGillivray. He was giving an account of his days as a tyro screenwriter, specifically the occasion when he was contracted to write a screenplay for a producer who lived in deepest Surrey. Only after travelling down there to discuss the project did he realise something he should have cottoned on to much sooner: he had signed up to deliver a porn film. David headed the article, 'Guileless In Esher'.

His piece came out around the same time as a report that a film company was about to make a movie entitled *The Rolling Stones Story*. According to Wardour Street sources, they had contacted all the major casting agencies to advise, 'Let him who is without sin cast the first Stone.'

I was always intrigued by Variety's 'physical' acts – the acrobats, contortionists, jugglers and adagio dancers. Some of them had been performing the same ten- to fifteen- minute routine for more than twenty years and, as a result, had developed a kind of physical self-awareness it was hard to find a parallel for elsewhere.

Warren, of Warren, Latona and Sparks, told me, 'During every second of our act, I'm in touch with every single part of my body. At any given moment, I can tell you exactly what my left eyebrow is doing and exactly what it will be doing next.'

In the black-and-white days of early Television, there were many verified reports of viewers changing into dinner jackets to watch the Sunday night play.

For its part, Television also did its best to make drama viewing as near the theatrical experience as possible. The plays would be presented in three-act form, with the acts separated by a formal intermission. During these, the BBC would show one of their specially shot 'Interlude' films, the most frequently chosen being 'The Potter's Wheel'. Other subjects of a similarly unthreatening nature included a kitten playing with a ball, angel fish swimming in a tank, a singularly placid waterfall and a slowly turning windmill, each providing a kind of non-commercial break.

As the final touch of theatre a warning bell would ring one minute before the next act began.

I have been putting off retirement for three or four years for fear of what I might find when I clear my desk Actually, I should refer to it as our desk, for it is the one Frank and I inherited from our days at Ted Kavanagh Associates and which we continued to work either side of all those years.

It was shabby even then, so one day, during the writing of *Seven Faces of Jim*, we decided to treat ourselves to a new one: something smarter, we agreed, and more in keeping with modern design. However, in certain important respects, its specifications had to match those of the present incumbents: namely, a wide top with knee-holes either side each flanked by two sets of drawers.

In those days, New Oxford Street was the place to go for this kind of purchase, being inhabited almost completely by office furniture showrooms. We walked the length of it without finding one of them able to supply what we were looking for.

Finally we fetched up at a small place where an elderly salesman listened politely to our requirements, then slowly shook his head. 'What you're describing,' he said, 'is what they call a Partners' Desk. Hardly anyone makes them any more because there're so few partners around these days.' He moved closer and his tone became confidential. 'There just isn't the trust about.'

We went back to the office and resumed work at the same desk I am writing on now. 'There just isn't the trust about' joined our private stock of cherished phrases.

While Frank went off to the Garrick or the Savile for lunch, I would often wander into Isow's and sit at the agents' table with the likes of Peter Charlesworth, Cyril Berlin and, occasionally, a very young Michael Grade. Their conversation was salted with tales of Variety's heyday and decline, all very much to my taste. One I particularly savoured was Keith Devon's hark back to a time when he was booking the Summer Season acts for a minor seaside resort on the East Coast.

As was generally the case, his proposals had to win the approval of the town's Entertainment Committee, a body drawn from the most important local tradesmen. 'The folk who live in this part of the world are my people. I'm one of them,' their chairman told him on one occasion. 'I know exactly who would go down well here. The kind of names they'd flock to see would be either Frank Sinatra or Eddie Calvert.'

'I give you my word,' Keith said. 'You will have one of them.'

Isow's, with its comfortable red leather chairs, most of them adorned with the gilt autograph of some top-of-the-bill star, was London's nearest equivalent to New York's Lindy's. Its owner, the corpulent Jack Isow, was generally unobtrusive, confining himself to grunted welcomes and muttered directions, except for an occasional display of almost bravura rudeness. Lew Grade and Val Parnell, responsible for ATV's *Sunday Night at the London Palladium* often lunched there the following day and on one such Monday I saw Lew beckon Jack over to tell him, 'This soup is almost cold.'

'And your show last night wasn't so fucking hot,' replied mine host.

Another pleasant Isow's moment happened one Saturday lunch-time, while I was at a table for one with my novel and a chicken in the pot. A waiter came over with a menu card and said, 'The lady over there wonders if you would sign this for her?'

Endeavouring to give the impression that this was the sort of thing that happened all the time, I took out my pen and signed. Then, furtively, I watched the waiter take the card across the room to an elegant blonde woman sitting by the window. I saw her take the card and inspect the signature. She then rose from the table but, before leaving, she looked again at the card. Then, quite deliberately, she tore it into four pieces, dropping them on the table.

As soon as she was gone, I called the waiter back and asked, 'What was all that about?'

'She thought you were Arthur Miller,' he replied.

The odd thing was, I felt even more flattered.

One of the most accomplished people I ever worked with was Sid Colin, a gentle person of wide and diverse talents. Prior to becoming the scriptwriter for many top radio and TV shows, he had been the theatrical cartoonist for *The Tatler*, played guitar in the Ambrose Orchestra and the Ambrose Octet, for whom he had been the singer on many of their hit records, composed such wartime favourites as 'If I Only Had Wings', toured Europe with The Squadronnaires and was an acknowledged expert on Picasso.

Frank and I spent a lot of time with him, though I'm told that the sight of the three of us walking along Conduit Street with him in the middle tended to attract attention, owing to what Sid called his 'extreme lack of tall'.

He was often summoned to 'gag up' British film comedies of that era, a sideline he greatly enjoyed. For one Norman Wisdom movie, he told us, he had suggested a little scene that would involve Norman taking over as an orchestral conductor. When they invited him to come down to Pinewood and watch the scene being filmed, he wandered into the sound stage to find that for this one short gag, they had built a sizeable section of what looked like a huge concert hall, on the rostrum of which no less than thirty-two musicians in full evening dress were sitting tuning up.

Delighted, Sid advanced towards them and, spreading his arms wide, declaimed, 'You are all figments of my imagination.'

Knowing me to be someone who has had an interest in parodies ever since I was involved in churning them out for cinema organ interludes, Ronnie Cass drew my attention to one of the neatest he had come across. It was written by Alan Sherman and based on the Gershwins' 'Our Love Is Here to Stay'. Its first lines are:

It's very clear
Your mother's here to stay

And from there on, you stick with the original wording:

Not for a year
But ever and a day

And so on, without altering a syllable all the way through to the penultimate line. Unfortunately, the Gershwin estate has banned its use in public.

In the days of live TV, there were no retakes, no out-takes, no second chances. If an actor in a Television drama made a mistake, if he fumbled his words or forgot them, if he walked into the scenery, or lit his nose with a cigarette lighter, it was witnessed by the entire viewing population.

But it was witnessed sympathetically. That was the difference. Performer and audience were still united in a common bond of wonder at the modern miracle by which any sort of picture was transported to their blank glass rectangle.

The most frequently told tale of those days was of the veteran TV actor who would advise his colleagues, 'If you forget your lines, don't panic, just keep moving your mouth, the people at home'll think it's the sound gone wrong again.'

I find that more and more of my conversations nowadays begin with the words, 'Many years ago.' And they tend to end, 'Which was a lot of money in those days.'

'For a Variety comedian,' Ted Ray told me over a pre-*Looks Familiar* drink, 'the vital turning point in your career comes when audiences greet you in a state of what you might call "laughter readiness". Prior to that, all your energies have had to go into overcoming their laughter resistance.

'It can take years,' he said. 'But once they decide to accept you as funny, for the rest of your life they'll start smiling the moment they see your name in the programme. Some agents call it "The Acceptance Factor". Personally,' he added, 'I've had it from birth.'

Of all the tasks Frank and I set ourselves during our time together, none caused us more brow-furrowing, knuckle-gnawing and sleep deprivation than the stories we had to invent for the last round of *My Word!*. As mentioned previously, these were fictional and heavily punned accounts of the circumstances in which familiar quotations or sayings were first uttered.

In the early years of the programme, they came to mind fairly trippingly, but as series succeeded series, listeners began recognising the tricks we employed and it became increasingly difficult to prevent them from getting to the 'twist' before we did. Consequently, in addition to the ongoing search for another well-known line susceptible to cunning punning, we now had to find ways of shaping its storyline so as to disguise the direction in which we were heading.

Over the last ten years or so of *My Word!* this problem began to weigh upon us more and more heavily, occupying a quite disproportionate place in our lives. Some weeks it would seem there was not a quotable line we had not already utilised or discarded and, as the day of each recording came nearer, we would be ringing each other up in a state of despair that approached panic.

'Got anything yet?'

'Not a glimmer.' ('No tag Lima? Story about flying to Peru with incorrect baggage labels?' the other's over-exercised brain would begin configuring.)

Somehow we always managed to come up with something in time but there were days when it was a close-run thing. I recall one occasion when inspiration did not come my way until four in the afternoon and the recording session began at half past six.

During those years of travail, only once did either of us hit on a line early in the week. For Frank, fortune smiled one night while he was driving home after the broadcast. Suddenly, the idea for the following week's story leaped into his mind, fully formed and quite unprompted. For an entire six days he enjoyed total freedom from the tyranny of quotation chasing and vowel mangling. (The story was for 'Goodbye, Mr Chips' which is related on page 158.)

My own period of remission came about while I was listening to a radio quiz. A contestant was asked for the origin of the phrase 'I think, therefore I am.' There and then, just as suddenly as happened with Frank, I 'saw' that line in an entirely new formulation. More or less word for word this is how the story shot up from the depths and presented itself:

I think, therefore I am

Although that was the line that launched René Descartes on his meteoric rise to stardom, what he actually wrote was something slightly different. So I can't tell you the pleasure it now gives me to put the record straight, if only for his sake.

I say that because life was not all roses for this seventeenth-century philosopher. In the first place, he'd been saddled with an unfortunate Christian name, and even though the French pronounce it '*Re-nay*', it was still something of a liability for a growing lad in those rough times. Secondly, when he came to manhood he married this real granite-block of a wife. Although Mme Descartes brought some property to the marriage, the truth is she was several years his senior, had the disposition of an untipped taxi-driver and was an inveterate picture-straightener. Every time Descartes sat down to work on a crystalline aphorism, in she'd come, still in her rollers, with 'I'm sorry, but I need this room for a social gathering' or 'If you don't mind, kindly shift your philosophy kit to the shed.'

275

It is hard to think of a way in which she could have been other than a millstone to any aspiring philosopher. Even in their more intimate moments, when he managed to steel himself for an attempt at lovemaking, her invariable response was the phrase which Gershwin was later to put to such melodious use, 'Descartes, take that away from me.'

You may wonder then, how was it, in such an unpromising work-environment, that René still managed to make No.1 among philosophy's all-time chart-toppers? Well, as I've indicated, it's all down to the widespread misunderstanding about his line 'I think, therefore I am.' And to trace the exact origin of that I must take you back to the New Year's Eve party which Madame Descartes threw to celebrate the advent of 1636.

As it was to be an informal affair, she'd decided to serve their guests a buffet meal, 'buffet' being a French word meaning 'we've got more people than chairs'.

As she also intended it to be a late do, with no one even arriving till around 11 p.m., she ran up an enormous bunch of that Gallic imitation of bacon-and-egg flan they call quiche. Not the large, family-sized ones, but those small individual versions so affectionately celebrated by Yvette Guilbert with 'Just a leetle love, a leetle quiche.'

However – and you'll be glad to know we're now getting somewhere near the point of all of this – Madame made it clear to René that although the quiches were all to be put out on the sideboard beforehand, 'the one thing I don't want to see is people helping themselves in advance and treading their crumbs into the Aubusson. So I'm relying on you to see that nobody starts digging into them until at least one hour after we've seen the New Year in. Then they can take plates and eat properly.'

Ironic, isn't it? The founder of the Cartesian School of Philosophy relegated to the position of a Securicor guard for bacon-and-egg flans. As he himself said to Father Dinet – I haven't mentioned him before but he was the Jesuit priest who was just about the only real mate René had at that time – 'I can't think this is in any way advancing my career. Being sat down here at the sideboard till one o'clock in the morning. That's no way to get any philosophising done tomorrow; I'll be like a limp rag.'

To which the good Father made an extremely practical rejoinder: 'Well, why don't you use this as working-time? Take a writing-instrument and, while you're sitting here, set your mind for lofty thoughts. Then, if any crop up, jot them down on a paper serviette.'

'Nice thinking,' said Descartes. 'Give us a borrow of your quill then.'

It worked extremely well. For the next hour or so the two friends sat quietly by the sideboard and Descartes was able to get off quite a few zingers relating to corporeal rationality. It was while he was fashioning an eternal verity regarding adventitious volition that he glanced up and, to his horror, saw what had happened. Father Dinet had helped himself to a quiche and was absently munching on it.

Just as Descartes was about to exclaim, 'Watch it, mate! They're not supposed to be eaten yet', he became aware of something else. There, well within earshot, stood his wife! There was only one thing to do.

Stealthily, Descartes took another serviette, scribbled his warning on it, then – equally furtively – pushed the serviette under the priest's nose.

Thus it was the whole 300-year-old misunderstanding originated. That message, the one that Father Dinet was later to publish to the world as 'I think, therefore I am' was, in fact, only a reference to the time-ban on the bacon and egg flans.

All it actually said was:

'I think they're for 1 a.m.'

After one of the *Looks Familiar* programmes, a woman who had been sitting in the front row of the studio audience approached me with an autograph book, 'Would you, please?' she asked. 'For my little boy?'

As I was writing, she added, 'Would you make it "To Peter". He's your biggest fan. Never misses you on *Call My Bluff.*'

I said, 'That's Frank Muir.'

'Oh.' She took the book and inspected it. 'Well, I don't suppose it matters,' she said. 'He can't read yet, anyway.'

GLOSSARY
AND INDEX

Adair, Hazel: writer, producer and actress. Wrote ITV's first ever serial *Sixpenny Corner* (1955) and BBC Television's soap *Compact* (1964) plus umpteen other Television programmes and screen-plays. Joint chairman with DN of The Writers' Guild of Great Britain and at the Guild's first Awards Dinner opened the dancing with Lew Grade. xx, 177

Adler, Larry: American star musician; acknowledged as world's leading virtuoso of the harmonica, which he always called a mouth organ. Noted raconteur, wit and friend of the Gershwins, he was a frequent guest on *Looks Familiar*. 17–18

The Adventures of Robin Hood: American movie (1938) starring Olivia de Havilland and Errol Flynn, directed by Michael Curtiz. 194–5

Alexander's Ragtime Band: Twentieth Century Fox movie (1938), with Alice Faye, Tyrone Power and Don Ameche sharing out twenty-eight Irving Berlin songs. 189

All Quiet on the Western Front: best-selling novel (1929) by Erich Maria Remarque about the experiences of ordinary soldiers in World War One. 111

All The Best: DN's farewell programme (2006); anthology of favourite clips from the various ITV shows he presented over the preceding years. Produced by Simon Withington and directed by Bill Morton. xxii

Ameche, Don: (Pronounced A'mee-chee) toothily-handsome American movie actor usually cast as dapper, moustached leading man in musicals such as *One in a Million* (1936) and *Alexander's Ragtime Band* (1938).
116–17

Amis, John: broadcaster, essayist, classical music critic and accomplished *siffler*. Cousin to Kingsley; Frank Muir's partner on *My Music!* (1967–94).
xx, 165–7

Amis, Kingsley: eminent novelist, City of London schoolmate and *Looks Familiar* panellist. His many books include *Lucky Jim* (1954) and *The Riverside Villas Murder* (1973).
183, 202, 213

And So To Bentley: live TV comedy series (1954), written by Frank Muir and DN, featuring Dick Bentley, Peter Sellers and Bill Fraser.
xix, 134–5

Andrews, Eamonn: Irish broadcaster who became BBC sports reporter, then chairman of the highly successful TV panel game *What's My Line?* (1951-63).
125–6

Andrews Sisters, The (Patty, LaVerne and Maxene): American recording and movie trio whose close-harmony singing made them favourites with the troops during World War Two. They sold 90 million records, including such hits as *Bei Mir Bist du Schön*, *I'll Be with You in Apple Blossom Time* and *Rum and Coca-Cola*.
119

Andy Hardy Movies: series of fifteen low-budget movies made by MGM between 1937 and 1947 about the almost intolerably loveable Hardy family. Set in a small town in America's Midwest, it starred

Lewis Stone as the father and Mickey Rooney as the volatile teenage son whose succession of girlfriends included Judy Garland and Ann Rutherford (the object of Eric Morecambe's most fervent adolescent reveries).
10

Angers, Avril: comedy actress and stand-up comedian. Started career as a Tiller Girl and appeared in a multitude of radio and Television shows between the forties and seventies, as well as many movies and stage shows.
xix

Animal, Vegetable, Mineral?: TV quiz programme (1952–9). Three experts had to identify objects from British museums. Regular panellists included Julian Huxley and Sir Mortimer Wheeler.
133

Are You Being Served?: bawdyish TV sitcom (1972–85), written by Jeremy Lloyd and David Croft, it achieved consistently high ratings, with a cast that included Mollie Sugden (as Mrs Slocombe), John Inman (as Mr Humphries) and Frank Thornton (as Captain Peacock).
8

Ascent of Man, The: landmark thirteen-part TV documentary series (1973). Presented by Dr Jacob Bronowski, it offered a comprehensive and remarkably comprehensible picture of the rise of man as a species.
129

Asimov, Isaac: prolific Russian-born American author who wrote or edited over 500 books. Particularly noted for his fifties and sixties science fiction works including his *Foundation* series and the Galactic Empire series.
84

Askey, Arthur: diminutive and enormously popular comedian. He came to fame with radio's *Band Wagon (1938)* and went on to star in many movies and stage musicals. His best-known catchphrases were 'Before your very eyes!' and 'I thank you!' (pronounced 'Ay-thang-yoh!').
187, 243

Astaire, Fred: Hollywood star of the first magnitude, for my money the screen's most appealing entertainer. His dancing, singing and diffident good humour graced such movies as, to list only my favourites, *Top Hat* (1935), *Roberta (1935)*, *Follow The Fleet* (1936), *Swing Time* (1936), *Shall We Dance* (1937), *You Were Never Lovelier* (1942) and *The Band Wagon* (1953).
109

At Last the 1948 Show: TV comedy sketch series (1967), generally quoted as the forerunner to *Monty Python*. It starred Graham Chapman, Marty Feldman, Tim Brooke-Taylor, John Cleese, and 'the lovely Aimi MacDonald', with DN involved as 'Script Referee'.
xx

Attenborough, Richard: actor, director and producer. After starring in such milestones of cinema as *In Which We Serve* (1942), *Brighton Rock* (1947) and *The League of Gentlemen* 1960), went on to play the lead in *The Bliss of Mrs Blossom* (1968).
xx

B

Bags of Panic: three RAF revues written by DN, with music by Ron Rich. Performed in various locations across France, Belgium, Holland and Germany, they featured, among many others, Bill Fraser and Eric Sykes.
55–6

Baker, Phil: American thirties and forties accordion-playing vaudeville comedian. Went on to appear in several Hollywood movies.
230

Ballantyne, R. M.: Scottish children's author. Works include *The Coral Island* (1857) and *The Settler and the Savage* (1877).
209

Barbara with Braden: BBC Television series (1953) written by Frank Muir and DN and starring Barbara Kelly and Bernard Braden.
xix

Barker, Ronnie: comedian, actor and writer. First appearance in a TV series was with Jimmy Edwards in *The Seven Faces of Jim* (1961). He came to prominence in sketches with John Cleese and Ronnie Corbett in *The Frost Report* (1966–7); then, after starring in several more TV series, he achieved the full flowering of his many talents with *The Two Ronnies* (1971–87).
xx, 144, 149

Barnett, Lady Isobel: regular panellist on BBC Television's *What's My Line* (1951–63). Originally a practising doctor.
126

Bassey, Shirley: International singing star; first West End appearance taking over from Vera Lynn in *London Laughs* (1952).
xix

Bath-night with Braden: one of a series of BBC radio programmes starring Bernard Braden, written by Frank Muir and DN.
xix

Baum, Vicki: Austrian novelist who emigrated to America. Wrote novel *Grand Hotel*, later adapted as an all-star MGM movie (1932).
210–11

Bedtime with Braden: evolved directly from BBC radio programme *Breakfast with Braden* (1950), starring Bernard Braden. First of the Braden radio shows to feature his wife, Barbara Kelly.
xviii

Ben Abdrahman Wazzan troupe: forties Variety acrobatic act.
71

Benchley, Robert: American humorist, newspaper columnist and movie actor. Wrote for *The New Yorker* and *Vanity Fair*, member of the Algonquin Round Table in the twenties.
49, 50

Benny, Jack: American comedian and movie actor. Became popular with British troops with his American radio series broadcast via the Forces Network and later his TV series, seen on the BBC. Made several successful London Palladium and Royal Variety appearances. Master of the long pause and impassive stare.
117–18

Bentine, Michael: comedian, writer and early Goon. A brimming well of comic invention, he was responsible for TV's *The Bumblies* (1954) and *It's a Square World* (1960).
xviii, 185

Bentley, Dick: Australian-born comedian; starred with Jimmy Edwards and Joy Nichols, who was subsequently replaced by June Whitfield and Alma Cogan, in the BBC radio series *Take It From Here* (1948–60). Earlier, *Bentley In London* (1946) was a series of fifteen-minute radio interviews recorded in London for transmission in Australia, with scripts by DN. *Gently Bentley* (1951) was a radio series recorded in Australia, with scripts by Frank Muir and DN, who later wrote the TV series *And So To Bentley* (1954), in which Bentley was supported by Peter Sellers and Bill Fraser.
xvii, xviii, xix, 75, 81, 115, 134, 221–2, 235

Berlin, Cyril: agent for among others Ted Rogers, Des O'Connor and Lonnie Donegan.
269

Berman, Shelley: American comedian and writer who made many appearances on *The Ed Sullivan Show* (1958-69) but came to fame in the UK via his best-selling comedy LPs.
147

Bernstein, David: one of the UK's most creative advertising practitioners, with whom many agreeable hours were spent toying with such notions as The College For The Advancement Of Minor Skills and A Festival Of Schmalz.
21

Best House in London, The: movie (1969) starring David Hemmings and George Sanders; director Philip Saville, screenplay DN.
xxi, 240–1

Between Times with Braden: TV series evolved from BBC radio programmes *Breakfast with Braden* and *Bedtime with Braden*, all starring Bernard Braden.
xviii, xix

Big Noise, The: BBC Television sitcom (starring Bob Monkhouse as a neurotic, teenager-hating DJ). Written by Frank Muir and DN.
xx, 149

Black, George and Alfred: theatrical impresarios, whose father, also George, was one of London's most powerful producers. They operated a flourishing theatrical business, put on some of Blackpool's most lavish *Summer Shows* and their involvement with Tyne Tees (1957) brought them into the world of Television.
231, 139

Bliss of Mrs Blossom, The: movie (1968) starring Shirley MacLaine and Richard Attenborough; director Joe McGrath, screenplay DN and Alec Coppel.

xx

Bluett, Kitty: played Ted Ray's wife in radio sitcom *Ray's a Laugh* (1949–61).

75

Bobrick, Sam: American author, composer and songwriter. Co-author with Ron Clark of the Broadway play *Norman, Is That You?* (premiered 1976). Other works include Elvis Presley's 'The Girl of my Best Friend' and episodes of the TV series *Bewitched* and *The Flintstones.*

226

Bonn, Issy: comedian, singer and, later, theatrical agent. His picture appears on the sleeve of The Beatles' *Sergeant Pepper's Lonely Hearts Club Band* album.

62

Bottoms Up!: movie version (1960) of *Whack-o!* TV comedy series. Screenplay by Michael Pertwee, additional dialogue by Frank Muir and DN; starred Jimmy Edwards as blustering, bullying, totally unscrupulous headmaster of Chiselbury School, For The Sons Of Gentlefolk.

xx

Boys Will Be Boys: comedy movie (1935) directed by William Beaudine. Screenplay by Val Guest; starring Will Hay.

186

Bracken, Eddie: American movie actor and comedian. Appeared in a host of theatrical and TV productions between 1940 and 2002.

188

Braden, Bernard: Canadian-born TV presenter, actor and comedian. Married Barbara Kelly (1942). BBC radio series include *Starlight Hour* (1948), *Breakfast with Braden* (1950), *Bedtime with Braden* (1950). BBC Television series included BAFTA Award winning *On The Braden Beat*, the first effective consumer affairs programme, (1962–7).
xviii, xix, 101–2, 106

Brazil, Angela: author of forty-seven novels, all schoolgirl stories; titles include *The Madcap of the School* and *Jill's Jolliest School.*
209

Breakfast with Braden: Saturday morning BBC radio comedy series (1950) hosted by Bernard Braden, written by Frank Muir and DN. Featured Benny Lee, Pearl Carr, Nat Temple and his orchestra.
xviii, 101

Briers, Richard: gifted comedy actor. TV career launched by appearance in three of seven episodes of BBC's *The Seven Faces of Jim* (1961), which led to a starring role in *Brothers In Law* (1962). This was followed by a host of major TV roles, including *The Good Life* (1975), *Ever Decreasing Circles* (1984) and the drama series *Monarch of the Glen* (2000).
xx

Bromfield, Louis: popular American novelist, author of *The Rains Came, Wild Is The River* and *Mrs Parkington.*
210–11

Bronowski, Jacob ('Bruno') Dr: mathematician, scientist and Television presenter, best remembered for *The Ascent of Man* (1973). Brother-in-law of Sid Colin.
129

Brooks, Mel: American writer, comedian, director, composer and lyricist. One of the few to win Oscar, Grammy (three times), Emmy (four times) and Tony (three times) Awards.
146

Brothers in Law: BBC Television comedy series (1962) starring Richard Briers; adapted by Frank Muir and DN from the book of the same name by Henry Cecil.
xx, 150

Brough, Peter: ventriloquist who, against all logic, starred with his dummy, Archie Andrews, in the long-running radio success *Educating Archie* during the forties and fifties.
80

Brown, Teddy: American Variety star of unusually wide girth who topped British bills in the thirties and forties, playing the xylophone with surprising grace and skill. A Holborn Empire favourite.
32

Bruce, Lenny: controversial American comedian and satirist. He achieved iconic status in this country with his LPs, recordings and a stint at The Establishment.
147

Buchanan, Jack: one of *Looks Familiar's* most potent nostalgics. Handsome, debonair, he was the essence of 'matinee idol' starring in many musical shows and movies where his lazy singing voice and graceful soft-shoe routines dented the psyche of an entire female generation.
124, 188

Buona Sera, Mrs Campbell: United Artists movie (1968) starring Gina Lollobrigida, Shelley Winters, Phil Silvers, Peter Lawford, Telly Savalas and Lee Grant; directed by Melvin Frank, written by Melvin

Frank, DN and Sheldon Keller. Nominated for three Golden Globes including Best English Language Foreign Film.
xxi, 144–5, 147, 193

Butlin, Billy: Holiday camp pioneer; opened this country's first camp in Skegness (1936), thence to Clacton, Filey, Barry etc.
78

C

Cahn, Sammy: one of America's most illustrious lyric writers. Won Oscars for lyrics of 'Three Coins in the Fountain' (1954), 'All the Way' (1957), 'High Hopes' (1959) and 'Call Me Irresponsible' (1963). Guested on *Looks Familiar*.
88, 192

Call My Bluff: BBC Television panel game based on word definitions. Its glory days were between 1965 and 1988 when, with Robert Robinson presiding, Frank Muir captained one team and the other was headed by, at various times Robert Morley, Patrick Campbell and Arthur Marshall.
130, 278

Calloway, Cab: energetic scat singing American band leader, who led the most commercially successful African-American orchestra of the thirties.
25

Calvert, Eddie: trumpet-playing star, first encountered as a member of the BBC orchestra accompanying *Take It From Here's* early programmes. Toured Variety as 'The Man with the Golden Trumpet' when his recordings of 'Oh Mein Papa' (1953) and 'Cherry Pink and Apple Blossom White' (1955) became No. 1 hits.
270

Campbell, Patrick: third Baron Glenavy. Journalist and TV personality with severe speech impediment which he deployed to great effect. 130

Caplan, Sidney: Musical Director, Holborn Empire, before it was bombed (1941) and then at the Town Hall Music Hall, Watford. xvii, 32, 256

Cantor, Eddie: sprightly American vaudeville entertainer who achieved movie success in the thirties with his rolling-eyed renditions of such perennials as 'Makin Whoopee', 'If You Knew Susie' and 'My Baby Just Cares For Me'. 10

Capricorn One: American sci-fi movie (1978), starring Elliott Gould. Its premise was based on a reporter discovering that Man's first space flight to the Moon was a carefully engineered hoax. 243

Carr, Pearl: lead singer in The Keynotes who went on to play comedy roles in most of the Braden programmes. After she married Teddy Johnson (1955), they became a successful double act and performed for England in the Eurovision Song Contest. xviii, 106

Carter, Jimmy: thirty-ninth President of the United States of America (1977–81). Awarded the Nobel Peace Prize (2002). 257, 263

Cartier, Rudolf: Austrian-born BBC TV drama producer and director, whose notable contributions included *The Quatermass Experiment* (1953), together with its various sequels and several distinguished *Play of the Month* productions. 252

Caryll & Mundy: Variety double act. The duo of Billy Caryll and Hilda Mundy were in George Black's *Crazy Week* that opened at the London Palladium in November 1931 and was the precursor of the Crazy Gang shows.
32

Cass, Ronnie: Welsh composer and writer. With his partner, Peter Myers, he devised and wrote most of the successful West End intimate revues of the fifties and sixties. Went on to compose much of the music for the Cliff Richard films *The Young Ones* (1962), *Summer Holiday* (1963) and *Wonderful Life* (1964). In addition to writing several TV plays, he worked with Tom Jones on more than seventy TV programmes and with another Welshman, Harry Secombe, on the religious series *Highway*.
272

Castle, Roy: Variety-nurtured entertainer renowned for his versatility as a comedian, singer, tap-dancer, player of many musical instruments, actor and, latterly, presenter of *Record Breakers* (1972–93).
xxii

Cecil, Judge Henry: English County Court judge (1949–67) and author. His novel *Brothers in Law* (1955) was made into a movie (1957) and he later collaborated with Frank Muir and DN to turn it into a TV series. They also worked together on another legal series, *Mr Justice Duncannon* (1963).
xx, 150, 152–3

Chamberlain, Neville: British Prime Minister (1937–40). Noted for umbrella-carrying and signing the Munich Agreement (1938) with Adolf Hitler and his 'Peace in our time' speech on his return to the UK.
31

Charles, Hugh: English lyricist. Wrote 'There'll Always Be an England' (1940) and Bud Flanagan's recording success 'Strollin''. Aide to Jack Hylton.
218

Charlesworth, Peter: English theatrical agent representing the likes of Clive Dunn, Frankie Vaughan, Joan Collins and Lionel Blair.
269

Cavalcade of Variety Acts: book written by Roy Hudd, with full title *Roy Hudd's Cavalcade of Variety Acts: A Who Was Who of Light Entertainment 1945–60* (1998).
32

Chesterton, G. K.: author, poet, prolific journalist, noted in his day for his employment of paradox. Major works included *The Man Who Was Thursday* (1908) and a series of detective stories about Father Brown, a Roman Catholic priest.
214

Chocolate Soldier, The: operetta (1908) by Oscar Straus based on George Bernard Shaw's *Arms and the Man* (1894).
26

Christmas Night with the Stars: annual BBC radio gala, recorded live till the year Jimmy Edwards hosted it. Thereafter recorded.
96–8

Clark, David: producer, director and writer at Thames Television; produced most of the *Looks Familiar* programmes.
184, 191, 192

Clark, Ron: American writer; with Sam Bobrick, wrote the Broadway play *Norman, Is That You?* (1976). Other works include the

screenplay of *The Revenge of the Pink Panther* and individual episodes of many American TV series.
226

Clooney, Rosemary: American popular singer; starred in *White Christmas* (1954). Hits in the UK included 'This Ole House' (1954) and 'Mambo Italiano' (1954).
192

Colin, Sid: scriptwriter, musician, composer, cartoonist and author. Guitarist and singer with the Ambrose Orchestra, Ambrose Octet and the Squadronnaires. He was a cartoonist for *The Tatler* before turning to scriptwriting. Radio scripts included *Starlight Hour* (1948), with Frank Muir and DN, *Ignorance Is Bliss* (1946) and episodes of *Educating Archie* and *Ray's A Laugh*. Among the songs he composed were 'If I Only Had Wings' (1940) and 'Friends And Neighbours' (1954). He provided scripts for TV's *The Army Game* (1957) and *Up Pompeii* (1970), the screenplay for the movie *Carry on Spying* (1964) and wrote a meticulous biography of Al Bowlly.
xviii, 79, 84, 104, 129, 233, 271

Collins, Jackie: 400 million-plus selling novelist, she began her career as an actress; sister to the more famous Joan.
xix

Coming to You Live: book bringing together behind-the-scenes memories of the early post-war days of British television, collected and presented by DN, Sybil Harper and Norma Gilbert (1985).
xxii

Complete and Utter My Word! Collection, The: book (1983), written by Frank Muir and DN.
xxii

Compton, Denis: England (1937–57) and Middlesex cricketer. Scored 5,807 runs and took 25 wickets in 78 test matches, as well as playing football for Arsenal FC (1936–50) scoring 15 goals in 54 first team appearances.
229

Confessions of a Door to Door Salesman: movie (1973) written by DN cowering behind the pseudonym Nicholas Roy.
xxi

Connor, Kenneth: comedian and actor. Starred in *Carry on Sergeant* (1958) and subsequently a further sixteen *Carry On* movies, as well as numerous comedy radio and TV shows.
xix

Cook, Joe: American vaudeville comedian, entertainer and actor. Appeared in several twenties and thirties Broadway shows and movies.
70

Coppel, Alec: dramatist (*I Killed The Count)* and screenwriter; co-wrote screenplays of *The Bliss of Mrs Blossom* (1968) and *The Statue* (1971) with DN.
xx, xxi

Coren, Alan: top-flight humorist, satirist, broadcaster and columnist. Edited *Punch* (1978–87). Made regular appearances on the BBC panel shows *Call My Bluff* and *The News Quiz.* He wrote about twenty books including *The Collected Broadcasts of Idi Amin.*
111, 225

Coral Island, The: novel (1858) by Scottish children's author, R. M. Ballantyne.
209

Cummings, Robert: American actor and light comedian star of successful US Television series *The Robert Cummings Show*. Bob Monkhouse liked to think of him as a role model.
201

D

Dancing in the Moonlight: Ronnie Barker's autobiography (1993).
149

Daniels, Paul: Top-of-the-bill stage and TV magician whose performances place a strong emphasis on comedy odes.
244

Davidson, Jim: Australian former band-leader; did a stretch as Head of BBC Radio Light Entertainment.
104–5

Dawson, Les: fondly remembered north country comedian. Affecting a lugubrious countenance, dodgy piano solos and the occasional outburst of high-flown rhetoric, he starred in his own radio and TV series throughout the seventies and eighties.
200

Day, Frances: American-born star of thirties and forties British musicals and farces. Vivaciously blonde, she enjoyed a wide following among that sector of the audience demographics then known as 'the tired businessman'.
xix

Dee, Sandra: American film actress and wife of singer Bobby Darin (1960–7). Made movie debut aged fifteen in *Until They Sail* (1957), winning Golden Globe as Most Promising Newcomer (1958).
233

Dehn, Paul: screenwriter. Formed lasting partnership with James Bernard, with whom he co-wrote the Boulting Brothers' movie *Seven Days to Noon* (1950), which won them the Oscar for Best Screenplay. Other credits include *Goldfinger* (1964), four *Planet of the Apes* films (1970, 1971, 1972 and 1973) and *Murder on the Orient Express* (1974).
xviii

Delmer, Sefton: British journalist. Born in Germany, he joined the *Daily Express* becoming head of its Berlin bureau in the early thirties and then the Paris bureau (1933). After covering the Spanish Civil War and the Nazi invasion of Poland, he was recruited into the British Political Warfare Executive (1940).
3

Denis Norden's Laughter File: series of ITV programmes (1991–2005), made up of 'the funny bits left in the bottom of our nets after we've trawled the Television channels for out-takes'.
xxii

Denis Norden's Trailer Cinema: one-off ITV programme (1992); anthology of cherished B-movie trailers from the forties and fifties.
xxii, 249

Devon, Keith: gravel voiced Variety agent, for many years a member of the Bernard Delfont Agency.
269–70

Dhéry, Robert: innovative French comedian and producer; brought London a touch of Parisian theatricality with his comedy revue *La Plume de Ma Tante*.
xxii, 244

Dixon, Pat: pioneering radio producer; besides bringing the BBC its

earliest regular jazz programmes, he was also in at the start of *The Goon Show*. Produced *In All Directions* (1952) written by Frank Muir and DN, and *Third Division* (1949) written by Frank Muir, DN and Paul Dehn.
xviii, xix, 108

Doctor Dolittle: movie musical (1967) starring Rex Harrison.
241

Donegan, Lonnie: the 'King of Skiffle', arguably Britain's most influential recording artist before the Beatles. No.1 hits include 'Cumberland Gap' (1957), 'Puttin' on the Style' (1957) and 'My Old Man's a Dustman' (1960); he got to No.3 with 'Does Your Chewing Gum Lose Its Flavour on the Bedpost Overnight?' (1959).
119

Dos Passos, John: influential American novelist, contemporary of Hemingway; a confessed 'social realist', his novels include *Three Soldiers*, *Manhatten Transfer* and the ground-breaking *USA* trilogy, with its use of newsreel and film-camera techniques.
49

Doyle, Jack: Irish boxer and singer known variously as 'The Singing Boxer' and 'The Gorgeous Gael'.
26

D'Oyly Carte, Bridget: granddaughter of theatrical impresario Richard D'Oyly Carte, founder of the D'Oyly Carte Opera Company of which she became head (1948–82).
90–1

Dreiser, Theodore: American writer of the thirties, whose bulky novels included such gritty best-sellers as *Sister Carrie* and *An American Tragedy*.
49

Duffy's Tavern: American radio comedy series, written by Ed Gardner, used as the basis of Frank Muir and DN's *Finkle's Café* (1956) produced by Pat Dixon.
xix

Dullea, Keir: American movie actor, specialising in nervous tension. Movies include *The Hoodlum Priest* (1961) and *2001: A Space Odyssey* (1968).
233

Dunaway, Faye: American movie actress, appeared in *Bonnie and Clyde* (1967) and played erotic chess with Steve McQueen in *The Thomas Crown Affair* (1968).
233

Durbin, Deanna: Canadian movie actress and singer. Born 1921, by 1935 was the world's most highly paid female star. Films include *Three Smart Girls* (1936), *Mad About Music* (1938) and *That Certain Age* (1938).
10, 205

E

Educating Archie: BBC radio series of the forties and fifties with ventriloquist Peter Brough and his dummy Archie Andrews; over the years featured Hattie Jacques, Max Bygraves, Harry Secombe, Warren Mitchell, Bruce Forsyth, Tony Hancock, Dick Emery, Robert Moreton and Julie Andrews. The writers included Eric Sykes, Sid Colin, George Wadmore, Marty Feldman, Ronald Wolfe and Pat Dunlop.
80

Edwards, Jimmy 'Professor': handle-bar moustached comedian, MA and Wartime RAF pilot, awarded DFC in 1942. Made his professional debut at the Windmill Theatre (1946), adopting the schoolmaster persona he maintained throughout his career. Began in BBC radio the same year in *Navy Mixture*, then starred with Dick Bentley and Joy Nichols, later replaced by June Whitfield and Alma Cogan, in more than 300 editions of *Take It From Here* (1948–60). On BBC Television he also starred in sixty-three editions of the sitcom *Whack-o!* (1956–72), later made into the movie *Bottoms Up!* (1960); *The Seven Faces of Jim* (1961) followed, then *More Faces of Jim* (1962–3).

xix, 81, 92, 97, 100, 103–5, 112, 115, 120, 133–4, 186, 203, 231–2, 264

Emney, Fred: hugely rotund character actor and comedian. Star of BBC Television's *The Fred Emney Show* (1956).
77

Evans, Norman: northern comedy star, with three Royal Variety Performances to his credit. Beloved for his 'over the garden wall' character, a moon-faced, toothless, precariously bosomed house-wife, gossiping over the garden fence.
264

***Every Home Should Have One*:** comedy movie (1970) about a sales-man tasked with finding an erotic way to market frozen porridge. Directed by Jim Clark, written by Marty Feldman, DN and Barry Took, starring Marty Feldman.
xxi

Exton, Clive: prolific TV and movie writer, one of the original con-tributors to that sadly missed segment of TV programming, the one-off play. His credits range from *Armchair Theatre* in the sixties and *Doomwatch* in the seventies to the later Agatha Christie drama-tisations and the movie *Isadora* (1968).
179

F

Fawcett, Eric: one of Alexandra Palace's small band of pioneering producer/directors who took on every type of TV programme, from studio Variety shows to outdoor cattle shows.
124

Faye, Alice: American movie actress and singer; the star of many Hollywood musicals, she became a Forces pin-up during World War Two. Movies included *You're A Sweetheart* (1937), *Alexander's Ragtime Band* (1938), *Hollywood Cavalcade* (1939) and *The Great American Broadcast* (1941). In *Hello, Frisco, Hello* (1941), she introduced the soulful 'You'll Never Know,' which became a standard.
188–90

Feldman, Marty: impish, bulging-eyed comedy star. After writing scripts with Barry Took – *Around The Horne* and episodes of *The Army Game* – he co-wrote and made his first starring appearance in *At Last The 1948 Show* (1967). He proved equally successful as the solo star of further TV series, which led to the lead part in a movie, *Every Home Should Have One* (1970) and thence to Hollywood. He was establishing his name there when, tragically young, he died while making *Yellowbeard* (1983).
xxi, 233

Ferber, Edna: American best-selling writer whose many novels include *So Big* (1924, Pulitzer Prize), *Saratoga Trunk* (1941) and *Show Boat* (1926), from which came the musical of the same name.
49

Fiddler on the Roof: American musical; first produced in London in 1967, starring Topol and Miriam Karlin.
228

Field, Sid: comedian. One of the few to make consecutive appear-ances in Royal Variety Performances (1945 and 1946). His movies, *London Town* (1946) and *The Cardboard Cavalier* (1947), do no justice to his comic artistry.
27, 66–7

Fields, Dame Gracie: affectionately known as 'Our Gracie' her singing and comedy made her Britain's top Variety and movie star through-out the twenties and thirties. Her movies ranged from *Sally in Our Alley* (1931) to *Holy Matrimony* (1943).
12

Fields, W. C.: American vaudeville and movie star, with an oratorical style as individual as his nose. He began as a juggler, but went on to write and perform in such classic comedy movies as *It's a Gift* (1934), *My Little Chickadee* (1940) and *Never Give a Sucker An Even Break* (1941). Played Micawber in *David Copperfield* (1935).
70, 259

Finch, Peter: London-born actor with Australian parents. Grew up in Australia before returning to Britain, where his movie successes included performances in *Sunday, Bloody Sunday* (1971) and *Network* (1976).
75

Finkle's Café: BBC radio series (1956) produced by Pat Dixon, written by Frank Muir and DN and starring Peter Sellers, Sid James, Avril Angers and Kenneth Connor. Based on the American programme *Duffy's Tavern*, written by Ed Gardner.
xix

Fisher, John: TV producer and author of *Funny Way to Be a Hero* (1973).
32

Fitzgerald, F. Scott: classic twenties American novelist and short story writer who served brief stretches as a screenwriter. *This Side of Paradise* (1920) was his first novel and other notable works include *The Great Gatsby* (1925) and *Tender is the Night* (1934).
252

Flanagan, Bud: English comedian and acknowledged Crazy Gang leader; with his partner Chesney Allen, popularised and possibly immortalised the song 'Underneath the Arches'.
188, 216–17

Flynn, Errol: Australian-born American movie actor noted for swashbuckling roles and multi-coloured private life. Typical movies were *Captain Blood (1935), The Charge of the Light Brigade* (1936), *The Adventures of Robin Hood* (1938), and *The Adventures of Don Juan* (1948).
194

Forbes, Bryan: movie director, actor. Writer and founder member of The Writers Guild. Wrote screenplay of *The Angry Silence* (1960) and directed movies as diverse as *The Stepford Wives* (1974) and *International Velvet* (1978).
173

Ford, Gerald: thirty-eighth President of the United States (1974–7).
257

40 Years of ITV Laughter: ITV special (1995) written and presented by DN.
xxii

Fowler, P. A. (Bill): General Manager, Trocadero, Elephant & Castle, in the forties.
7, 15–16

Frank, Melvin: American screenwriter, and latterly movie director and producer. Beginning as a Bob Hope gag writer, he teamed with Norman Panama to write, among others, *My Favorite Blonde* (1942), *White Christmas* (1954) and *The Road to Hong Kong* (1962). As producer/director, *A Touch of Class* (1973) and *A Funny Thing Happened on The Way to the Forum* (1966). With DN, wrote screenplay for *Buona Sera, Mrs Campbell* (1968).
xxi, 147, 188, 192–6, 236, 262

Franklin, David: panellist on *My Music!* (1967–94).
00, 00, 00, 00

Frankau, Gilbert: popular novelist, author of *World Without End* (1943) and the *Peter Jackson, Cigar Merchant* series.
211

Fraser, Antonia Lady: historian and novelist. Probably best known for her biography *Mary, Queen of Scots* (1969). DN's partner on *My Word!* (1979-90).
xx

Fraser, Bill: comedy character actor with wide stage experience; appeared in *Bags of Panic, Here's Television* (1951), also *And So to Bentley* (1954). Other TV series include *The Army Game* (1957) and *Bootsie and Snudge* (1961).
xix, 52–6, 134–5

Frisco, Joe: American dancer, vaudeville performer and comedian renowned for his (false) stutter.
187–8

Frost, David: broadcaster, writer and businessman. Hosted groundbreaking, satirical BBC Television series *That Was the Week That Was* (1962–4), produced and directed by Ned Sherrin. Subsequent shows included *The Frost Report* (1966–7), *Frost on Friday*

(1968–70), *The David Frost Show* (1969–72) and *Breakfast with Frost* (1993–2005); a frequent transatlantic traveller, his genius was said to consist of an infinite capacity for taking planes.
130, 242

Fry, Stephen: actor, presenter, novelist and beaming polymath.
192

Funny Way to Be a Hero: book by John Fisher (1973).
32

G

Galton, Ray: scriptwriter, whose partnership with Alan Simpson made them Britain's top comedy writing team. The duo's best-known works are BBC radio and Television's *Hancock's Half Hour* (1954–9 and 1956–60 respectively) and *Steptoe and Son* (1962).
186

Garland, Judy: iconic American singer and movie star. Starring roles included *The Wizard of Oz* (1939), *Meet Me in St Louis* (1944), *Easter Parade* (1948) and *A Star is Born* (1954).
10, 89

Gently, Bentley: Australian Broadcasting Corporation radio series (1951), starring Dick Bentley; commissioned to mark ABC's silver jubilee. Written by Frank Muir and DN with much material reworked from UK shows starring Bernard Braden.
xix, 106

Geraldo: big band leader, who progressed from Geraldo's Gaucho Tango Orchestra to the Geraldo Concert Orchestra (1940); spanned over 2,000 broadcasts.
xviii

Gershwin, George and Ira: American brothers, whose twenty-year partnership as composer and lyricist, provided some of the most durable contributions to popular music; among them 'Oh, Lady Be Good', 'Somebody Loves Me', 'They Can't Take That Away From Me', 'The Man I Love' and 'I Got Rhythm'.
272, 276

Glums, The: family comedy sketches introduced to BBC radio's *Take It From Here* in its fourth season (1950–1). Revived for two seasons as part of London Weekend Television's *Bruce Forsyth's Big Night* (1978–9).
xxi, 94–5, 232

Golding, Louis: Manchester-born novelist, whose most popular works were *Magnolia Street* (1932), *The Camberwell Beauty* (1935), *and Mr Emmanuel* (1939).
210

Gondoliers, The: Gilbert and Sullivan operetta (1889).
88

Gone with the Wind: novel by Margaret Mitchell set in the south at the time of the American Civil War (1936); made into an epic ten-Oscar movie (1939) starring Clark Gable and Vivien Leigh.
200–1

Goodman, Lord Arnold: Heavily built lawyer and political adviser. Credits include Chairman Arts Council of Great Britain (1965–72), Chairman of British Lion Films, the Housing Corporation, Newspaper Proprietors Association, Director of the Royal Opera House and Sadler's Wells and Governor of the Royal Shakespeare Company.
209–10

Gray, Eddie: his name was generally preceeded by 'monsewer', owing to his tendency to address the audience in fractured French. A legendary figure in Variety folklore, he was a comedy juggler, much given to muttering, who frequently found himself swelling the ranks of the Crazy Gang.
32, 187

Great Escape, The: American movie (1963) and regular Christmas treat, it starred Steve McQueen, James Garner and Richard Attenborough in a World War Two story about Allied soldiers seeking to escape from a German POW camp.
43

Green, Benny: jazz saxophonist, writer and broadcaster. Appointed columnist for *New Musical Express* (1955) and later jazz critic to the *Observer*, a position he held for nineteen years. He was probably best known as broadcaster on programmes such as Radio 4's *Stop the Week* and *Kaleidoscope* and his Sunday afternoon record programmes on Radio 2 (1983–98).
233

Greene, Graham: author, novelist and travel book writer. Best known of his fictional works are *Brighton Rock* (1938), *The Power and The Glory* (1940) and the movie *The Third Man* (1949).
29, 131

Guest, Val: prolific writer, director and producer for over fifty years. Married to Yolande Donlan, he wrote movies for Will Hay, Arthur Askey and the Crazy Gang, with screenplays that include *Good Morning Boys* (1936), *Oh, Mr Porter!* (1937), *Alf's Button Afloat* (1938), *Band Wagon* (1939), *The Ghost Train* (1941) and, in a departure from his usual genre, one of the best British science fiction movies *The Day the Earth Caught Fire* (1961).
186

Guilbert, Yvette: French music hall singer and actress. Painted by Toulouse-Lautrec while performing at the Moulin Rouge in the eighteen nineties. Best known over here for her song, 'Just a Little Love, a Little Kiss'.
276

Hancock, Tony: comedian and comedy actor, star of BBC radio and Television's *Hancock's Half Hour* (1956–61). A complex and ultimately tragic figure, he was at his unparalleled best with Galton and Simpson scripts.
xix, 72, 144

Harris, Mai: wrote the English subtitles for many French and Italian films including Roger Vadim's *Et Dieu ... Créa la Femme* (1956) starring Brigitte Bardot.
235

Havilland, Olivia de: British-born American movie star, sister to Joan Fontaine, her winsome, heart-shaped face adorned many box-office successes, including *The Adventures of Robin Hood* (1938), *Gone with the Wind* (1939), *Hold Back the Dawn* (1941), *To Each His Own* (1946) and *The Snake Pit* (1949).
193–4

Hawes, Tony: scriptwriter. Wrote for *The Des O'Connor Show* (1964–8), *Des O'Connor on Stage* (1969), *Des* (1972) and *The Two Ronnies* (1972). Voice behind the conveyor belt on BBC Television's *Larry Grayson's Generation Game*. Married Stan Laurel's daughter.
233

Hay, Will: in his role as a bumbling schoolmaster starred in Variety,

with a series of classroom sketches featuring Graham Moffatt and Moore Marriott. Incorporating these into his first movie, *Boys Will Be Boys* (1935), he played a series of variations of the character in such incomparable farces as *Oh, Mr Porter!* (1937), *Convict 99* (1938), *Ask a Policeman* (1939) and *The Black Sheep of Whitehall* (1941).
186

Haynes, Arthur: Variety and TV comedian, star of *The Arthur Haynes Show* (1957–66), written by Johnny Speight.
xix

Hemingway, Ernest: classic American novelist and short story writer. His first success came with *The Sun Also Rises* (1926), retitled *Fiesta* in the UK, which was followed by *A Farewell to Arms* (1929), *For Whom the Bell Tolls* (1940) and *The Old Man and the Sea* (1952).
252

Hemmings, David: actor, later director and producer. Dubbed 'the acceptable face of the sixties', he first came to public attention in *Blowup* (1966), which was followed by *Camelot* (1967), *Barbarella* (1968), and *The Charge of the Light Brigade* (1968). Also starred in *The Best House in London*.
xxi

Henderson, Dickie: one of the most graceful and stylish comedians of his era, he began in Variety and went on to become a popular Television performer, compering *Sunday Night at the London Palladium* (1959 and 1966) and starring in his own series, *The Dickie Henderson Show* (1971), which ran for a hundred episodes.
200

Henry Hall's Guest Night: BBC radio series launched in 1934, featuring the trademark introduction, 'This is Henry Hall speaking and tonight is my guest night.' The programme continued to be broadcast through World War Two and beyond, notching up nearly a thousand editions.

61

Here's Television: BBC TV one-hour special (1951) written by Frank Muir and DN, directed by Michael Mills and starring Ian Carmichael, Bill Fraser, Sid James and Clive Morton.

xviii, 127–8

Hill, Benny: inventive and often under-rated comedian and writer. *The Benny Hill Show* began on BBC TV in 1955 and, after moving to Thames, ran until 1989. The Thames Television one hour episodes were edited into half-hours and sold to 140 countries including the USA, making it Britain's most successful comedy export.

xviii

History of the Holborn Empire: radio series (1942, six episodes). DN's first scripts for the BBC.

xvii, 32

Hitchcock, Alfred: portly English-born director of classic suspense movies, including *The Man Who Knew Too Much* (1934), *The 39 Steps (1935)*, the *Lady Vanishes* (1938), *Rebecca* (1940) *Foreign Correspondent* (1940), *Notorious (1946)*, *North By North-west* (1959) and *Psycho* (1960); made cameo appearances in most of his movies.

5

Hobley, Macdonald: born Falkland Islands. During BBC Television's post-War period, one of its most frequently seen 'announcers', as presenters were then called. Hosted the first *Come Dancing* (1949) and chaired the radio series *Does the Team Think?* (1954).

127–8

Holloway, Stanley: actor and entertainer. Remembered for his character and comedy roles particularly that of Alfred P. Dolittle in *My Fair Lady* (1964).
89

Hollywood Cavalcade: movie (1939) starring Alice Faye and Don Ameche.
189

Hope, Bob: English-born American comedian, 'king of the one-liners', noted for his cameraderie with Presidents, his readiness to entertain the troops anywhere at any time and the large retinue of gag-writers he kept in continuous employment. A former vaudeville dancer, he became one of Hollywood's top-grossing stars, turning out a string of hit comedies, ranging from *My Favorite Blonde* (1942) and *The Paleface* (1948) to the award-winning *Road To* movies, in which he was teamed with Bing Crosby and Dorothy Lamour. This in addition to his never-ceasing output of radio and TV series and specials, all of them assiduously studied by aspiring gag-writers the world over.
116, 262–3

Hopkins, John: TV scriptwriter and dramatist. A notable contributor to *Z Cars*, TV's first long-running police drama series (1962–78). His quartet of plays *Talking to a Stranger* (1966), in the *Theatre 625* series, were a peak-point in TV drama.
179

Horse Feathers: film (1932) starring Marx Brothers with screenplay by S. J. Perelman.
225

Houdini, Harry: Hungarian-born world-renowned American magician and escape artist. One time president of the Society of American Magicians.
24, 254

How to Be an Alien: dire TV series (1964) written and presented by Frank Muir and DN, based on George Mikes' book (1946).
xx, 143–5

Hudd, Roy: Variety entertainer, actor and comedian. A regular on BBC radio's *Workers' Playtime* (1941–64) and starred in *The News Huddlines* (1976–2001). Came to prominence in satirical BBC Television series *Not So Much a Programme, More a Way of Life* (1964). Acted in character roles in *Coronation Street* (1966) and the Denis Potter TV serials *Lipstick on Your Collar* (1993) and *Karaoke* (1996). Wrote *Roy Hudd's Cavalcade of Variety Acts: A Who Was Who in Light Entertainment 1945–60* (1998).
32

Hutch: stage name of Leslie Hutchinson, a top-billed Variety performer, who accompanied himself at the piano, while singing popular songs in a beautifully modulated, if slightly mannered, style. Something of a heart-throb among the debs of his day.
32

Huxley, Sir Julian: scientist, educationalist, writer, humanist and broadcaster. Appeared on many radio and TV shows. Regular panellist on BBC Television's *Animal, Vegetable, Mineral?* (1952–9).
133

Hyams Brothers, The (Mr Phil, Mr Sid and Mr Mick): built, owned and operated the splendiferous palaces of CineVariety, Gaumont Super Cinemas. 'The last of the great showmen.'
xvii, 4–6, 8–12, 14, 17, 20, 24–5, 37

Hylton, Jack: Bolton-born dance band leader and impresario. After leading a successful stage and recording band in the thirties, he turned to production with *Peter Pan* followed by Crazy Gang shows. Subsequent major London productions included *Kiss Me Kate* and

Porgy and Bess. At one time, he was reputed to be the owner of fifteen West End theatres.
25, 71, 217–18

I

Ignorance is Bliss: BBC send-up of radio panel games (1946), imported from the USA. Stewart MacPherson preceded Eamonn Andrews as question master, while the panel included Harold Berens, Gladys Hay and Michael Moore.
79

In All Directions: first radio sketch show series the BBC allowed on air without a written script (1951). Devised and put together by Frank Muir and DN, it starred Ustinov and Peter Jones doing all the voices and most of the sound effects. Produced by Pat Dixon.
xix, 108–9

In On the Act: TV series (1988), looking back on Variety. Written and presented by DN.
xxii

Instone, Anna: Head of BBC Gramophone Records Department (1941).
32

It'll Be Alright On The Day: TV one-off shown on Cup Final day, 1983. DN at Wembley exhibiting all manner of sport-related out-takes and bloopers.
xxi

It'll Be Alright on the Night: long-running TV series, originated by London Weekend Television (1977–2006). Compiled, written and presented by DN, each programme consisted of out-takes and

bloopers culled from world-wide sources. Principal producers were Paul Smith, Paul Lewis and Simon Withington, with the direction mainly in the hands of Bill Morton.
xxi, 196–206

Isow, Jack: owner of Isow's, a New York-style deli restaurant in Soho, popular with the show business and boxing fraternity. Among those who ate there frequently enough to have their names embossed in gold on the backs of the red leather chairs were Jack Solomons, Walt Disney, Danny Kaye and Frank Sinatra.
270

It's That Man Again (*ITMA*): forties radio comedy show starring Tommy Handley and written by Ted Kavanagh. A proven morale-booster for the Home Front throughout World War Two.
77

J

Jacques, Hattie: English comic actress, part of the original *ITMA* team. Stage debut 1944. Toured with the Young Vic (1947–8). Appeared regularly in BBC radio programmes *ITMA* (1948–9) and *Educating Archie* (1950–4). Television debut in *The Tony Hancock Show* (1956) and after an appearance in *Carry on Sergeant* (1958), had parts in twelve further *Carry On* films, most notably playing hospital matrons. Her ideal partnership came when Eric Sykes cast her as his sister, Harriet, in his long-running TV series, *Sykes And …* (1960).
263

James, Jimmy: high on any list of funniest comedians. Harassed by two gormless sidekicks, his pained facial contortions and surreal asides made him one of the jewels in Variety's corn.
32, 103

James, Sid: South African-born comedy actor with a face like a cheerful kneecap. Bore the burden of most of the *Carry On* films; also supported Hancock in *Hancock's Half Hour* (1956) and starred in his own TV series, *Citizen James* (1960–2) and *Bless This House* (1971–6).
xix

Jay, Manny: Variety agent, on floor above Hyman Zahl.
71

Johnson, Nunnally: American producer, screenwriter and director. Nominated for Oscar for Best Writing, Screenplay for *The Grapes of Wrath* (1940) and *Holy Matrimony* (1943). Other notable films include *Jesse James* (Original Screenplay, 1939), *Rose of Washington Square* (Writer and Producer, 1939), *How to Marry a Millionaire* (Producer and Screenplay, 1953), *The Three Faces of Eve* (Director, Producer and Screenplay, 1957) and *The Dirty Dozen* (Screenplay, 1967).
252–3, 255

Johnston, Johnny: singer and music arranger and publisher. Founded music publisher Michael Reine Music (1946). Wrote and performed as a member of the Keynotes' theme to BBC radio's *Take It From Here* (1948). Known as 'King of the Jingle' after forming Johnny Johnston Jingles (1956).
137–8

Jones, Peter: comedy actor, playwright and broadcaster. Best known as a panellist on BBC radio's *Just A Minute*, for his role in the BBC Television comedy sitcom *The Rag Trade* and as the voice in the BBC Television series *The Hitchhiker's Guide to the Galaxy* (1981).
xix, 108–9

Joyce, Teddy: Canadian orchestral leader of the thirties in Great Britain. Played the violin. Orchestra appeared at the Kit Kat Club,

London. Known as the 'Stick of Dynamite' because of his boundless energy.
25–6

Junkin, John: radio, TV and film performer and scriptwriter, and was the voice of the chimp 'Mr Shifter' in the long-running PG tips tea TV advertisement.
233

Kamen, Milt: American comedian and scriptwriter. Discovered Woody Allen. Writer on US TV Sid Caesar's *Your Show of Shows* (1950).
241

Karlin, **Miriam**: actress best known for films *A Clockwork Orange* (1971), *The Millionairess* (1960), *Fiddler on the Roof* – London stage production (1967) and film (1971) and as the militant shop steward in TV's *The Rag Trade* (1977).
228

Keller, Sheldon: American composer, writer and songwriter. Co-wrote *Buona Sera, Mrs Campbell* (1968).
xxi, 93, 144

Kelly, Barbara: Canadian-born actress, presenter and TV personality, best known as one of the original panellists in *What's My Line.* Married Bernard Braden in 1942 and co-starred in husband's radio and Television series including *Bedtime with Braden* (1950).
xx, xviii, xix, 126

Kentish Lad, A: Frank Muir's autobiography (1997).
98, 264

Kerr, Deborah: movie actress. Starred in *Major Barbara* (1941) and *The King and I* (1956). Received Oscar nomination for Best Actress in a Leading Role six times for *Edward My Son* (1949), *From Here to Eternity* (1953), *The King and I* (1956), *Heaven Knows Mr Allison* (1957), *Separate Tables* (1958) and *The Sundowners* (1960).
117–18

Ketèlbey, Albert: composer and conductor; orchestral pieces include 'In a Monastery Garden' (1915) and 'In a Persian Market' (1920).
30

Knox, Ronald: theologian, writer, broadcaster and friend of Evelyn Waugh. Also wrote several detective novels.
3

Knox, Teddy: comedian, half of double-act Nervo and Knox. Member of the Crazy Gang; wrote screenplay and composed music for the movie *Okay for Sound* (1937).
219

Kossoff, David: actor. Debuted at Unity Theatre (1942). Acted in BBC Radio serial *Journey into Space* (1953). Starred as hen-pecked Alf Larkins in TV sitcom *The Larkins* (1958). Movie appearances include *The Bespoke Overcoat* (1956) and *Mouse on the Moon* (1963).
174

Kostelanetz, Andre: Russian-born American composer of easy listening music, conductor and recording artist selling in excess of 50 million records.
102

L

La Bohème: opera (1896) by Giacomo Puccini.
78

Larkins, The: TV sitcom (1958–60 and 1963–4) created and written by Fred Robinson.
174–6

Last Night of the Paris, The: final radio show to be recorded at the BBC's Paris studios in Regent Street.
234–5

Laughter by Royal Command: TV programme (1993) written and presented by DN; based on Royal Variety shows from 1960 onwards.
xxii

Laurel and Hardy: Probably the most durable of Hollywood's comedy duos. British-born Stan Laurel, who debuted as a comedian in Glasgow (1906), and American Oliver Hardy, who began as a boy soprano at the age of eight (1900). They made their first movie, the silent *The Lucky Dog*, in 1921, followed by over seventy shorts. Their first sound feature was *Hollywood Review of 1929* (1929), which led to a further twenty-seven features culminating in *Atoll K* (1951).
10, 233, 256

Lawford, Peter: British-born American movie actor. Member of the 'Rat Pack' and brother-in-law to President John F. Kennedy. Made over eighty movies including *Buona Sera, Mrs Campbell* (1968).
xxi

Leacock, Stephen: An unlikely combination of economist and humorist. British-born, he lived and worked in Canada, his best

known collection of comic pieces *Literary Lapses* (1910).
108

Lee, Benny: Scottish comedy actor and singer. Took part in BBC radio's *Breakfast with Braden* (1950) and, with Michael Bentine, Judith Chalmers, Clive Dunn and Ron Moody, *Round the Bend* (1957–60). Made guest appearances in many TV sitcoms and series. xviii, 106

Legends of Light Music: Radio 2 series (1995–7) written and presented by DN.
xxii

Lejeune, C. A. (Caroline Alice): first regular film critic; *Manchester Guardian* (1922–8) followed by thirty-two years at the *Observer*.
133

Life with the Lyons: BBC radio (1950–9), and BBC Television (1955–60), starring the American Lyon family comprising Ben Lyon, his wife Bebe Daniels and their children Barbara and Richard. Also Molly Weir.
143

Legman, Gershon: wrote *The Rationale of the Dirty Joke: An Analysis of Sexual Humour* (British edition, 1969).
246

Le Mesurier, John: notable supporting actor. Appeared in numerous films including *Brothers in Law* (1957) and *The Fiendish Plot of Dr Fu Manchu* (1980, with Peter Sellers), also Tony Hancock's films and TV series. Probably best remembered as Sergeant Arthur Wilson in *Dad's Army* (1968–77).
243

of Dover' (1940), 'We'll Meet Again' (1942) and 'Auf Wiederseh'n Sweetheart' (1952), which also earned her a No. 1 hit in America.
xix

M

McCrea, Joel: rugged American movie star, whose films include *Wells Fargo* (1937), *Foreign Correspondent* (1940) and *Ride the High Country* (1962). Married to actress Frances Dee.
5

McGillivray, David: actor, director, producer, playwright, screen-writer and film critic. Wrote screenplays for Norman J. Warren and Pete Walker's horror movies. Presently writes for the stage and pro-vides material for Julian Clary.
267

McGiveney, Owen: starred in Variety as a quick-change artist; later became an actor in several Hollywood movies.
67

McGrath, Joseph: Scottish movie and TV director and producer, whose credits include James Bond's *Casino Royale* (1967), *The Bliss of Mrs Blossom* (1968), and the Peter Cook / Dudley Moore series *Not Only ... But Also* (1965).
xx

MacLaine, Shirley: notable American movie star. First film was *The Trouble with Harry* (1955), followed by *The Apartment* (1960), *The Bliss of Mrs Blossom* (1968) and *Terms of Endearment* (1983), for most of which she either won or was nominated for awards. Sister of Warren Beatty.
xx

MacLean, Quentin: highly-respected cinema and church organist. Played the organ at Westminster Cathedral and in cinemas, including The Trocadero, Elephant and Castle. Frequently on radio, where he performed UK premiere of Hindemith's 'Concerto for Organ'. Later emigrated to Canada.
29

Magnet, The: British boys' comic launched in 1908 featuring the story of Greyfriars School, whose most notable students included Billy Bunter and the boys of the Lower Fourth. Ceased publication in 1940 due to wartime paper shortages after 1,683 issues.
215

Marks, Alfred: versatile comedian and singer with an unusually good bass voice. Appeared in many TV series, including his own *Alfred Marks Time* (1956), as well as making notable contributions to stage and movies.
xviii, 99

Marriott, Moore: character actor. Best remembered for his portrayal of the aged Jeremiah Harbottle in films made with Will Hay including *Oh, Mr Porter!* (1937) and *Ask a Policeman* (1939).
186

Martin, Mary: American movie and stage star. Broadway debut in *Leave It to Me* (1938) and was immediately contracted by Paramount Pictures. Notable performances in the Broadway musical *South Pacific* (1950) and *Peter Pan* (1955).
116

Marx, Groucho: American comedian who, with his brothers Chico, Gummo and Harpo, made fifteen comedy movies. As a solo performer his greatest success was as the host on the US radio and subsequently TV show *You Bet Your Life*.
225

Maschwitz, Eric: writer, broadcaster, lyricist and broadcasting executive. Lyrics include 'A Nightingale Sang in Berkeley Square' (1940), 'These Foolish Things' (1941) and 'Room Five Hundred and Four' (1941). After writing several musicals and the screenplay for *Goodbye, Mr Chips* (1939), he became Head of BBC Light Entertainment (1958–63).
52, 146

Mason, Edward J.: King Edward VII lookalike, he created and wrote, with his partner Geoffrey Webb, the long-running radio series *Dick Barton, Special Agent* (1946–51). When this finished, they went on to fill the same early evening slot with an everyday story of country folk they entitled *The Archers* (1951–). With Tony Shryane he then created a number of panel games including *Guilty Party, My Word!* (1957) and *My Music* (1967–94).
157

Matthau, Walter: American movie actor who came to prominence in his Oscar-winning movie *The Fortune Cookie* (1966) and *The Odd Couple* (1968).
256

Matthews, Jessie: actress, dancer and singer. Appeared in Rodgers and Hart's *Ever Green* (1932) and the film adaptation, *Evergreen* (1934). It featured her singing 'Over My Shoulder', which became her personal theme song. Played Mary Dale (1963–9) in the long running BBC radio soap, *Mrs Dale's Diary* (1948–69).
265

Maupassant, Guy, de: French novelist and short story writer (1850–93).
214

Maxwell, Charles: BBC radio producer working primarily for the BBC

General Forces and BBC Light Programmes. Programmes produced include *Navy Mixture, Take It From Here* (1948) and the last two episodes of the first series of *Beyond Our Ken* (1958).
81, 87, 90, 99–100, 114.

Melly, George: singer of good-time songs, author and raconteur. Wrote three volumes of autobiography, *Owning Up* (1965), *Rum, Bum and Concertina* (1977), *Scouse Mouse* (1984) among ten plus published books.
113, 151

Midweek: BBC Radio 4 programme presented by Libby Purves (1983–).
247

Mikes, George: Hungarian-born author of *How to be an Alien* (1946) which poked gentle fun at the English.
xx, 143, 145

Miller, Arthur: one of the greatest of American playwrights. First successful play *All My Sons* (1947), followed by *The Crucible* (1953) and *A View From The Bridge* (1955). His tragedy *Death of a Salesman* (1949) won the Pulitzer Prize. Wrote screenplay of *The Misfits* (1961). Married Marilyn Monroe (1956) and subsequently divorced her (1961).
271

Miller, Sir Jonathan: member of the ground-breaking *Beyond the Fringe* team (1960). Also distinguished himself as a neurologist, author, producer, director, humorist and presenter. Editor and presenter BBC Television's *Monitor* (1964–5). Many productions at English National Opera since 1974. Wrote and presented BBC Television's *The Body in Question* (1978) and *States of Mind* (1983).
151

Miller, Max: comedian. Known as the 'Cheeky Chappie', his jaunty white Stetson, flowered plus-four suit and jokes purportedly as bright blue as his wickedly rolling eyes, he earned the right to describe himself as 'the pure gold of the Music Hall'; first topped the bill at the Holborn Empire (1926), thereafter a member of Variety's comedy elite. Made many successful movies.
32

Milligan, Spike: writer and comedian, completely changed the landscape of radio comedy with *The Goon Show* (1951–60), and did much the same thing for TV with *A Show Called Fred* (1956) and the *Q Series* (1969–80). Appeared in many films and made a memorable Ben Gunn in *Treasure Island* at the Mermaid Theatre in 1961, 1973–5.
236

Mills, Michael: pre-war sound effects assistant who became BBC first specialised Light Entertainment producer at Alexandra Palace. Responsible for many prestigious shows. Later Head of Light Entertainment.
252

Modley, Albert: chuckling, gravel-voiced northern comedian. A Blackpool favourite (*On With the Modley*), he also starred in many pantomimes, primarily at the Alhambra, Bradford. Can be seen in the movie *Up for the Cup* (1950).
264

Moffatt, Graham: character actor. Best remembered for movies made with Will Hay including *Oh, Mr Porter!* (1937), *Where There's a Will* (1936) and *Ask a Policeman* (1939).
186

Monday Night at Seven: successful radio magazine series (1938)

featuring *Inspector Hornleigh Investigates,* the magician Sidani performing card tricks on the radio, and Ronnie Waldman's 'deliberate mistake'.
80

Monkhouse, Bob: comedian and writer with an unparalleled mastery of every comedy technique. With his ex-school friend Denis Goodwin, wrote many radio series including material for Bob Hope. As a solo entertainer he was a matchless cabaret performer and scored with his own TV series *The Bob Monkhouse Show* (1983–6). After making a success of *Candid Camera* (1960–1), he hosted many game shows beginning with *The Golden Shot* (1967–75), then on through *Family Fortunes* (1978–83) and *Bob's Full House* (1984).
xviii, xx, 149–50, 233, 241

Moodie, Douglas: TV producer and director, responsible for *Dixon of Dock Green* (1955–63), *Whack-o!* (1957) and *More Faces of Jim* (1962).
232

More Faces of Jim: BBC Television series (1962) starring Jimmy Edwards.
xx

Morecambe, Eric: comedian who, when fifteen, formed lasting duo with Ernie Wise in touring stage show *Youth Takes a Bow* (1941). West End debut in revue *Strike a New Note* (1943). With BBC Television's *Morecambe and Wise Show* (1968–78) and Thames Television's *Morecambe and Wise Show* (1978–83), they became Britain's best-loved comedy pair and a must-see for Christmas night.
149

Moreton, Robert: comedian, enjoyed success on *Educating Archie* and *Variety Bandbox,* with readings from his 'Monster Fun Book'. Catchprase 'Get in there, Moreton.'
xviii, 213

Mount, Peggy: stage and film actress best known for playing battle-axe characters. Television debut in the sitcom *The Larkins* (1958–60 and 1963–4). Subsequently appeared in many other TV programmes and in movies.
174

Movita: eye-catching Mexican-American actress and wife of Jack Doyle. Appeared as Tahitian girl, Tehani, alongside Clark Gable in *Mutiny on the Bounty* (1935).
26

Mr Justice Duncannon: BBC Television comedy series (1963) written by Frank Muir and DN with Henry Cecil; a spin-off of *Brothers in Law.*
xx

Mrs Dale's Diary: (1948-69) First post-war soap on BBC radio.
265

Muir, Frank: comedy writer, author, radio and television presenter and DN's long-time partner. In addition to co-writing many radio and TV series, he appeared in several long-running panel games and was the author of a succesion of *What-a-Mess* children's books, *The Frank Muir Book: An Irreverant Companion to Social History, The Oxford Book of Humorous Prose,* a novel *The Walpole Orange,* and his autobiography *A Kentish Lad.* Throughout all these he wore a pink bowtie.
xviii, 14, 80, 85, 124, 136–7, 159, 231, 278

Navy Mixture: radio programme (1943–1947) 'blended to suit the taste of the Royal Navy'. Its final episodes, produced by Charles Maxwell, featured young Australian newcomer Joy Nichols and another newcomer 'Professor' Jimmy Edwards delivering 'a light-hearted lecture'. When Dick Bentley started making guest appearances, it became the seed bed for *Take It From Here*.
81

Newhart, Bob: American stand-up comedian and actor noted for his comedy albums such as *The Button-Down Mind of Bob Newhart* (1960) that won him the Grammy Award for Album of the Year. This was the first of twelve albums.
147

Nicholas Brothers, The: American highly acrobatic tap dancers. Appeared in nightclubs, concerts, on Broadway, on TV and in films including *The Great American Broadcast* (1941), *Sun Valley Serenade* (1941) and *Orchestra Wives* (1942). They also made several successful appearances at the London Palladium.
67

Nichols, Joy: Australian comedienne and singer who moved to London (1946) and was given a major role in the last series of *Navy Mixture* (1947) which led to a starring role in *Take It From Here* (1948). In 1952 she was replaced by June Whitfield and Alma Cogan when she left the cast to marry American musical comedy performer Wally Peterson. Later appeared on Broadway in supporting roles in *Redhead* (1959–60) and *Darling of the Day* (1968).
81, 113, 147

Nixon, Richard: thirty-seventh President of the United States of America (1969–74). Only one to resign from office.
257

No, No Nanette: stage musical (1925); later, a movie starring Anna Neagle (1940), directed by her husband Herbert Wilcox.
102

Norman ... Is That You?: a Broadway comedy (1976) co-authored by Ron Clark and Sam Bobrick.
226–7

No Trees in the Street: Play (1959) by Ted Willis.
218

Niven, David: actor; a polished light comedian and gallant hero in films such as *The Charge of the Light Brigade* (1936). After service in World War Two, he spent the next thirty years as an urbane leading man in films such *As Around the World in Eighty Days* (1956) and *The Statue* (1971). Won an Oscar for *Separate Tables* (1958).
xxi, 191

O'Casey, Ronan: actor who starred in the TV series *The Larkins*, (1958–60 and 1963–4) and in films including *Trouble in Store* (1953) and *The Beverly Hillbillies* (1993).
174

Of Mice and Men: novel (1937) by John Steinbeck; later a play then a movie starring Burgess Meredith and Lon Chaney Jnr.
100

Oh, Mr Porter!: movie (1937) roughly based on *The Ghost Train*, starring Will Hay with Moore Marriott and Graham Moffatt; screenplay by Val Guest and Marriott Edgar.
186

Oh, My Word!: collection of *My Word!* stories (1980) by Frank Muir and DN.
xxi

Olgo, the Mathematical Genius: one of those out-of-the-way talents that were an integral part of Variety's appeal.
23

Oliver's Twists: radio comedy series starring Vic Oliver which teamed the writing talents of newcomer Frank Muir and veteran Dick Pepper.
81

O'Riordan, Shaun: actor, director and producer. Made TV debut in *The Adventures of Robin Hood* (1955). Played Eddie in the TV sitcom *The Larkins* (1958–60 and 1963–4). Served a term as Religious Programme Director.
174

Orkin, Harvey: American television writer and theatrical agent representing Richard Burton and Peter Sellers. A notable wit, he wrote several episodes of *The Phil Silvers Show* (1955) and was a frequent guest on *Not So Much a Programme, More a Way of Life* (1964).
151

Owen, Alun: Welsh playwright primarily writing plays for one-off drama series such as ABC's *Armchair Theatre* (1959–62), including *No Trams to Lime Street* (1959). On the strength of this he wrote the screenplay for the first Beatles' film, *A Hard Day's Night* (1964).
179

Ozzie and Harriet Show, The: popular American Television sitcom (1950–66) starring Ozzie and Harriet Nelson and their real-life family.
142–3

P

Pagan, Bobby: theatre organist. Played Wurlitzer organ at Troxy Cinema, Commercial Road, from opening (1933) until he moved to Trocadero Cinema, Elephant & Castle. Signature tune, 'Pagan Love Song'.
11, 30, 254

Panama, Norman: American comedy writer, screenwriter, producer and director, partnered Melvin Frank (1936–66). They jointly wrote the screenplay for *Road to Utopia* (1946) starring Bing Crosby, Bob Hope and Dorothy Lamour. On his own, Panama wrote *Road to Hong Kong* (1962).
193

Park, Phil: theatre organist at the Regal Edmonton cinema in North East London. The Christie organ was installed there in 1934 and remained in use until the cinema was redeveloped in 1984, when it was moved to its present home in the Memorial Hall, Barry, South Wales.
28

Parker, Dorothy: American short-story writer and poet, noted for her caustic wit ('Brevity is the soul of lingerie' and 'If you want to know what God thinks of money, just look at the people he gave it to.')
200

Parnell, Val: producer and impresario. Became Managing Director (1945) of the Moss Empires theatre-owning group. Appointed Managing Director Associated Television (ATV) (1956) which was particularly associated with weekend Variety entertainment. Lent his name to *Val Parnell's Saturday Spectacular* (1956–61) and *Val Parnell's Sunday Night at the London Palladium* (1955–65).
270

Payne, John: American film actor and singer. Best remembered for his singing in musicals such as *Tin Pan Alley* (1940) and as lead in *Miracle on 34th Street* (1947).
233

Payne and Hilliard: married comedy duo of Tom Payne and Vera Hilliard, one of Variety's most reliable middle-of-the-bill comedy duos.
66

Perelman, S. J.: American humorist, essayist, travel writer and screenwriter. In addition to the movie *Horse Feathers* (1932) wrote screenplay for another Marx Brothers' movie, *Monkey Business* (1931), and also for *Around the World in Eighty Days* (1956). His travel writings, parodies and diverse essays appeared in *The New Yorker* and many other magazines throughout the twenties and thirties, and in 1943 he wrote the book of the Broadway musical *One Touch of Venus,* with music by Kurt Weill and lyrics by Ogden Nash. It ran for over 500 performances.
49, 225, 253

Pertwee, Michael: playwright and screenwriter. For TV he wrote *The Grove Family* (1954) and episodes of *Alfred Hitchcock Presents* (1960), *Danger Man* (1964), *The Saint* (1967) and *The Persuaders* (1971). His screen credits include *Laughter in Paradise* (1951), *Top Secret* (1952), *The Mouse on The Moon* (1962) and he co-wrote with Frank Muir and DN *Bottoms Up!*, the screen version of *Whack-o!*
xx

Pick of the Pilots: six-episode TV series, each drawn from unsold pilots which had never made it to the Television schedules. Written and presented by DN. Directed by Terry Kinane.
xxii

Porter, Cole: American composer and songwriter. Musicals include *Kiss Me Kate* and *Anything Goes*. Songs include 'I Get A Kick Out of You', 'I've Got You Under My Skin', 'Let's Do It', 'Night and Day' and 'What Is This Thing Called Love'.
219

Powell, Dilys: distinguished *Sunday Times* journalist, doyenne of film critics. Author of ten books, including *Remember Greece* (1941) and *The Golden Screen: Fifty Years at the Films* (1989); regular panellist on *My Word!*
xx, 16–17

Purves, Libby: journalist, author and radio presenter whose regular programmes include Radio 4's *Midweek*. A columnist for *The Times*, named Columnist of the Year (1999), she is also the author of eleven novels including *Mother Country* (2002) and *Love Songs and Lies* (2007), in addition to children's stories and travel books.
247

Q

Quant, Mary: fashion designer. During the sixties her clothes became extremely fashionable; their geometric simplicity and colours together with her miniskirts were a part of the 'swinging sixties'.
233

Race, Steve: composer, musician and radio and television presenter. Wrote soundtrack music for several films including *Calling Paul Temple* (1948). Initially played the piano for BBC radio panel games such as *Whirligig* (1950) and *Many a Slip* (1964). Host in more than

500 editions of *My Music*, providing most of questions.
xx, 165, 171

Randle, Frank: north country character comedian, a major attraction in Blackpool seaside shows before World War Two with his portrayal of a cackling, wheezing, randy old man. Made a series of films including *Somewhere in England* (1940) and *Somewhere in Camp* (1942) for which he also wrote the screenplay with John Blakeley and Arthur Mertz.
264

Rathbone, Basil: South African-born actor famous for portrayals of Sherlock Homes in fourteen films between 1939 and 1946, and as swash-buckling villain of the piece in such movies as *The Adventures of Robin Hood* (1938) and *The Mark of Zorro* (1940).
191

Rattigan, Terence: playwright. His best-known play is *The Winslow Boy* (stage, 1946; film, 1948). He also wrote *The Browning Version* (1948) and *Separate Tables* (1954). At the same time as serving in the RAF as a fighter pilot in World War Two he wrote screenplays for several propaganda films including *The Way to the Stars* (1945).
115

Ray, Ted: Liverpool comedian who spent years in Variety with his 'Fiddling and Fooling Act' in which he portrayed an inept violinist. His fusillade of Bob Hope-style one-liners adapted so well to radio, his *Ray's a Laugh* took over the *ITMA* spot in 1949. His ready responses made him a welcome chat show guest as witness his frequent appearances on *Looks Familiar*.
185, 273

Read, Al: northern comedian and master of 'observational' humour. With his catchphrase 'Right monkey' he appeared in the Royal

Variety Performance (1954) and led the popular BBC radio programme *The Al Read Show* (1951–5). Stage shows included *You'll Be Lucky* (1954) that ran for twelve months at the Adelphi Theatre, London.
103

Red Hot & Blue Moments: (1940) touring review starring Sid Field.
27

Remarque, Erich: German-born novelist. Won international acclaim with *All Quiet on the Western Front* (1929) about ordinary soldiers' experiences of World War One.
111

Rich, Buddy: American drummer and band leader. Played with many bands including Artie Shaw, Tommy Dorsey, Harry James, and Les Brown, as well as with his own band.
192

Riverside Villas Murder, The: pastiche detective novel by Kingsley Amis (1973).
183

Robards, Jason: award-winning American movie actor who won Oscars for his roles in *All the President's Men* (1976) and *Julia* (1977).
233

Robertson, Arnot E: novelist and film critic. Author of eleven books and regular panellist on *My Word!*
xx

Robeson, Paul: American actor, bass singer, writer, athlete and civil rights activist. Played professional American football to pay way through Columbia University Law School. Appeared in London production of musical *Show Boat* where he made his performance of 'Ol' Man River' the definitive version. Appeared in eight movies including *Sanders of the River* (1935) and *The Proud Valley* (1940). 255–6

Robinson, Eric: orchestral conductor and composer regularly seen on post-war Television; presented his own *Music for You* featuring The Eric Robinson Orchestra. 124–5

Robinson, Fred: Writer. Creator of TV sitcom *The Larkins* (1958–60 and 1963–4). Other output included ABC Television series *Just Jimmy* (1964–8) starring Jimmy Clitheroe and *Vacant Lot* (1967) starring Bill Fraser and Alfie Bass. 174–7

Robinson, Robert: radio and Television personality, journalist and novelist. Hosted *Call My Bluff* (TV, 1966–8), *Ask the Family* (TV, 1967–84), *Brain of Britain* (radio, 1973–2004) and *Stop the Week* (radio, 1974–92). He was also one of the hosts on *Not So Much a Programme, More A Way of Life* (TV, 1965) and his novels included an outstanding detective story *Landscape with Dead Dons* (1956). 151

Rodgers, Richard: American composer of many top-flight musicals including *Ever Green* (1932), *Pal Joey* (1940), *Oklahoma!* (1943), *Carousel* (1945), *South Pacific* (1949), *The King and I* (1951), *The Sound of Music* (1959). 266

Romance, Viviane: exceptionally appetising French dancer and actress. Debut as a dancer at the Moulin Rouge. Elected Miss Paris (1930). Film debut with cameo role in *La Chienne* (1931). Starred in *Naples*

numbers, toured Variety and became resident comedian on *Variety Bandbox* (1945–9). Further radio series included *Variety Fanfare, Hip Hip Hoo Roy* and *Happy Go Lucky*. In 1957, he became the first comedian to appear on TV.
110, 213

Rubinstein, Artur: Polish-born virtuoso pianist and composer. Widely recognised for his interpretation of the music of Brahms and Chopin.
166–7

S

Sahl, Mort: Canadian-born American stand-up comedian and actor, who was an innovator in the realm of topical satire and among the first to achieve worldwide popularity through the medium of comedy LPs.
147–8

Sanders, George: Russian-born English movie actor. British movie debut *Find the Lady* (1936). Made his first American film, *Lloyd's of London*, that same year. Won Oscar as Best Actor in a Supporting Role for *All About Eve* (1950), and starred with David Hemmings in *The Best House in London* (1969).
xxi

Sanders of the River: movie (1935) based on the popular Edgar Wallace novels; old-style colonial adventure story, with Paul Robeson as Bosambo, a local Nigerian native chief, alongside Leslie Banks as the British District Commissioner, Sanders, fighting gun-runners and slavers.
256

Savalas, Telly: American actor. Best known for roles in *The Dirty Dozen* (1967), *Birdman of Alcatraz* (1962), *On Her Majesty's Secret Service* (1969) and as TV's Kojak (1973–90), with his lollipop and 'Who loves ya baby?'
xxi

Saville, Philip: actor turned TV director/screenwriter. During the sixties he directed several important television plays, including Harold Pinter's *A Night Out* (1960), *The Madhouse on Castle Street* (1963) and the still talked-about *Boys From the Blackstuff* (1982). Also directed *The Best House in London* (1969).
xxi

Secombe, Sir Harry: Welsh comedian, actor, singer and presenter knighted in 1981. Alongside Spike Milligan and Peter Sellers, he was part of the immortal trio who constituted *The Goon Show* (1951–60). Featured in West End stage musicals, most notably *Pickwick* (1963), *The Four Musketeers* (1967) and *Oliver!* (1968). Also presented BBC Television's *Songs of Praise* and ITV's *Highway*.
xviii, 63, 171

Schwartz, Arthur: American composer, responsible for the melodies of many popular songs and Broadway musicals. With his lyric writing partner Howard Dietz, he provided us with 'I Guess I'll Have to Change My Plan' (1929), 'You and the Night and the Music' (1934), 'That's Entertainment' (1953) and, perhaps his most lasting contribution, 'Dancing in the Dark' (1931).
116–7

Scott James, Anne: journalist and author. Wrote for *Vogue* and *Picture Post* then edited *Harper's Bazaar* (1945–51). Later woman's editor *Sunday Express* (1953–7) and columnist *Daily Mail* (1960–8). Mother of Max Hastings. In 1967 she married Osbert Lancaster. Succeeded Nancy Spain as panellist on *My Word!* in 1964.
xx

CLIPS FROM A LIFE

Sellers, Peter: actor and comedian. Discovered when doing impressions of film stars at the Windmill theatre, his first broadcast was in *Showtime* (1948), scripted by DN. Went on to radio appearances in Frank Muir and DN's *Sellers' Market, Third Division, Finkle's Café* and, on TV, *And So To Bentley* (1954). Following *The Goon Show* (1951–60), he took to movies where after *The Ladykillers* (1955) and *I'm All Right, Jack* (1959), Hollywood claimed him. Now probably best known for *Dr Strangelove* (1963) and the five *Pink Panther* movies (1963–78).
xviii, xix, 134–6

Seven Faces of Jim, The: BBC Television show (1961) starring Jimmy Edwards, Amanda Barrie, Richard Briers and June Whitfield. Ronnie Barker made his TV debut in this series.
xx, 149, 268–9

Show Time: BBC radio Variety new talent programme (1948) written by DN and produced by Roy Speer. Newcomers on the show included Peter Sellers.
xviii

Shryane, Tony: radio producer. First producer of *The Archers* (1951–79), and then produced *My Word!* (1957) and *My Music* (1967) with Edward J. Mason.
157, 163

Silvers, Phil: American actor, entertainer and comedian. Best known for his role as Sergeant Bilko in the sitcom *The Phil Silvers Show* (1955–60).
xxi

Singleton, Valerie: radio and Television presenter. Best known as BBC Television's *Blue Peter* presenter (1962–75) and as *Nationwide* presenter (1972–6).
197

Speer, Roy: BBC radio producer responsible for *Beginner's Please*, DN's first post-War entry to broadcast writing; his *Show Time* series gave Peter Sellers his first break in broadcasting.
xviii

Speight, Johnny: scriptwriter and dramatist. First broadcast work was for BBC radio's *Mr Ros and Mr Ray* (1955) writing jokes for band leaders Edmundo Ros and Ray Ellington. First Television script was for *Great Scott – It's Maynard* (1955) featuring Terry Scott and Bill Maynard. Other TV series included *That's Life!, Says Max Wall* (1957), *The Arthur Haynes Show* (1957–66) and the first series of *Sykes and a ...* (1960), but he will be best remembered for *Till Death Us Do Part* (1966–75) featuring Warren Mitchell as Alf Garnet.
237

Squadronaires, The: British big band, originally the wartime No. 1 RAF Dance Band, formed in 1940. Players included trombonist George Chisholm, trumpeters Tommy McQuater, Cinton French and Kenny Baker, guitarist Sid Colin and pianist Ronnie Aldrich.
271

Squire Brown, Edna: genteel forties striptease artist whose act put doves to good use.
24

Starlight Hour: BBC radio Variety programme (1948) written by Frank Muir and DN with Sid Colin. Featured Bernard Braden and was the first radio series for Peter Sellers.
xviii

Statue, The: movie (1971) directed by Rodney Amateau and starring David Niven. Screenplay by Alec Coppel and DN. Dedicated to the proposition that all men are not created equal.
xxi

Sunday Night at The London Palladium: ATV Television Variety show (1955–67 then 1973–4) created by Val Parnell and sometimes winning as many as twenty million viewers.
270

Stern, Mike: colourful Petticoat Lane market trader.
75

Styne, Jule: London-born American composer whose successful musicals include *High Button Shoes* (1947), *Gentlemen Prefer Blondes* (1949), *Gypsy* (1959), *Bells are Ringing* (1956) and *Funny Girl* (1964). They gave us such songs as 'Diamonds Are a Girl's Best Friend', 'The Party's Over', and 'Everything's Coming up Roses'.
192

Swanson, Gloria: diminutive American movie star, primarily a silent movie actress appearing alongside the likes of Charlie Chaplin and Rudolph Valentino. Acted in a few talkies (e.g. *Music in the Air,* 1934) but only returned to her former eminence with Billy Wilder's *Sunset Boulevard* (1950).
187

Sykes, Eric: comedy writer and performer. Early career included writing Frankie Howerd's monologues in *Variety Bandbox* (1946) then the series *The Howerd Crowd* (1952) and *Nuts in May* (1953). An early TV appearance was with cast including Tony Hancock, Sid James, Donald Pleasence and Peter Sellers in comedy play *Orders Are Orders* (1954) which he also co-wrote. Other significant credits include the TV series *Sykes and a …* (1960–5), Sykes (1972–9), the multi-award-winning *The Plank* (1967), the play *Big Bad Mouse* in which he toured with Jimmy Edwards (1966) and as a voice in *Teletubbies* (1997–2001). Movies include *Heavens Above!* (1963), *Monte Carlo or Bust* (1969) and *Harry Potter and the Goblet of Fire* (2005). Autobiography *If I Don't Write It, Nobody Else Will* (2006).
51, 53, 55–6, 237

T

Take It From Here: BBC radio comedy series (1948–60) written by Frank Muir and DN (1948–59), starring Jimmy Edwards, Dick Bentley and Joy Nichols who was later replaced by June Whitfield (1953) and Alma Cogan. Initially a comedy and sketch show, a major segment was gradually transformed into a sitcom by chronicling the problems of the Glum family. In 1959 when Frank Muir and DN left to devote themselves to TV writing, the last series was written by Barry Took and Eric Merriman.
xviii, 85–90, 92–3, 96, 98–100, 105, 112–15, 120, 137, 229, 232, 264

Take My Word for It: A published collection of *My Word!* stories (1978).
xxi

Tarloff, Frank: American screenwriter most noted for *Father Goose* (1964) for which he won the Oscar for Best Writing, Story and Screenplay Written Directly for the Screen. Also wrote for TV including *The Dick Van Dyke Show* (1961).
140–1, 252, 263

Temple, Nat: big band leader and clarinet player. Formed Nat Temple Band in 1944. Chosen by Bernard Braden to feature in his radio programmes of the late forties and early fifties. He made many broadcasts; singers fronting the band included Julie Andrews, Anne Shelton and Frankie Vaughan.
xviii, 101–2

Temple, Shirley: American child star forever associated with the Good Ship Lollipop. Films included *Baby Take a Bow* (1934), *Bright Eyes* (1934), *Wee Willy Winky* (1937) and *Heidi* (1937). Ran for the US

Congress in 1967 and was appointed United States Ambassador to Czechoslovakia (1989–92).

10

Tesler, Brian: Television producer, director and executive. BBC Light Entertainment producer and director (1952–7) where he produced and directed *Barbara with Braden* (1953), *And So To Bentley* (1954) and *Fast and Loose* (1954). Transferred to ITV and later became senior Executive for Thames Television.

xix, 134

Third Division: BBC Third Programme experimental radio series (1949) written by Frank Muir and DN with Paul Dehn. Cast included Robert Beatty, Benny Lee, Patricia Hayes, Harry Secombe, Peter Sellers, Michael Bentine, Benny Hill and Robert Moreton. Produced by Pat Dixon. Introduced the sketch, *Balham: Gateway to the South*.

xviii

This Is Your Life: American NBC television programme (1952–61 and 1972) imported by BBC Television (1955–64) and presented by Eamonn Andrews.

265–6

Three Stooges, The: American vaudeville knockabout comedy act who later made several movies. Act consisted of the brothers Curly, Moe and Shemp Howard and Larry Fine and Joe Besser with a changing line-up over the years.

256–7

Took, Barry: comedian, writer and presenter of BBC's *Points of View* and Radio 4's *The News Quiz*. With Marty Feldman co-wrote *Round the Horne* (1965–8), also *Every Home Should Have One* (1970) with DN.

xxi

Toomey, Regis: American movie and Television actor. Appeared in over 180 movies, including such classics as *The Big Sleep* with Humphrey Bogart. Holds the record, along with his co-star Jane Wyman, for the longest on-screen kiss (three minutes and five seconds) in *You're in the Army Now* (1941).
254

Topol: Israeli actor and singer who came to fame with his role as Tevye in *Fiddler on the Roof* (1971) for which he was nominated for an Oscar.
228

Torch, Sidney: composer, conductor, orchestral arranger, pianist and cinema organist. Played in various London cinemas until appointed chief organist at Gaumont State Cinema, Kilburn (1937–40). Joined RAF (1940) and became conductor of the RAF Concert Orchestra. Post-war, he created and conducted the BBC Concert Orchestra and inaugurated *Friday Night is Music Night* (1953–), radio's longest-running live music programme.
29

Trinder, Tommy: trilby-hatted London comedian with popular catchphrase, 'you lucky people!'. Beginning as a Variety stand-up in revues *Tune In* and *In Town Tonight* (1937), he topped many Palladium bills and was a frequent broadcaster on radio and TV, becoming first compere of *Val Parnell's Saturday Night at the London Palladium* (1955–7). Many *Looks Familiar* appearances.
26, 256

Tynan, Kenneth: controversial English theatre critic and writer. *Evening Standard* critic (1952) who became prominent after moving to the *Observer* (1954). Champion of *Look Back in Anger* by John Osborne. Appointed literary manager National Theatre in 1963. First to use 'f' word on British TV (November 1965) resulting

in four House of Commons censure motions. Latterly wrote articles for *The New Yorker*.
151

Ullman, Liv: Norwegian actress born in Tokyo who came to fame in Swedish films (Ingmar Bergman's *Persona* (1966), *Hour of the Wolf* (1968), *The Passion of Anna* (1970) etc.). Moving to Hollywood, she starred in *A Bridge Too Far* (1977), *Autumn Sonata* (1978) and *Players* (1979).
233

Upon My Word: A published collection of *My Word!* stories (1974).
xxi

Ustinov, Peter: multi-talented, multi-voiced actor, dramatist, screenwriter, journalist and raconteur. First movie part was in *One of Our Aircraft is Missing* (1942). His first writing success was with the play *The Love of Four Colonels* (1951); on the screen he won two Oscars for Best Actor in a Supporting Role for his performances as Lentulus Batiatus in *Spartacus* (1960) and as Arthur Simon Simpson in *Topkapi* (1964). Also starred in BBC's first non-scripted radio series, *In All Directions* (1952).
xix, 108–9

V

Variety Bandbox: Sunday night, hour-long BBC radio series first broadcast in 1941, 'presenting the people of variety to a variety of people.' Producers included Bryan Sears and Joy Russell Smith, its comperes down the years included, among others, Hal Monty,

Derek Roy, Reg Dixon, Frankie Howerd and Arthur English.
61, 110

Vosburgh, Dick: accomplished American-born comedy writer and lyricist working in the UK. Wrote for many TV comedy shows including *The Frost Report* (1966–7), *The Two Ronnies* (1971–2), *The Kenny Everett Video Show* (1978) and was the author and lyricist for the musical *Windy City* (1982). With an unrivalled ear for the idiocies of popular song lyrics, he wrote and presented many outstanding radio programmes on this theme.
233, 259

W

Wadmore, George: comedy scriptwriter and gag writer for Ted Ray. Contributed to *Ray's a Laugh* (1949–61) and *Educating Archie* (1950–4).
92

Waldman, Ronnie: producer, radio and TV Executive who also presented programmes. While a Senior Executive for BBC radio, he was a presenter of *Monday Night at Seven* where he introduced the principle of the 'deliberate mistake'. On TV, he presented *Kaleidoscope* (1946–53). Was made BBC Assistant Head of Productions (1948–50) then BBC Head of Light Entertainment (1950–8). After that he became Business Manager, BBC Television Programmes (1958–60), General Manager BBC Television Enterprises (1960–3), then Managing Director Visnews Ltd (1963–77).
128, 141–2, 265

Wall, Max: droll Variety comedian, eccentric dancer and actor. After touring in revues and appearing on Variety bills and in panto, his radio break came with *Our Shed* (1946). In the sixties he became a

straight actor specialising in the plays of Samuel Beckett including *Krapps' Last Tape* (1975) and *Waiting for Godot* (1980). Remembered for comic character Professor Wallofski dressed in lank wig, black tights and ungainly boots.
32, 183

Wallace, Ian: Scottish bass-baritone opera singer. Sang at Glyndebourne and for Scottish Opera. Panellist on *My Music* (1967–94) taking part in every one of more than 520 editions.
xx, 165, 172

Waller, Fats: American jazz 'stride' pianist, organist, singer and songwriter. Hits include 'Ain't Misbehavin'' and 'My Very Good Friend the Milkman'. Appeared in films such as *Stormy Weather* (1943).
233

Waller, Jack: pre-World War One Music Hall entertainer from a penniless immigrant family, who became a composer of blockbuster musicals, theatre owner, impresario and millionaire. Among his successes was *Yes, Madam* (1934).
244

Waring, Peter: sophisticated comedy entertainer who rose through the ranks of Variety and The Windmill to star in radio and TV series *Variety Bandbox* and *Music Hall*. Tragically he was sent to jail in 1949 and committed suicide in his cell.
79, 229

Warren, Latona and Sparks: Variety act. Appeared in *Folies Bergère* (1951) at the London Hippodrome and in Canada at the Canadian National Exhibition in 1953.
267

Water Babies, The: animated cartoon film (1978) of the children's book by Charles Kingsley. Starred, among others, the voice of James Mason. DN wrote additional animation dialogue material.
xxi

Whack-o!: BBC TV sitcom series (1956–60) written by Frank Muir and DN. Built around Jimmy Edwards as boozing, bullying, blustering headmaster of Chiselbury School with (now unacceptable) penchant for corporal punishment.
xix, xx, 231–2

What's My Line?: by far the most memorable of all the BBC's early panel games (1951–63 and 1973–4). Hosted by Eamonn Andrews, its panellists included Lady Isobel Barnett, Gilbert Harding, Barbara Kelly, David Nixon, and, for one inglorious season, Frank Muir and DN. Its most memorable contestant was a 'saggar maker's bottom knocker', a worker in pottery firing.
xviii, 125

Wheeler, Sir Mortimer: eminent archaeologist, noted for his work at Verulamium (St Albans) and Maiden Castle (Dorset). Appeared as a panellist on the TV quiz show *Animal, Vegetable, Mineral?* in the fifties.
133

Where the Rainbow Ends: patriotic children's play (1911) written by Clifford Mills and John Ramsey.
32, 216

Whitfield, June: gifted actress whose talents have rescued more comedy half-hours than the commercial break. Made her broadcasting debut in *Take It From Here* (1953) and subsequently co-starred with more or less every leading comedy name in radio and

Television from Arthur Askey and Tony Hancock to the *Absolutely Fabulous* (1992–2005) team.
94, 112, 144

Who's Whose?: panel game devised by Frank Tarloff for BBC Television. Crashed on take-off.
140–1

Windmill, The: London theatre in Great Windmill Street, off Piccadilly Circus. During World War Two, it presented a continuous Variety show running from 2.30 p.m. until 11 p.m. in which the female participants were allowed to appear without clothes as long as they remained motionless. ('If you move, it's rude'). The roster of comedians for whom it smoothed the transition from serving in the armed forces to becoming professional performers included Tony Hancock, Harry Secombe, Jimmy Edwards, Barry Cryer and Peter Sellers.
124

With Hilarious Consequences: TV one-off featuring clips from Thames Television's twenty-one years of situation comedies.
xxii

Williams, Kenneth: comic actor and raconteur. Discovered in repertory (1954) by producer Dennis Main Wilson while casting BBC radio's *Hancock's Half Hour*. Appeared in *Round the Horne* radio series and many *Carry On* films. A favourite guest of all chat shows.
264

Willis, Lord (Ted): Television dramatist, screenwriter and an active Labour Party member. His *Woman in a Dressing Gown* (1957), *No Trees in the Street* (1959) and *Flame in the Streets* (1961) were BAFTA nominations for Best British Screenplay. Probably best

remembered for the *Dixon of Dock Green* (1955–63) series. He was the chairman of the Writers' Guild of Great Britain (1958–64). Awarded Life Peerage as Baron Willis of Chislehurst, Kent (1963).
173, 218

Wilson, Keppel and Betty: a deadpan duo, wearing short-skirted Egyptian dress whose soft-shoe dancing on sand, sprinkled by the glamorous Betty, was one of the staple Variety acts from the twenties to the fifties.
66

Winnick, Maurice: dance band leader, radio and Television impresario, whose thirties band enjoyed successful residencies at the Mayfair and Dorchester hotels. In the forties he acquired the rights to the American radio series *It Pays to be Ignorant* which he renamed *Ignorance is Bliss* and in 1951 bought the British rights to the American TV panel game *What's My Line?*.
79

Winslow Boy, The: stage play (1946) and movie (1948) by Terence Rattigan; based on the true story of a naval cadet falsely accused of stealing a postal order.
115

Winters, Bernie: comedian, who with his brother Mike enjoyed success as a Variety and TV double-act. Later, with his St Bernard dog Schnorbitz, became popular as a solo star and guested on *In On the Act* (1988).
xxii

Winters, Shelley: American actress who appeared in many movies including *The Diary of Anne Frank* (1959), *A Patch of Blue* (1965), both of which gained her Oscar nominations, *Buona Sera, Mrs Campbell* (1968) and *The Poseidon Adventure* (1972) for which she

received a Golden Globe. Observed that 'the winter of 1947 was so cold I almost got married.'
xxi

Wisdom, Norman: stage, screen and TV slapstick comedian, singer and actor given to uncontrollable laughter. After serving in World War Two he made his debut as the straight man to magician David Nixon wearing his trademark garb of sideways-on flat cap and a suit several sizes too small. Made eighteen successful comedy movies of which the best-known is probably *Trouble in Store* (1953), featuring the song 'Don't Laugh at Me (Cause I'm a Fool)'.
271

Woollcott, Alexander: notably acerbic American critic and commentator working on *The New Yorker* in the twenties and thirties.
49

Wolfe, Thomas: American writer whose lengthy novels *Look Homeward Angel* (1929) and *Of Time and The River* (1935) were extravagantly rhetorical celebrations of youth, sex and America.
49

Workers' Playtime: long-running radio Variety series (1941–64), produced by Bill Gates. It was broadcast live three times a week from factory canteens and halls around the UK.
61

Worth, Harry: comedy actor best known for the BBC Television series *Here's Harry*, later renamed *Harry Worth*. Ran for over a hundred episodes in the sixties.
226

Wyman, Jane: American leading lady in forties movies. Appeared in *The Lost Weekend* (1945), *The Yearling* (1946) and *Johnny Belinda*

(1948). Still holds the record for the longest screen kiss (*You're in the Army Now,* 1941).
254

Y

You Can't Have Your Kayak and Heat It: first collection of *My Word!* stories (1973).
xxi

You Have My Word: another collection of *My Word!* stories (1989).
xxii

Young, Joan: a former Music Hall star, she enjoyed successful acting roles in many West End productions, including playing Mrs Antrobus opposite Vivienne Leigh in Thornton Wilder's *The Skin of Our Teeth* (1950). In movies, her favourite role was supporting Ingrid Bergman in *The Inn of The Sixth Happiness* (1958) and, most famously she took on Jimmy Edwards and Eric Sykes in the lengthy worldwide tour of *Big Bad Mouse* (1966 onward).
228

Z

Zahl, Hyman: leading Variety agent representing many of the top stars of the period from the thirties to the sixties.
xvii, 61–5, 70–1

Also available as an audiobook from

HarperCollinsAudioBooks

www.harpercollins.co.uk